Gods, Gloves, Pop-Ups, & Ponies

A LOOK AT THE CHARACTER FOUND PLAYING YOUTH BASEBALL.

...AND A RUN AT THE 1975 PONY LEAGUE WORLD SERIES

by: Chris Smith

BANYAN · TREE · PRESS

BanyanTreePress.com

Gods, Gloves, Pop-Ups, and Ponies

A LOOK AT THE CHARACTER FOUND PLAYING YOUTH BASEBALL.
...AND A RUN AT THE 1975 PONY LEAGUE WORLD SERIES

ISBN: 978-1-936449-26-2
Library of Congress Control Number: 2012944607

LEGAL NOTICE
This is a work of non-fiction.

Cover & Interior design by David Prescott of DPMediaPro.com

DEDICATION

This work is dedicated to all the coaches who put in the long hours helping to create great athletes and great young men.

And to Mr. Meeder, Mr. Faulk, Coach Schachtel, Coach Klein and my father, Lester Smith, all great coaches who had a hand in helping me become the man I am today.

And thank you to my wife Mary who understands and fosters my passion for this great game.

Lastly, thank you to Baxter for being there with me for every word.

Table of Contents

INTRODUCTION

Early spring in the foothills of the Rocky Mountains is no time to be thinking about baseball. However, when the snow starts to melt and the infield dirt starts to poke through the white blanket of winter, my thoughts are powerfully drawn to the diamond. It can be any old rough-cut patch of dirt and grass, I don't care, for the long winter baseball drought has me itching to get back out on to the field to teach the game of baseball and to mold some young baseball minds. I am a high school baseball coach who has a real need to be on the field presenting the game I love to stubborn minded fourteen- year-old freshman boys. All the frustrations from last year, and the previous years, magically melt away over the winter months. With the arrival of the new spring, I am refreshed and ready to once again take on the challenge of teaching this great game to kids who are beginning to understand the deeper mysteries of the game of baseball, and who are embarking on the journey of sorting out their teenage world.

The young men who come out to the barely thawed field in the shadows of the looming Flatiron Mountains are excited about continuing their tutelage in the ways of baseball. However, the one thing they do not realize is their time spent learning about hitting and fielding will also include a healthy helping of lessons on character, humility, poise, pain, and what it means to be a member of society. These large concepts will be swirling around the field while I help them connect their minds with their stubborn body parts. We will be working hard to hopefully create a fluid path to physical grace, and at the same time, we will be developing mental toughness through winning and losing. Once again I am anxious to introduce these young men to the struggles of being a great player and to awaken the excitement of discovering the amazing people they can be.

March is a tough month in Colorado to start high school baseball; the ground is as locked and frozen as these player's young minds. March brings winds and wet weather that can make a season last forever, but with the end of the school year fast approaching, it's now or never. During my years growing up in the Chicago area back in the 70's, we didn't even consider March as a starting time for baseball. We looked on with envy as the pro teams went to Arizona and Florida to bask in the sun and throw to their hearts content. In Chicago the snow and cold weather off of Lake Michigan left the raw black dirt infields hard with permafrost. No nail drag could penetrate the quick-frozen undulations of rock hard dirt clods which by March were cracked and brittle, crying for water to loosen their marble-hard stature. Frozen waves of uneven gray/black playing surface lay waiting to launch grounders into unprotected eyes and plastic protected regions down below. No, the spring in the Midwest comes even slower than in the foothills of Boulder, Colorado, so March is as good a time as any to start another year of baseball. Our fields are beginning to come around from all the sunshine we receive with only the most shaded areas stubbornly retaining their winter frost. Now is the time, I am ready, the boys are chomping, so its outside we go; bundle up, it's time to start.

My first job as the freshman/sophomore baseball coach is to help pick the spring teams; to begin the process of creating great baseball players and fine young men of character. Out of the sixty or so kids who have come out to the field today, it is the coaching staff's job to create three teams; varsity, junior varsity, and my team, a compilation of the best freshman and sophomore players. A tall order indeed, but with the rebirth of the Earth comes fresh optimism from a coach who has seen it done. I bolster my optimism as I steal a glance at the crew strolling through the gate.

The players straggle in one by one with bags in hand and anxiety in tow. The varsity players and the kids from last year swagger into the dugout knowing what's in store for them this season. The young freshmen "newbies" are wide-eyed, shy, and self conscious. Although they have had most of the year to acclimate to the halls of the school, having to display their athletic ability in front of their peers sends them tumbling back to those painful first days of school. The slow disjointed process of teenagers getting dressed and ready to play begins. The clothes they wore down the hallways today, the ones that already look half removed for the way they hang and drape all over their gangly frames are shed, and are replaced with baseball gear that hangs in the same disheveled manner. More than one kid is told to hitch up his pants and cover his underwear so he can actually take a full stride without being restrained by polyester pants stretched to their limit. We coaches mill about talking about this prospect or that kid from the year before. We wait because the process to get ready seems to drag on forever, burning the daylight that disappears behind the Flatirons way too quickly this time of year. Finally the boys start to pop out of the dugout in ones and twos, clomping and dragging their shiny new spikes and the gloves they hope will serve them well.

The odd mixture of boys that will be mine to mold are a group of kids who have played together on and off for years. These wannabe superstars are a mixed lot which fall into several different categories. They fall into three groups: we have the "sort of want to play" group: kids who have been playing for years and just keep playing because they always have; then there are the kids who woke up that morning and thought baseball would be "fun to take up;" and finally there are those kids who have been told by their parents to "get involved in an activity:" reluctant participants who would rather be home with a control console in hand. The shuffling and milling around begins with most kids standing awkwardly, not quite sure of how to be around the varsity talent and inspecting coaches. The "sort of want to plays" know they should be doing something right now but don't want to be too forward. The "think it would be fun" bunch are smacking their gloves and punching each other. And the "told to get involveds" are just waiting for the gun to go off or the directive to be made so they can begin the involving. Altogether they do not look like much.

It is my task to take this group of miss-matched young men and develop their athletic talents into a group that can play the game of baseball. The talent is there, hidden somewhere beneath the gawky exterior of their ill-fitting youth. I will do my best to teach them the game of baseball, the mechanical acts of throwing, hitting, and playing the game. Together we will learn the science of what to do and where to go on each particular play at any given moment.

Those who make the team will have the opportunity to absorb the inner workings of the game of baseball far beyond the scope of their understanding to this point in their career. As an added bonus to this bounty of baseball knowledge, I will also share with them the lessons of life which the game has taught me in the forty years I have been playing. This game has helped create the person I am today through the many lessons learned while on the field, around my teammates, listening to coaches, and being on the bench. I am now at the point in my life where I am able to understand all the game has taught me and I am grateful to be able to give back to the game which has given me so much. The lessons are sneaky, hard, and swift, but with the right preparation and a willingness to take a punch, the blow can be rather pleasant.

I know being a freshman baseball coach may not seem like a very glamorous or rewarding position; some have even questioned the sanity of taking such a post. The pay is really nothing to get too excited about and the headaches of coaching such a squirrely group are innumerable. The reason to take on the challenge year after year is for the love of seeing the game played well and for the look of satisfaction from a kid who has gone far beyond his limits.

I have so many clear memories of the faces of kids coming off the field after they made a play that neither they nor I thought they could make. The look of pride and joy as they trotted in from the scene of amazement will stay with me in my memory scrapbook for all time. I can picture all those light bulb moments of realization when the lessons on hitting finally take hold and a kid actualizes the movements we have been working on for six weeks. To see a young man drive the baseball into the gap and tear around the bases ending up next to me on third base with a goofy grin on his face is payment enough for a baseball junkie like me. Or better still seeing the look of understanding fall across the team when my talk about humility and sportsmanship is negatively demonstrated by an opposing player who goes off on an umpire and starts jumping around looking foolish and crazed, driving my point home better than I ever could with words. Every day from now until the middle of the summer, I am allowed the opportunity to teach the game of life through the workings of the game of baseball. I will expose these young men to the lessons the world has to offer in the microcosm of a seven inning game. Together we will understand the similarities of having a tantrum in the bosses' office to controlling our temper on a blown call by the ump. We will see that rather than dumping the girl of their dreams with rude behavior and typical teenage crassness, we will instead develop a sense of style, class, and confidence through winning and losing ballgames and in turn win the girl's heart. The world of baseball is gracious enough to teach us the hard and soft of the world, but it is our job to pay attention to the lessons and to work hard learning the game at all times.

The boys have done their best to look like ballplayers, dressing how they think they should, emulating their favorite player, purchasing the latest and greatest gear in the hopes that shiny shoes will give them the edge they need to succeed. Down the left field line an aspiring talent looks like a young Manny Ramirez with his baggy pants and overblown extra-large shirt. However, as Manny has some muscle hidden inside his parachute pants, this young man simply looks like he woke up in his pajamas and stumbled out to the ball field. His throwing partner is a bit more put together with his new shoes, new hat, just out of the wrapper batting gloves, still creased shirt, and blinding white pants. If I hadn't actually seen him move, snagging his new spikes on a slight bump in the turf, I would have sworn he was a mannequin at Dick's Sporting Goods.

Watching all the hard-pressed efforts from the boys to impress the wandering coaches, the thought runs through my mind that so many young men have come before these guys with far less nice gear and yet those same hopeful young men achieved far more on the field than these guys may ever hope to. However, the hope in these boys' eyes is enough for me to wipe away the knowledge that their grandest dreams for baseball most likely will never happen. The look in their eyes is enough for me to get excited and to think of all the possibilities for success that lie ahead. I know there are great things ahead for these young men. Perhaps there is a budding superstar on the field today; many of my former players have gone on to achieve great success at the higher levels. What I do know is that these young men will have an experience this spring which will move them forward in their lives in a positive way. They may not all become the next Manny, thank God, but at this point in the season, we are still tied for first and these boys are all superstars in spirit.

Chapter 1
Finding the Game

My first introduction to the game of baseball was not the Hollywood story of yesteryear in which my old uncle Mortie, the hard nose, cigar-chomping, mythical he-man, takes me under his wing and brings me to the emerald-green field of a young boy's dreams. No, as a young boy of seven living in the elm draped suburb of Wilmette, Illinois, just north of Chicago, we lived just an L-train ride from Wrigley Field, home of the Cubs, and a scary car ride from Comisky Park, site of the less appreciated White Sox... and baseball was not on my radar. Those venues meant nothing to me in my insulated white-bread world near Lake Michigan because my sports world had not expanded past those sturdy elms. I lost my best friend to the moving van the previous summer and I was in search of my next friend when Jonathan Cullen moved in down the block.

Jonathan was a rough and tumble kid, built solid, yet swift. His tank-tough physique was very different from my sinewy-quick frame which always seemed to leave me wanting for competition in games of chase and agility. We quickly became friends during my seventh year, becoming a perfect complimentary pair just like Abbot and Costello, Laurel and Hardy, or Jenkins and Hundley, the dynamic battery mates of the sixties and seventies Cubs. Jonathan's thick legs were twice the size of my scrawny arms, and his thick wavy black hair offset my constantly flipping blond locks. Jonathan's house, a large fire-engine red expanse that sat as a landmark on the corner of Lake Street and 8th, was always filled with the chaos and mayhem of his squabbling younger sisters and a younger brother who never would leave us alone. My house was more staid and quiet, with one older brother and a mother who constantly battled the demons of disorder, never wanting us to enjoy indoor life when the sun was up. Living a block apart, we might as well have been from different countries, for the way our two worlds worked. However the variance of our two settings gave us innumerable options when it came to the kind of day we would decide to spend together. Did we want to run wild or did we need boundaries? Should we torment our siblings or sit and watch the Cubs game? Whatever the setting, the chemistry was always clear and reactive. When we got together, we would run and play and tackle and create a world so physical and pure that keeping track of us was well beyond any two moms' ability to keep up. Thankfully back in 1967 moms didn't even try to keep track of their kids in the giant playground of middle-class suburbia.

Jonathan and I were of the baby boom generation, a tidal wave of kids created from the release of young men from the second World War. The kids from that generation of procreation ruled the orderly blocks of suburban America en mass. The area where we lived was home to a hive of kids fifty strong. Every home, including ours, had at least two kids and the families with only two were clearly the minority. Most houses had three or four kids, but when you threw in a few Catholic families, you had two teams ready and available for any activity you could think of. When my mom kicked my in-the-way butt out of the house, all I had to do was look around to see two, three, or ten kids available to start the latest adventure, game, battle, or trouble.

Many of my days were spent on the "lot" next to the Kennedy's house. That open space of ground, a full house-sized "lot" which had somehow been spared from the developers' need to fill in all of suburbia with stucco, seemed to have been placed in the middle of our block by a divine hand. Everywhere you looked houses filled the landscape, prosperity and stability reigned throughout the land, yet on our one block there sat a full size lot, empty and pristine as if a park commissioner had declared the site open space. Year after year the lot remained open, a grass Mecca drawing kids out of their homes to the open field to run and play. Situated in the middle of our block, just off the alley which ran behind the two rows of street-facing houses, most kids could look out their windows and see if anyone was playing at "the lot." Just walking onto the lot with a football in hand was like dropping an Alka-Seltzer tablet in water, the rush of activity was instantaneous. It was as if kids were just waiting at their windows for the first sign that the game was on.

The Catholic family next to the lot, which numbered eight strong, was usually the first to arrive, no doubt anxious to escape the bedlam of a house too full. The three Hogan kids, John, Jimmy, and Audrey, kids who would always leave the game crying at some point, were the next to make their way onto the field. They would usually be followed by the Tomes kids, Rob, my age and a friend through high school, a friendship that would somehow survive his inability to have any heroic moments on the field of play; his brother John, the real athlete of the family and a top pick, and his twin Betsy. Next door to me, and within eye line of the field, was the Warden family. Although their house was plagued with a majority of girls, the Warden kids, Matthew, Mary, and Pam, were always ready to add a touch of tomboy to the mix. Other assorted kids and characters filled the lot with their varied energy during the humid summer days and crisp fall afternoons. There was an explosion of youthful play around our neighborhood which is hard to find these days in our over-organized world of parent-driven kid activities. Together we played well into the evening until the unique sound of each kid's house bell or bellowing mom filled the air. The jangle of bells from our house cathedrals beckoned each child to return home. A failure to come was followed by a last call from a very serious mother or annoyed father. As the lot emptied, the dusk of the evening re-absorbed the kid-juice which had spilled out, and the still of night gave the lot a twelve hour chance to recover.

CHAPTER 2
THE JOURNEY BEGINS

The 700 block of Washington Avenue had its own sports world going on and didn't really worry itself with the professional sports realm. The Cubs and White Sox, Bears and Blackhawks, were only a mild influence on the block. Because none of those "professional" teams seemed capable of producing a championship let alone a winning season there was very little buzz about their performance from the adult world. My father was a very well-educated Ph.D.-toting human resources director for Blue Cross Blue Shield in Chicago. Sports were only on his radar in the form of glancing at the sports page in the morning or catching a quarter or two of a lopsided Bears game on the occasional Sunday, or a ridiculous Saturday outing to watch the Northwestern Wildcats get pummeled by Michigan. Other than a passing interest in order to be current at the water fountain, I believe my dad simply saw the beauty of the struggle but was not particularly interested in giving it any more thought. Every day he rode his bicycle the five or six blocks past the orderly and equally isolated streets of Elm, Oak, Lake, and Forest to take the L-train to the city. At the end of the day, he would bicycle home from the station to his manicured home, his two kids, and a wife with dinner on the table.

Baseball was not a part of his life—yet. Baseball was not a part of my life either, until Jonathan came along. My journey into the baseball world began one spring day when Jonathan mentioned to me he was going to play Little League baseball. Since my best friend was going to play baseball, I guess that meant I would play too; I mean how hard could it be? I figured the two of us would be teammates for life and we would rule the world of this Little League thing together.

Saturday rolled around and we made our way to the Wilmette Sport Shop for Little League sign-up. The Sport Shop would become a regular stop for all things sports in my years to come. Old wooden floors, an inviting bell attached to the door, and the smell of new mitts and bicycle chains filled the air. I was in awe of how much stuff they could pack into such a small store. Everywhere you looked the space was filled with the in-season gear du jour. One wall was devoted to baseball mitts; catchers' gloves, first basemens' mitts, outfield gloves all lined up and orderly, all stiff and ready to be molded. Racks of shirts and pants and athletic supporters gave the shop a "boys only" feel. Even the overhead space was filled with overflow merchandise and stuff too big to navigate around. High above, near the ceiling fans, the air was river-like as boats and paddles, duck blinds, and tents hung suspended in a crazy upside down camping world. On top of all the gear covering every sport popular to kids in the 60s there was also a full bike-repair facility in back. The bike guys stood at tortured work benches with tiny drawers, clamps, and myriads of strange tools scattered about, no doubt for pulling chains hopelessly wedged into sprockets from our attempts to mimic the antics of our favorite daredevil, Evil Kneivel. A real work-drenched smell emanated from that back room which the store owners allowed us to walk into without anyone blinking an eye. By the time I was in full-bloom sports adolescence, I felt like a regular there, having developed that "Norm from Cheers" familiarity with the place. When I walked into the Sport Shop, I knew the gear I needed was in stock and ready for purchase. The money I earned from many sweaty afternoons pushing a lawnmower around a neighbor's yard was burning a hole in my pocket, ready to be spent on the new hat or glove I had been scouting for days. The Sport Shop was a place of comfort for a long time, always there to show me the latest and greatest gear which would surely make me the best ballplayer around.

The sign-up for Little League was my first big-money responsibility as well as my first exposure to public sales. Armed with my twelve dollars and my sign-up sheet, I made my way to the Sport Shop where I presented both to one of the many employees mustered for this banner day in Wilmette. With all hands on deck, the cramped Sport Shop never looked so important and industrious. Parents and kids jostled to turn in their money and their sign-up sheets in exchange for the twelve round Little League supporter decals which were to be sold for one dollar apiece as a declaration to our parents of our undying commitment to the baseball cause. Everyone was anxious to receive their decals. We were poised at the starting gate to get back to our neighborhoods in order to be the first to knock on our neighbors' doors. Woe to thee who arrived late and had to trail in the wake of those who were first on the street and first to buzz in at the neighborhood houses. Nothing was more demoralizing to a decal seller than to see the 1967 Little League logo affixed to the window of a neighbor who was sure to be a dollar bill. The hordes of kids who were your teammates on the empty lot and who were always there to be your friend and to spend your summer afternoons were now your sales competition, and the fighting was fierce. To come home after a long hard day pounding the pavement with five decals remaining was hard to take, when the deal with my folks was any decals left would come out of my allowance. Five dollars to go and, as far as the eye could see, the front porches of Wilmette were festooned with decals reading, 1962, 1963, 1964, 1965, 1966, and there it was, 1967. Luckily my parents agreed that seven sold was a fine demonstration of my desire to participate. My lesson in sales and responsibility was learned and my allowance was paid in full. The tryouts were just around the corner and I had no idea what to expect.

CHAPTER 3
WARMING-UP

The collage of mis-matched high school players stand before me in their patchwork of officially licesened clothing and just-out-of-the-box shoes; they look to me to start the first day of practice, to start their careers as high school athletes. At the ages of fourteen and fifteen, these kids are still doe-eyed enough to be respectful of an adult even when their MTV disregard for authority and the adult world tries to seep through. After a couple of wardrobe corrections, an adjusted hat, a cinching of falling pants, I have them ready to begin. How does one begin to guide a young man through the maze of information he experiences on a daily basis? How does a budding young man navigate the myriad images of bad behavior he sees on TV and that he is exposed to on the endless social networks? How does one begin to counsel a raw youth about the intense scrutiny he feels from his peers as well as from himself? What is the formula for success in an age so complicated with new technology and so muddled with messages of self worth tied to things and money? How do I help these young men to see through the murky quagmire of their developing minds to the clear world on the other side? Why, sports and fundamentals, of course.

The boys who arrive on my field come to me filled with so many mixed messages about how best to field and to swing and to throw and about how to succeed on the field, that the only way to cut through all the mixed-up information is to stop and start anew. The game of baseball is about connecting with another player with a baseball. If you can throw the ball to your teammate with a certain degree of accuracy, there is a chance something good is going to happen--- simple. To see where we are in the connecting department, the boys gather up their ammunition and seek out their targets. The search for that first great connection begins with players pairing up and loosening arms that until recently have been used primarily for video games. As the balls start flying I head for cover.

The guys who have played forever and who have it all figured out lead the way with throws both strong and dangerous. These "seasoned" players are the guys who have played the game for a number of years and feel pretty comfortable with their abilities. These guys can be the hardest to work with because their skills have been taught by trusted coaches and dads. To undo the work of prominent influences in these young men's lives is tricky. Although these guys will make up the core of the team, their willingness to accept the new ways of this coach will be instrumental to our success. My job will be to demonstrate the value of all that I teach and to demonstrate success through these good players. When they succeed the rest will follow.

The marginal players, the ones not as sure of their abilities, the ones told through the years that they are average in not so many words, are tentative, erratic, and also dangerous. The middle of the pack kids are the bread and butter in a coach's search for success stories. These are the guys who have either never had a good coach, or they have been late in putting together all their physical components. Many of these guys want to play well, desire to be good, but have never been in front of the right guy to help them succeed. A good number of these kids have been too small or too skinny or have just been awkward in their youth. But it's funny how the body can sort itself out through the years.

There are innumerable ugly duckling stories when it comes to sports, and with the right coaching and guidance, a young gawky kid can become the smooth field-stud he has always wanted to be. The best part about this segment of young athlete is that they bring big hearts to the ball park. Give me a kid who wants to work hard, wants to be at the field, and who loves the game, and I can succeed right alongside him. I usually get a good batch of this kind of player, for which I am quite thankful. I know a good portion of these kids will only play another year or two and move on to something else, however there are always a couple of these kids who will put in the time, pay attention to the instruction, and work their way to the top to become the athlete they always wanted to be. Not only do these kids succeed on the field but they also succeed as people because they learn to respect the process of becoming great.

Then there are the kids who just woke up and decided this is the day they will become ballplayers. This group of young men is working to find that first connection with a teammate and it is not going well. The game of baseball is such a fine motor skill activity that it requires an endless numbers of repetitions for the body to become comfortable with a given motion. The act of throwing and catching involves innumerable muscles and rotations; from the feet to the hips, up to the torso, out to the arm, all the way down to the final tips of the fingers. Because these muscles haven't been fired in sequence over and over, thousands of times, the pathway in the brain is too vague and the ball rarely flies true twice in a row. On top of all that, there is the act of tracking and catching the darn thing as it sails toward your face; now that would be a connection to remember. Add one of the most difficult activities in sports, hitting, and you have an immense challenge for a young athlete to decide to undertake.

To ask a kid, or better yet, for a kid to ask of himself, to put on a glove and try to catch up on all the repetitions he has fallen behind is asking a lot. However, there are those kids who can catch up once they surround themselves with a group of like-minded motivated individuals and a coach who can show them the right way to shortcut the process. Will these guys be the best? Only time and desire will tell.

Finally there are the kids who aren't sure why they are here, the ones told by their parents to play, or who have played for years but don't know why. These opaque guys are having a grand time messing around and they too are dangerous. For the most part, it is hard for a kid to know why he is doing anything at any time of the day. Ask any child at any time of the day what and why they are doing something and the usual response is, "I don't know." The act of self analysis is difficult for the average adult to undertake so it is not surprising that a young man is unclear about his likes and dislikes. Ask any adult why they do the job they do or why they watch so much TV and the same refrain is often heard. The sleep-walking adolescent is not a particularly rare thing, but try it on the baseball field and someone is going to get hurt.

My challenge with the unclear, as well as with all the other guys, is to help them to awaken to the world around them and their place in it. Part of being a member of a team is the being part. The young men on this field will learn some lessons about being responsible, being on time, being accountable, being better each day, being awake for their part in the making of this team. Given the material at hand, this is a tall order and tough task. But the team is picked and the process has begun; the warm up of their rusty arms continues until all are in agreement that they are tired of chasing the balls around the field and the madness stops.

Why are we here playing this game which is so simple on paper yet so difficult to execute? What possible satisfaction could come from struggling to master all the fine motor skills required to send a ball flying through the air? What compels us to want to work so hard to be able to roam hard to our left, spear a sharply hit ground ball, plant, pivot, and throw out a runner by a step? Who in their right mind would expend the effort to learn to drop step and open up to the right, sprint hard to the wall and leap up and rob someone of an extra base hit? Surely the thought of spending hours doing repetitive drills and working tirelessly with your teammates for weeks and then losing gut wrenching close games and pulling out nail biting victories is totally pointless, right?

Well, as the guys hustle back from their warm up, I look at each young man and see the satisfaction that each one feels for the great job they did warming up. I realize there is no other place I would rather be than right here trying to conjure up all the baseball moments and feelings which will keep us here working hard, getting us ready for the season at hand. The reason to be here… the sound of the ball, the feeling of being a part of something, that first good contact, and for me, the chance to reveal what the game really has to offer, a peek at who these young men can be if only they let the game speak to them.

CHAPTER 4
LEARNING THE LESSONS

For many of these young men, the lessons of life have been brought to them by well- meaning parents who have studied books and passed on translated lessons from their own parents. The cycle of life continues with lessons of manhood and conduct passed down from generation to generation. Kids endure traditional lectures, and endless harangues about behavior and ethics, these lectures are time honored traditions which rarely inspire and more often go completely unheard. The result is continued bad behavior and careless acts which bring parents to their knees, wondering and whining to other parents about why the message hasn't sunk into little Bobby's thick skull. Many a night has been spent commiserating with other parents around barbeques and card tables about the inability of young people to "get it." "Why can't he get it when I tell him that if he wants to get anywhere in this world he is going to have to study and get good grades!" How comforting it is for the parent listening to hear the same lament from another parent going through the exact same misery they are. How often does a parent sit up at night wondering whether or not their child is the only bonehead who can't seem to "get it?"

The struggle to make your child into a sensible well-mannered citizen of the world is one that has plagued well-intentioned parent for years. How often have we heard a parent say they had their own struggles as a youth, and then the familiar tag, "And look how well I turned out." What we all seem to forget is that we too were the glassy-eyed youth who knew everything and who had "it all" figured out. All of us have events in our lives that define us, that made us, that helped us "get it." The thing we are trying to "get" is an understanding of the way things work in the world and some insight into how to handle that knowledge. You can call it maturity, but I don't think we as parents, or as adults for that matter, really know what that word means. We view maturity as simply a growing process in which age somehow defines our progress along a path. Maturity is really more about our ability to recognize the requirements the world has for us and our ability to make decisions based on those requirements, moving us forward in a positive way. What we want for our young people is for them to find a little understanding each day about this complex world so they can develop their own way of handling themselves. As much as we want to teach and show our children what the world is all about, we know deep down that they will have to experience learning the way we did, by getting dirty and doing life.

Most of us in our youth moved ourselves through the maturation process with events that made us cringe and flinch. Sometimes the memories cause us shame, sometimes a small smile, sometimes amazement at the understanding it brought us. A memory of old loves, risky behavior, defiance, mistakes, and wrong turns fill us with the path markers that led us to the people we have become. Rarely do we think back and remember a great lecture our parents gave us. Unfortunately those well-meaning speeches never really set us on the path to understanding and greatness. However, some of the lectures we listened to after our mistakes and life experiences did have some bearing on the lesson learned and whether the experience really needed to be lived again.

Many of us draw from another set of experiences that have been instrumental in the creation of our being. These experiences did not require as many horrific lapses of judgment in order for us to learn the lessons which molded our character. For many of us, the sports fields of our youth were the training grounds for many of our character building moments. On those fields we were able to make dumb mistakes and try out the new understanding of who we are or want to be. The kid who is painfully shy in the classroom and hallways can have the courage to open up on the field and in the dugout. A person who is unable to be loose and free around girls and who is intimidated by the more powerful guys in the social order is often able to find his voice and style in the arena of the bus ride to an away game or in the huddle of guys needing to pull together to find victory. Leaving it all on the field and coming out victorious confirms to the young man that the risk of letting go is worth the reward. On the sports fields we are allowed to extend ourselves and see if the skin we are wearing fits right or if we need to find a new tailor.

Allowing a player to make the mistakes and create the player he feels he needs to be is important, but it is the coach's job to give feedback and to help the player hone and understand what is right with each play and what is wrong with each behavior. Making a mistake on the field is a lot better than making a mistake on the street, and with each mistake comes the responsibility of learning what the mistake has to offer.

The mistake having been made, having been looked at and squeezed for all the truth that can be had, must then be checked off as done and used and not to be repeated. It is the measure of the student and player that once the play is over not to revisit the spectacle of that travesty again. It is the measure of the coach to equate the travesty on the field in a given play with the horror that can occur to a young man if he makes the equivalent mistake in his life. The field is easy, life bites back hard.

CHAPTER 5
GODS, GLOVES, AND THE
FIRST COACH

My on-field journey to manhood had its own ups and downs, but the joy that came from exploring the game, and myself, was both subtle and sweet. Today the wonderful memories of the years spent on the diamond flash into my head at the oddest moments. Looking at the brand new glove of one of the hustling players on the field reminds me of all the gloves I have had in my day, the smell, the feel, the frustration.

My first glove did not serve me well. The smell of the leather and the promise of great things to come were all there, but the glove just didn't come together the way I had envisioned. From the minute I started to break it in, wrapping it tight with an old extension cord and piling ten volumes of the Encyclopedia Britannica on top, it just didn't behave. No matter how hard I worked at torturing the crease into submission it just wouldn't hold the way I needed it to. The problem with my game was without a doubt, no question about it, can't tell me differently, my glove. How in the world was I supposed to help my team when my Jerry Reinholdt model, piece of crap glove wouldn't cooperate? And for its inability to make me great, I let that glove know just how unhappy I was with its performance. I threw the glove on the ground, at the bench, at the ball. I left that good-for-nothing glove at games only to have coaches pick it up and return it to me mainly because my name was scrawled across the back for all to see... thanks a lot, Mom!

It was around this time of my glove discontent, the age of seven, when I was first introduced to a deity that would curse me and celebrate me for years to come. The wrath and benevolence of the most powerful force in my young life, and into my adult life, would be shown to me over and over. By kicking around the tool that should be my most trusted ally and partner, I was stirring up and angering the all-powerful, child humbling, athlete-exasperating baseball gods. The force of the baseball gods is not a power to be tempted or taken lightly. A combination of respect for the game and the karmic balance of life, create a force which must be respected to ensure the success we want on the baseball field.

The baseball gods smile down on those who adhere to the guiding principles of fair play, respect for all players and reverence for the game. The gods' wrath comes down hard on those who stray from the path of good sportsmanship and the pursuit of baseball purity. Many a player who has blasphemed the game by yelling at his pitcher for a walk or chastised a teammate for an error has had the gods' temper turned on them. The ball will find those who disparage others and it will create error after error or strikeout after strikeout until the offending supplicant repents and humbles himself to the game. My displeasure with my glove and my denial about the nature of my poor play turned the gaze of the baseball gods upon me and helped me to see the error of my ways. For finally realizing my poor play had nothing to do with my glove, but was more about the fact that I had no idea how to operate it, the gods rewarded me with my first savior, Coach Meeder.

My first Little League team was sponsored by Johnson's Pharmacy and we were coached by Big Mr. Meeder. Jim Meeder, a bowling ball-shaped classmate, was my teammate on Johnson's Pharmacy and his ever so patient father was the wrangler and teacher of our squirrelly squad. I was thrilled to be a part of a team, thrilled to be a part of something. My brother was involved with Boy Scouts and had come home with the uniform and the kerchief and those badges. Although a great organization, the whole notion of salutes and mottos and such just wasn't the kind of group I was looking for. Plus the fact of my being unable to sit still long enough to earn a patch made it clear to my parents that running around chasing a baseball was more the route for me. I was thrilled to be starting my baseball career, plus the new hat and uniform made up for the lack of a kerchief.

The owner of Johnson's Pharmacy, Mr. Johnson, was kind enough to let us know that for every game we won we would receive a free ice cream from his soda fountain. With this happy news, the gods were eager to demonstrate to us our first lesson in humility. Our desire for our ice cream bonus was the perfect introduction into what the game had to offer in the way of life lessons.

My first year in the big leagues, with my eye on the ice cream prize, netted not a single victory. We were 0-12 for the year. With that record a clear message was sent from the gods, it is not about the end prize, it is about what happens on the field and how you play the game that matters. Play the game for the sake of the game. All the prizes and rewards will come to you if you take care of business on the field. As long as you don't pick your head up from a ground ball and don't look any farther than the next play, you will receive the ball and all the accolades you deserve in due course. As a result of our on-field struggles, we kept our heads down and crossed the street whenever we walked by Johnson's Pharmacy. The thought of going into his store and suffering the eyes of shame was unheard of; I don't think I went into his store for years after just in case he had our team picture on the wall for identification purposes.

Mr. Meeder was our coach and the man who helped us engineer that memorable season. Coach Meeder had his hands full trying to coach us first timers in the basics of baseball, just as any coach at any level does. Every new group of kids, no matter the age, requires understanding, patience, and time in order to find the path to each player's ability. No two players are the same and no two players can be coached the same. The way to unlock the potential of each player comes from listening, watching, and matching a player's ability to learn new skills to the voice of reason he will hear the clearest.

Mr. Meeder did his best to hear the voices of reason on those late evenings in Gilson Park, just a stone's throw from the lapping waters of Lake Michigan. All of us kids spinning around, oblivious to the work at hand, must have been a nightmare to the affable father of Jim Meeder, an equally challenged baseball prodigy. Large and rotund, Coach Meeder had a way of wearing his kelly green Johnson's Pharmacy cap in a way that defied physics. It sat on his head but wasn't really pulled onto his cantaloupe-round head to any degree. Where my cap's edge butted against my ears, his sort of perched like a yarmulke at the pole of his head; it made me wonder if he used bobby pins to keep it in place. However, for all my study of Coach Meeder's hat tricks, the one thing this man had in abundance was patience. Calm and clear, Coach Meeder led us through the anxiety of our first days, guided us to the spark of our first baseball skills, and supported us through the longest winless season of my life. His coaching style was just what we first timers needed. Anything short of the extreme kindness and support he showed us and the respect he gave to the game would have sent us all running from this difficult game and into Cub Scout uniforms the next year.

A coach like Mr. Meeder is such a gift to a young man. Sure he is there to help teach the sport, but his secondary assignment is to instill confidence and a sense of self to the awakening young man. The game we are struggling to learn is about to teach us some not-too-subtle lessons in humility and failure, and the player who thinks he knows what it is all about, will be singled out by the higher powers for some special instruction. The gods will make sure that the young initiate is allowed to experience the many frustrations of the game; the errors, the strikeouts, and all the bizarre miscues that pop up at the most inopportune times. He will struggle to the breaking point of understanding his supposed greatness, and at the moment he realizes that he could be human is when a coach needs to step in and mediate between the baseball gods and his need to focus on the fundamentals. The player who wakes up to his limitations, and who really wants to play, needs to have a coach who will shows him the beauty of the game, the grace in which it can be played, and the joy that comes from fine execution. The player who doesn't want to be there, who seems to have had enough, needs a coach who can demonstrate that he wants to be his coach, and that he is there to share with the player his own love of the game. By showing the beauty of the game to his players, he demonstrates that the love of the game can make them feel good about themselves and about so much more in this life.

Mr. Meeder worked with me one hot summer day and told me I would make a pretty good pitcher. Singled out and off to the side, one on one, he patiently demonstrated the footwork required to toe the rubber and to maximize the energy in my scrawny little body. Over and over we worked to create some fluidity and grace in my delivery to the plate. I felt special not just for the attention given to me but for the chance to learn the mysteries of a motion I had only seen on TV watching the major leaguers. Here I was out on a real field learning to do what Fergie Jenkins learned to do when he was my age. But it took the love of a coach to bring me to that feeling of connection with the baseball spirit. Coach Meeder took the time to show me the mechanics of pitching, and in turn showed me the love he had for the game. I came home from practice that day and I gushed to my mom about pitching, showing her the love I now had for the game. Thanks Mr. Meeder, for giving me a little bit of your time. That afternoon you gave me a glimpse of the game and that glimpse kept me coming back for the next 40 years.

CHAPTER 6

RESPECT AND JOY

The weather holds clear and cool, a perfect afternoon for baseball at the foot of the Rocky Mountains. The boys don't yet realize what a treat it is to be out on the field away from all the distractions of the workaday world. The highlight of my day is getting out onto the field and forgetting all the little unpleasant moments that occur each day. I fret a bit through the course of the day thinking about my practice plan. Mainly I wrestle with thoughts about what I'm going to say and what skills we are going to work on. I struggle each and every day with the lesson plan, searching the vast stores of information for just the right lesson at just the right time based on where we are in the season, where we are in our development. The game of baseball, although simple in structure, is vast and intricate in its parts. My job is to boil down the different aspects of the game into a tolerable lesson that can be swallowed in a two hour dose. I lie awake in the morning and wonder throughout the day about what piece of the game we need to touch on to continue the construction of our baseball mosaic.

Here on opening day, the lessons and skills to learn are endless, but once again, the place to start is at the beginning with fundamentals. The building blocks of the game are the keys to success. If we can field, catch, throw, pitch, and run with a modicum of proficiency, we will be able to unlock the desire to excel. What we need to do is take the superstar, the sleepwalker, the force fed, and the ongoing player, and have all these varied types of individuals experience the world of success; give them a taste of what it means to succeed both personally and with their team. Once they touch success and experience the thrill of personally reaching a goal, no matter how small, then we can go on to work at reaching the larger pieces of what we came here to do; achieve success on the field and success with self will follow. Learn the game, learn thy self.

Looking at the fresh faces jogging in from the chaos of their warm-up, and all my wrestling with lesson plans quickly evaporates. I should know by now that once I hit the field, the spirit of the game will always take over. My mouth starts moving the minute I get onto the field, spewing the game I love in an endless dialogue. So much of the game is inside me that I have to work to censor myself so as not to completely overwhelm the kids with information and enthusiasm. I work hard to stay coherent and connected to the kids, using words, phrases, and jargon with which the kids can identify. This early in the season is not the time to introduce them to the mysticism of the game and the higher powers of baseball. For now I rein myself in and the kids weather another wordstorm of information and practical knowledge about baseball, hygiene, and the proper way to wear their hat. So with all eyes firmly fixed on me, at my insistence, we begin the budding new season with the first large concept for their consideration: respect.

Respect is such a big word, and the boys in front of me know very little about its true meaning. The only real exposure most of these kids have to the word comes in the form of respect your elders, a "be polite" mentality. Their experience with the concept of respect is to be quiet and subservient, don't be rude, be passive and accepting. To truly understand what respect means, one must experience all of its meanings. At the age of 50, I am still learning things about life that give me a whole new understanding and respect for my parents. The same can be said for my ongoing relationship with the game of baseball. I still show up at the baseball field and find new pieces of the game that increase my love and respect for the game. I am continually amazed at the way the game is able to create events and opportunities for young men to respect themselves, their teammates, and their opponents.

In baseball, respect has so many levels and nuances for the way it is displayed, demonstrated, and given. Through the multi-dimensional quality of respect, an understanding of the game and how it is played creates a person who is required to carry those principles beyond the game. You cannot help but respect the awesome velocity of an opposing pitcher's fastball and the audacity of a competent pitcher to throw a hard over-the-top curveball on a 3-2 count in a tight game.

The testament of such a performance requires the young player to take a little slice of humble pie back to his world. To know there are players in the world who have mastered the skills to play at the same level as you, and beyond, is to be aware of yourself and your place in the world. Respect for your fellow man and all he is capable of commands a respect for yourself as a human being. Once you have discovered the respect for yourself within the game, it is easy to start playing the game with respect for your opponent. I have seen pop flies head into the sky in a tight game with men in scoring position and the thought enters the disrespectful players mind to jinx the opposing fielder by yelling sharply or calling "I got it." The player who respects the game and his opponent will watch the play hoping for something good to happen but also knowing that the play will be made and the game will go on with more chances to come from your end.

A player learns to respect his opponent through the empathy he finds in playing the game. A player learns respect by feeling the game's powerful ability to shake himself, his team, and the other team's players into submission. Over and over, the flow of the game gives each player the choice to be in tune or not with the unwritten rules of the game; rules which are heavy on right actions, sportsmanship, honor, and respect. Do I argue this call? How do I deal with the badgering voice of the opposing catcher? Should I slide spikes high to get back at the shortstop because of a hard tag earlier in the game? Should I let the coach know that Tommy has been hanging out with some questionable people before the games?

The power of the game is its ability to teach us aspects of life by allowing us to succeed and fail in the relative safety of the field. We succeed and fail by learning how to use the experiences gleaned from the ball field to help create a person who is capable of picking himself up after a difficult failure and putting himself back in line for another game. Through this trial by fire a person is forged who has the courage to persevere on the field and who is capable of dealing with the inequities in his life.

The big messages will come in time, but for right now I want the boys to simply respect each other and their coach by showing up for practice on time. A fundamental lesson for any individual or team is a respect for the commitment each has made to themselves and to their teammates to be here. If we fail to acknowledge that we have made a commitment to each other, then the time we spend out here is simply more me time.

Playing on a team is not like playing a video game at your house. Walking out to the field, packing your gear, running, throwing, and being present is a gift you have given to yourself and to all those around you. The act of being on the field is a great present you have spent the time and energy to bring to the party. The trick is to get all of the partygoers to bring the same size present.

The player who lives and dies for the game brings everything to the party; their present is in the biggest box. The first to arrive and the last to leave, they are the kids who have the first little tickle of awakening, the first inkling that there just might be more to the game than the stick and ball. They have a hunch this game is going to get big and they are curious to see what will become of it. The quick flashes of pure joy they experience when making that smooth backhand stop in the hole and throwing a speedy runner out by a quarter of a step is not enough. These are the players who want that feeling more and more. These are the players who are starting to feel the buzz just from showing up. They know the real thrill will not happen unless they show up and get out there; they know that the more they practice the better they will get, and the better they get the greater the chance the ball will find them, and that's when they will get their next fix of baseball joy. The more joy they find the easier it becomes to find it. Soon the routine play becomes joy, soon the batting cage becomes joy, and soon the act of lacing up your spikes becomes joy. The player who wants to be here, who has to be here, knows there is something right about it all and he is dying to dig deeper to find out what more he can discover.

Not all these guys are equally as eager to be here every day after school for two hours. For the unsure players, the thought of being at practice and on the field is easier than actually being here. For the player who has simply been doing baseball unconsciously for years, the guy who still doesn't understand his relationship with the game, the time spent at the field is just another tedious chunk of time. The unconscious fellow arrives at the field in a heap of sighs and a too heavy bag which seems to him a ball and chain that he has been toting around to ball fields for years. Somewhere down the line a father or coach encouraged, prodded, or begged the child to pursue the game. Knowing no better, and with little control of his life, he found he had some talent for the sport so he accepted his lot. Once headed down the path, and with a couple of moments of glory along the way, he found he was stuck with the game. It is my task to help this baseball-Eyore find not just another moment of baseball glory, but also to help him find a way to illuminate the value of his time spent out on the field and the connection of field time to his lifetime.

Many of the boys who show up at the field have slogged their way through countless years of Little League and junior programs, however their personal baseball spark really has never caught hold. In this over-busy fast-paced world of ours we tend to organize the fun for our children to the point where they rely too heavily on their parents for their next life experience or boredom-busting fun. We do not empower, or better yet, demand that our kids take ownership of their fun. For a kid to really find the joy in sports, they need to find it on their own.

Too often the game never finds its way home and into the backyard. Where are the buddies out throwing the ball and creating new games with rubber balls bought at the local sports shop? When a boy needs a schedule to announce when it's time to have fun, then we have lost the route to joy. The task I have with the boys going through the motions is to find the path back to the joy of being on the field. I tell all the kids that being on the field is their time away. For two hours after school they can come here and yell and spit and run and play and get good at something. Their parents aren't here to nag them, their teachers and school work are forgotten, and that fight with the girlfriend will just have to wait. For this slot of time in the afternoon, you are allowed to be loud, joyous, and free. Some will take me up on the offer; others won't even know what being joyous means. The most I can do for these boys is offer them a place to come that gives them the potential for freedom and the opportunity for joy. I am here every day ready to demonstrate, coach, and play, because I too need the freedom from my daily cares and who doesn't need more joy?

CHAPTER 7

PREPARATION AND

SPORT SHAME

To this day I can't believe how far I had to ride my bicycle to get to practice. What could my mom possibly have been doing that she couldn't take me to practice? The idea that someone else needed to make sure I had fun never entered her head or mine. Two or three times a week, I put on my practice gear, packed my glove, got on my bike with my rubber spikes hanging from the handlebars and I peddled what seemed like ten miles, but was actually more like four, to baseball practice. Living and riding my bike in the suburbs of Chicago was like riding through an endless tree-shrouded park. Street after street was lined and covered over with a canopy of elm, oak, and maple trees. I rode with the anticipation of the practice ahead, happy to be on my way to play. I never took the same way twice, but invariably the route home was the path of least resistance after a strenuous practice with the large mouth of Mr. Faulk.

Mr. Faulk was what you would call a yelling coach. Rarely did you receive baseball instruction from Mr.Faulk in conversational tones; it was always at full volume. Mr. Faulk's son Robert was on the team, which was usually the case in Little League, and the only reason we had a coach at all.

Robert wasn't a particularly good baseball player, giving his best effort some of the time, but receiving the lion's share of the noise most of the time. Even though Mr. Faulk was a continuous yeller, I never really felt as though he was personally upset with me. I certainly was not the only one singled out for his high- volume instructions, any and all were subject to his high-decibel communications. And even though more than one kid was sprayed with the spittle of Mr. Faulk's disapproval, we all felt in the end that he really did care for us. We saw that Robert didn't seem to mind the emphasized emotion pouring out of his father, so we figured he probably didn't really feel as mean as he sounded. Mr. Faulk was just a yeller. When we won he yelled, when we lost he yelled. When we did just what he wanted us to do he yelled and when we screwed up he yelled. He just had to yell, it was just his way.

My father came up to me after a particularly loud game and had this concerned look on his face and wanted to know if I was okay after all the abuse I was exposed to. I didn't know what to say, we were just playing and Mr. Faulk was just coaching. Thinking back I suppose his methods weren't all that healthy for us or for himself. As a coach, when you are constantly yelling at your players, everything you say tends to take on the same level of importance, nothing really gets emphasized and the kids simply focus on the volume.

Yelling does have its place in sports, simply because there are high-stress emotional situations, however personal abuse or put downs do not. Mr. Faulk tended to get a little too excited all the time, and the fact that his boy was on the team seemed to fuel his desire for all of us to do well and perhaps put out his fire.

Thinking back on Coach Faulk, I have to believe he was simply a control junkie and father who wanted what was best for his kid and for the team. However, the problem with sports is that we are unable to control ninety percent of what happens on the field, so if you are into control and overly invested in the outcome of the game, you will most likely have a problem with your emotions. The only thing we can really control on the field is what we do with our bodies, how we handle adversity, and what we do with the outcome. In order to put ourselves into the best position to take on the uncontrollable and to handle the inevitable adversity, we need to brace ourselves and prepare for the diabolical fun the game is about to dish out.

How we prepare physically for the game and the season is up to each player. The hard work of endless drills, running, and repetition that a player puts in during the course of the spring months will no doubt pay off during the games in May and into the summer season. The average joe ball player has a hard time seeing the forest for the trees when the early season workouts begin. "Long term" and "down the road" are terms the young person has a hard time conceptualizing. I have a hard enough time getting young players to put a snack and a jacket in their gear bag for their hunger and for the snow flying in the third inning. Unfortunately the preparation for that doubleheader we will play in June starts in March, however, the thought of those games is lost to most players in early April.

How we prepare for a game a day and an hour in advance can also be tough to fathom for the average fifteen year old. Warming up muscles seems to be second in importance to warming up mouths full of stories of Susie in math class. Every year I watch the boys stumble off the bus after a long bumpy ride to the far corners of Denver with the thought that they have spent an hour with no idea of what is to come on the field. The endless drone of the bus and the excitement of missing that last period math class creates a layer of crud on the psyche of my players which is hard to scrub off before the first pitch. Some are able to run, stretch, and throw their way through the fog to find their game face, while others don't find it until we climb back aboard for the ride home. Focusing our thoughts on the task ahead requires the player to once again want to experience the joy of making the play that can't be made.

Everything comes to those in the increments to which they desire them. Big effort brings big rewards. I believe that is a law of the universe and I know the baseball gods demand it. Any player can have a day where they put in a minimal effort, take the field, and in one shining moment have the game winning ball get inexplicably stuck in their glove, and by accident become the hero. The gods will give you that moment where you do the least and achieve the most, simply as a test to see if you are paying attention and to see if you are willing to want that moment again. Most likely that player will not see the same outcome again any time soon. The next time, the ball will tip off his glove because he isn't ready on the pitch and the ball will get by him and roll to the wall. The player will come into the dugout scratching his head, moaning about how he almost had it, or, "If only I had just..." Those moments of excellence and success are given to you to see if you have it in you to do what it takes to pursue more baseball joy.

How we handle the moments of adversity are the result of all the elements of our baseball makeup and personality. We all bring our constructed personalities to the game, and we build our baseball self on top of and along side that base personality. As we play the game, we learn to accept the ups and downs of the game whether we understand the reasons for the flow or not.

Some players begin to understand the way the game goes, and they work hard to insulate themselves from the turbulence by being prepared. Preparation takes away some of the uncomfortable feelings players go through after a loss or individual error. There is no worse feeling than when the game lands on your shoulders and you aren't ready or fully prepared to make the play presented to you. Your teammates may rally around you to make you feel better. They may pick you up the way good teammates do, but inside you know and have to live with what really happened. The player with strong game-heart hates the deception of the moment and doesn't want to have to feel that way again. He knows he wasn't prepared and no one can make him feel better or take away the thought that he let his team and himself down. The player with heart becomes a changed man and works to eliminate the possibility of having to experience the icky feeling of sport shame, demanding more of himself and his teammates so they don't have to experience that remorse again.

CHAPTER 8
WINNING, LOSING, AND CHARACTER

How we handle the results of a game is also in our control. Having prepared ourselves mentally and physically for the game, and having learned to avoid sport shame through focus and attention, we should have no trouble with a ten-run mercy killing by the state champs, right? Well, maybe. Winning and losing are funny things; neither is easy and both require a concentrated effort to feel comfortable on the ride home. Losing is never easy, never fun, and rarely feels good.

The response to a loss is pretty straightforward, don't like it, and don't want to feel it again. Each player needs to review his part in the game and make sure that his game was sound and that he was clear about the role he played in the loss. When a team loses, the story is usually clear about what went wrong and what can be done better. Each player needs to be honest with himself about what he could have done better to further the cause in creating a victory. The main component in reviewing a loss is the honest assessment by each player about the role they played in the game.

Rarely is a game lost on one play. I have had to console so many young players who unfortunately happened to be the last guy to touch the ball in a mad dash play to throw a guy out at the plate or to try to get the last out on the mound. I have been the guy that has to pat the back or put my arm around the guy who had the final strikeout with men in scoring position. I am the one who has to help the miserable victim in an attempt to assuage the notion that he was the reason we didn't win the ball game. The truth of the matter is the last pitcher inserted into the game who gives up a base hit in the final inning, which happens to score the winning run, is not the cause of the loss. However, if that pitcher was thinking about Susie and joking with the warm-up catcher before the inning started instead of preparing himself to do the best job he could for himself and his team… then maybe he was at fault. But generally there are a myriad of moments throughout the course of a game which could have gone differently if only a player had been a bit more tuned into the events at hand. Again, all of the participants in each of these moments must honestly access their part in the play and determine whether they could have done more to help their team. The bus ride home will be long and quiet for all those players with true hearts, for they will know inside whether or not they had a hand in derailing the game; lesson learned…maybe.

Winning has its own special set of issues which each player with true heart and a respect for the game must contend with. If you happen to be on the giving end of a ten-run mercy killing of your cross-town rival, the obligation to yourself and the game is a heavy one. What if that cross-town rival beat the crap out of you the last time you played, and in the course of the game they were not very respectful to your team or to you? The comments made about your pitcher and about your girlfriend Susie who was sitting in the stands did not sit too well. In fact, because of the way the game played out, your team became highly motivated to get back at those bums for the way they ran rough shod over your team.

How does a player handle the next game to be played? The emotions involved in a large magnitude game with a lot on the line are difficult for a young man to handle. The need for revenge and honor are real emotions which require our attention. The actions of our rivals have stirred us up to the point of distraction, to the point where anger is the only emotion ruling us. To win baseball games, we must play for ourselves, our team, and for the game. If we approach the game with attention to solid mental and physical preparation, the results will be a quality effort with acceptable emotions and feelings which in turn will make for a good night's sleep.

The same feeling of sport shame and queasy disgust can follow a player after a big win just as with a big loss. If we go out and bad mouth the opposing pitcher and find the shortstop's girlfriend to taunt, then we become the same thug that tore the last game apart. By allowing our emotions to rule our spirit we may win the game, but the next time the teams meet we will be on the receiving end of a motivated team which wants nothing more than to tear us down.

Every victory brings with it the responsibility of being a player who is proud of how he represented himself on the field and who is respectful of the other team no matter how that team conducted themselves. Too often I have to watch an opposing team display the negative abusive attitude of its coach. The loud-mouth macho man who is more interested in his win-loss record and how he looks on the field instead of how his players play the game is a way too familiar sight. Does he win baseball games? Sure he does, but at what cost?

I believe a coach can be intense and compassionate at the same time. He can be aggressive and benevolent without giving away his manhood. Those are the behaviors a player needs to mirror from his coach. Rising above the primal emotions of big ego, anger, and selfishness is not easy and it starts with the coach. Presented with a Neanderthal team across the diamond, a coach must lead the way so his players don't fall prey to playing the game of attack, anger, and loss of control. The players need to take care of their emotions because we cannot control what kind of jerk the other guy is going to be. The only thing we can control is how we play the game. The goal for the player interested in maturity and growth is to play with heart, respect, and dignity, so that win or lose, the ride home is shame free.

The level of maturity all this high-minded thinking and behaving requires is generally beyond the scope of most young men. Hormones, peer pressure, and exposure to the tirades of professional athletes create a world which allows for the emotional outburst to be okay. It is the one or two special guys which every group of players produces who need to be the messengers of civility. Leaders are those players who are best able to model the emotions and actions of a person beyond the examples most young men are exposed to.

Leadership is a trait foreign to most young men. However, when these fledgling adults see actions that are brave and true from their teammates, they will naturally gravitate toward them. Sticking out and sticking up for principles of truth, honor, and decency are scary thoughts which most young men shy away from in a group setting; something as simple as picking up the helmets without being told or chasing a foul ball over the fence before being assigned the duty are huge acts of bravery in the adolescent world. And the player who voices a concern to the coach in front of the group can take on mythical proportions in the eyes of the less brave.

We all have the desire to be a hero and a leader, but acting on those feelings is a hard boundary to cross for a person who is making his way through the mine field of youth. However, most kids are willing to be a disciple of a higher way of thinking as long as the general consensus is in favor of flying that flag. The dynamics of a team usually allow that once the better players are on board with a given ideal the rest will follow. When the "too cool for anything" superstar shortstop realizes the team is adrift without any team guidance and steps up to lead, the other players are more than willing to jump aboard. And once the players realize the game requires a larger investment than just their own small interests that is when the game takes on a brighter light. The higher principles of the game start to mirror the higher principles of life; the lessons on the field begin to guide the young men in the conduct of their lives.

A few of the players will feel the game has something special to offer them, so illuminating the message and demonstrating its worth is not a tough sell, and in turn the message will be carried to the disciples. For all the players the lessons of honor, respect, and dignity are lessons which will have to be demonstrated through multiple wins and losses.

Wearing these large concepts is a heavy mantle that requires fortification and strengthening of character. The game is more than willing to demonstrate the need for a player to raise himself up, doling out never- ending blows and tests to his psyche. As a coach it is my job to point out the ways in which each player can conduct himself in these tough-testing situations, and it is my job to require certain principles of sportsmanship and decency be carried out by all.

CHAPTER 9
A COACH'S
RESPONSIBILITY

The tone a coach sets for the game and for his team is paramount to the development of his player's character. Leadership is modeled by the coach, as is honor, respect, and a love for the principles of the game. Everything starts at the top, so a coach needs to be on guard at all times in both manner and speech.

Mr. Faulk was not a coach who necessarily demonstrated restraint and composure at all times, yet he was successful and most of the time got his point across. I take with me onto the field all the coaches who have helped me and inspired me as a player and person. The best advice I received when I started coaching was to take all the good aspects of the coaches I have had through the years and combine all those good qualities together. The coach I am today is a testament to not only all those good qualities but also to the bad elements in the coaches I have had and who I have observed.

Not all coaches are the same and not all coaches have the same style. There are plenty of great coaches who used loud demonstrative methods and fiery temper to convey strength and passion. Often you hear of a coach who is known for his impassioned loud style on the field but who is known by his players to be a caring well-meaning mentor to all. The balance between emotion and composure, passion and abuse, crazy and calm is a balance with which all coaches must struggle.

Every coach is faced with the uncertainty of the game combined with the disjointed and uncertain play of his players. The ability of seemingly normal and generally talented young athletes to go brain dead at the most inopportune times is an unending source of dismay for all coaches. Many pre-game chats between coaches turns into a swapping of can-you-believe stories that get wilder and wilder with each coach leaving the discussion feeling that they don't have it so bad after all.

Every coach needs to find the style that suits him best and use it to its full effect. Trying to be something you are not is never a wise decision in sports or in any other venue. The quiet guy comes across as fake and forced when he tries to be the hot head. The passion a coach feels for the game needs to come to the surface in whatever form is natural for him given who he is. I am by nature an analytical guy who is very competitive when it comes to sports. I will get worked up in the course of a game and I work to keep my emotions in check when dealing with umpires and boneheaded plays. On the other hand, I will discuss at length with a player about a mechanical issue or proper procedure on a given play until I see the light go on in his head or until he has heard enough from me and his eyes beg to be let go in order to digest the material.

As a player, my competitive nature would get me worked up and impassioned throughout the game; as a coach, I have to restrain those emotions and work to keep myself in check for the good of the team and as a model for the boys. I am not saying that emotions have no place in the game, but a controlled approach more often than not will get you farther. I have yet to see a call by an umpire be reversed after a coach came out of the dugout and argued and screamed and fussed. At the same time, I have yet to see a call by an umpire be reversed after a coach came out of the dugout and discussed politely the decision made by the esteemed gentleman in black. However, I have seen an umpire give me a call later in a game because I treated him with decency earlier in the game. And I have seen an umpire work with my kids, talking to them to inform them about rules and decisions made because we all treated him with respect.

Being emotional with a player can be a tricky situation which requires knowledge of the player and control of tone. Knowing your players is critical to how you address issues of attitude, talent, discipline, behavior, conduct, and all aspects of game comportment. Not all kids will respond to the same approach when it comes to presenting information about their play or behavior.

The more talented kids are not always interested in your assessment of their play because for their whole career they have been praised and coddled by fawning coaches and grateful teammates. Sometimes the talented ones need to fall hard to be willing to accept the coaching they need. The struggling superstar is ripe for the lessons you have been waiting to give. So when the big slump comes or the gods seek them out on the field for that three error inning, you have to be ready with the words they need. The speech isn't about how good you are and to keep your chin up, the speech is about respect. The gifted athlete has an obligation to respect the game and his talent by working harder than anyone else because he has a gift. Realizing the game gets harder the higher you go is a lesson that the best need to learn in order for them to wake up from their privileged run.

Dealing with the multiple personalities that come to the park every day is an ongoing learning experience for the coach. Balancing the lessons each individual player needs to learn with the complex emotions a child growing up in our society today must deal with is a tough task. The socioeconomic differences, multiple parents, and various learning issues are all factors which make the job of a coach who wants to have an impact that much more challenging. Yet, if you pay attention to the interaction of the kids in practice, the banter on the bench, and the response of the individual to the adversity and success on the field, the picture becomes clear as to what a kid can handle and what his character is really made.

The sensitive kid who doesn't handle the kidding on the bus well is not going to excel when a coach calls him out in front of the team. In turn, the loud mouth on the bus who dishes out the digs is in need of a lesson in humility and will most likely accept and respond to the instruction from a well-meaning coach. A coach needs to have his eyes and ears open at all times so he can tap into the energy of his team in order to use it most effectively to win games and guide players. Given all the areas of observation available to the coach, the path becomes clear as to what can be said and how the material can be presented to help a player become a man.

A person's actions on the field have consequences whether you are a coach or a player. We need to monitor our behavior on the field just as we do when we are in society. To simply react to situations as they come up does not elevate us in any way; it only creates actions for which we usually have to apologize. Just because we are on the field in this created world of sport does not give us license to behave in ways which are unacceptable to what we know to be right. Reaction to the ball is different than a reaction to an event. One is physical and the other is emotional, and we must learn to develop the instinct of the first and learn to harness the feelings of the second. If we are able to allow the flow of our physical self to happen in the moment, we will find great success on the field. However, if we do not harness and guide our emotions, we will have to deal with repairing our honor at every turn.

These principles apply to both the player and the coach. Too often I have had my own long ride home in which the nagging feelings of doubt and shame linger in my mind. Saying the wrong thing to a fragile player or reacting to the events on the field in a manner unbecoming to a coach always leaves a bad taste which is hard to wash away. The responsibility to encourage and further a kid instead of knocking him down is a duty that needs to be guarded at all cost. Never have I seen a kid excel at his sport with the fear of retribution in his mind.

The job of a coach is to guide, encourage, and teach each player. Discipline and admonition are a part of those precepts, but they must be used within a positive framework of teaching the sport and the person. A player knows when he has failed physically on the field, the question becomes how does he learn from it? The conduct and character of a player is modeled by his coach and teammates, and wavering from what is expected needs to be pointed out by his coach and teammates. The group will guide the conduct and the coach will encourage better play. The game will humble, and balance will be found.

Chapter 10
The March through Little League Begins

The lessons I learned from the field and my path to manhood continued after my painful time with Mr. Meeder and the winless season. Getting involved with the game was my first step on a long journey which eventually landed me on the high school practice field as a coach. But to get there, I was slowly seduced by the lure of the great play, the solid contact, and the bond of taking the field with a group of friends and fellow knuckleheads.

Little League was calling, the great American institution and training ground for little baseball hopefuls throughout the land. All across the country, kids were taking to their bicycles with gloves in tow, heading to ball fields to learn the trade. Even though I was winless in my first season I was back for more, hoping to at least find a victory.

Mr. Faulk was my C league coach in Little League. In the town of Wilmette, we had three levels of Little League, A, B, and C. Just like in the minor league farm system of professional baseball there was a parent team, the A team, which had a B and C team feeding into that highest team. I was selected to play for Heurter Post, the local American Legion chapter. Heurter Post was the A team, Lymon Sargeants was the B team and Kelly's Appliances the C team. Our primary color for all these teams was maroon. Maroon hat, maroon socks, and maroon lettering on our uniform. For the next three years, I could be tracked down in any crowd by the maroon hat which rarely left my head except for the winter months. I aspired to play at the A league level, but coming from a team that was 0-12 for a reason, I was relegated to the bottom C level. The goal was always to play with the top team, but my journey to the elite A league was not to be a swift one.

The story of my baseball career was one of slow and steady progress. I was not the gifted natural baseball player, however I was a well put-together little athlete. Tow haired and swift, I was undoubtedly one of the fastest kids on the playground. So fast in fact that the games of chase and mad dashes from adoring third grade girls offered no challenge and often left me all alone on the far side of the playground when, moments before, I thought I was being pursued. Lithe and quick, I was a first round pick in all games of kickball, dodge ball, and football. However my skills in baseball developed just as the designers of Little League had envisioned...methodical and measured.

Although blessed with the ability to run and jump with reckless abandon, the practiced skills of the baseball diamond required me to work hard and learn to be good. My year with Mr. Faulk in C league was one of loud instruction and hard work. My goal, in my second year of play, was to improve my batting skills, get my glove to work properly, and to earn some praise from the noisy one. By the end of the year, I had achieved some success in all these areas and was moved to the B league team to help in their playoff run.

The next year found me climbing onto the second rung of the Little League ladder, a solid B player, still working hard to get to the elite A league team. My tortoise-pace progress was just as it should be in the eyes of Little League even though it pained me to see others jumping ahead. I was not the phenomenal athlete that shows up at tryouts with more frequency these days. I had to work hard to progress through the system, but the work was fun and most of the time the work was done on the empty lot out back, at a friend's house, or in the backyard with my dad.

Jonathan, the friend who got me started on this baseball journey, was never a teammate of mine through most of my early baseball days. He was a stocky hardnosed kid who came from a household of four; a home in constant turmoil and chaos. Going to Jonathan's house was an adventure that a kid from an orderly house of two kids and a cat never quite got used to. The big red house on the corner always seemed to have some crisis or uprising spilling out its doors. The saving grace of the Cullen household was that it had five yards in which to play and endless games and adventures waiting to be invented and discovered. The dog yard, where they kept their drippy-eyed cocker spaniel, was a jungle of weeds and plants ripe for catching bees and wasps in killing jars. The front yard was the prime location for acorn fights which would escalate until someone cried. The side yard to the street was banked with a wall of hedges a mile high that offered the perfect cover for throwing snowballs at cars in the winter. The other side yard was our field for sport and activities such as full contact leaf catching, tackle hippity-hop, hot box (now called pickle), and of course our endless games of pitcher-catcher.

Jonathan was a catcher. He was the perfect catcher in so many ways. Built tough and strong, he had legs built for squatting. He looked like a catcher and loved the grit of being the dirt-ball behind the plate. We would spend hours in his side yard, playing pitcher and catcher, working on our stuff, developing our arsenal of pitches for batters that always struck out. We measured our distance, cut out a pitching rubber from a piece of plywood and pounded into the ground. We created the greatest imaginary battery the world had ever known on the greatest imaginary field there could ever be. As a pitcher we never got tired, never got into trouble, never had to have a visit by the manager, and we were always undefeated.

The other tool we used to help develop our young baseball bodies was the game of hot box also known as the game of pickle. We would buy these great rubber balls at the Woolworth store downtown that were perfect for the game. Perfect because, unlike hardballs, these balls would never end the game early due to a concussion or major eye contusion.

The game of pickle consisted of two bases, two basemen, and any number of runners. The object was to get from one base to the other without the basemen tagging you out, simple. As simple and somewhat boring as the game sounds, hours would go by in which endless running, throwing, sliding, diving, laughing, and cursing would happen. We had epic games of hot box at Tom Clark's house where my brother, two years older, and our neighborhood friend Tom Clark, also two years older, would do battle against Jonathan and myself. Tom's yard was set up perfectly for the game, and Jonathan and I would work on all of our baseball skills while teaching the older boys a lesson. Laughing and running all afternoon and into the evening, we were slowly getting better at the basic skills of baseball and at the same time learning the rules of sportsmanship and fair play. Although Tom and my brother were older than us, they were not as good as Jonathan and I in the baseball department, so we had to be careful in our taunts during their drubbing. If we were too aggressive, the game would fall apart, too much abuse and we would end up alone. So feelings were monitored and scores kept close which kept the game going well into the night.

Where are the games of pickle these days? How many kids are in their backyard pitching in the bottom of the ninth with the bases loaded, two outs, and the best hitter coming to the plate? Where are the games that teach us to be humble in play and careful with friend's feelings?

More and more the only time kids get together to play is when an adult has organized it and a fee has been paid. Unorganized play is where the first repercussions of kid's actions hit home. When your best friend has a problem with your behavior and you realize you need to fix the hurt or be alone, that is when you learn to negotiate the price of friendship. All the complexities of getting along with another individual become magnified when the dimension of sport is added. Not only do you have to deal with the personality of your friend at rest, but you have to deal with his sport personality. I have encountered many people who are mild-mannered easy-going guys on a sunny afternoon, but put them in a competitive situation and a whole different guy shows up.

The formation of one's sport-self has its roots in the games we played in our youth, and in how we were treated in those sport situations. Again, the better athlete has the responsibility of setting the tone for sport interaction at the early stage. Most young people are oblivious to the impact they have on the formation of the sport-self in others. Yet most kids feel that fair play makes for a better time, so it's important to regulate the quality of play to ensure everyone has an experience that promotes a healthy sport-self. If the great player rubs his greatness into everyone's face or abuses the mere mortal athlete with in-your-face antics then the game becomes tainted, the future games are in jeopardy, and the seeds of future poor-sports are sowed.

Given the diverse group of kids in my neighborhood, we accepted everyone into the pick-up games on the empty lot or in the street out front…even girls. The level of ability of each kid was a known value, and each kid knew where he stood in the hierarchy of sandlot play. However, knowing all the levels of play did not always make for fair and noble treatment. Kids are cruel at times, and the heat of the battle brings out the best and the worst of the sport-self.

Spirits and feelings are crushed on the fields of school yards throughout the country everyday. The sport-self of many young athletes is formed from the reaction of teammates to dropped passes, missed fly balls, strikeouts and unintended blunders. The slights, put downs, and disappointments of classmates and teammates form the basis for our future sport-self. So when Bill from the office invites you to play racquetball and he turns into the Tasmanian devil on the court and blows a cog when you call the winning point out, just know that sometime in the past little Billy probably suffered some indignation at the hands of the sport gods and insensitive uber-athletes.

Now that kids are more apt to get their sports feedback from an organized activity or gym class, it's important that coaches be prepared to mold the sport-self in a manner which makes the future racquetball game pleasurable. We are in the midst of the baby-boom coach craze in which all those sandlot players from the sixties are now in charge of coaching their children. We need to be careful not to perpetuate the damaged sport-self to the next generation. The coach and the gym teacher are now the primary sport educators in a kid's life, so it's imperative that they take care in the way they administer the life lessons sports have to offer. The old school methods of "suck it up" and "be tough" don't necessarily work with the youth of today. A play-and-learn approach can be the best way to teach younger kids. Let them experience the game, learn the game, and then direct the inevitable conflict in a positive way so all the participants understand the dynamics of resolving the fracas.

We also need to be careful not to go too far in the other direction and protect the young athlete from all forms of disappointment and self-reflection. The participation award is a prime example of insulating children from the reality of sport and in turn denying some of the lessons of life. Sports are activities which provide a child with an opportunity to grow as a person and learn more about how to handle adversity in their world. When we strive to achieve and in turn fall short of our goal a lesson is learned and discipline is created. The drive to excel usually starts with failure. Although telling a kid that just participating is great and wonderful it doesn't really motivate the child to want to work hard and achieve greatness. Just participating is not always what is best.

Many of the coaches that perpetuate this idea of participation is enough are sport-self damaged kids from the past who do not want others to suffer the way they did on the field of play.

The goal of the coach needs to be to teach the reality of sport and to strengthen the individual in their ability to handle the endless waves of success and failure. It is only when we are given all the information and are made aware of what is to come that we will be prepared to accept the feelings which will surely follow. Knowing the measure of success at the plate is 33% and that failure will occur roughly two out of every three times at bat needs to be known so the inevitable failure can be fully understood. We continue to strive forward because we know success is out there, but we also know it will take some pain to fully appreciate the joy of our success.

CHAPTER 11
HIGH SCHOOL PLAYERS

After a week of practice, the boys are no longer an immediate danger to themselves or to their teammates, for the most part. The tearing down of all the old habits and the diffusing of ingrained information from all the well-intentioned dad-coaches will take some time and will be an on-going process for much of the season. A player who has reached the high school level finds the game of baseball changes dramatically in speed and skill. Even though a good number of the kids have been playing on some of the competitive teams in the area, logging fifty and sixty games a year, the step to the high school level is big.

Several factors make high school ball a unique barrier for the young player. One factor is the intense rivalries and school affiliations which are now a huge new pressure for the boys. The pride of putting on the colors of your school and going up against the cross-town rival or the league powerhouse is a powerful emotion which requires close monitoring. By adding a level of expectation, we set up another source for emotional disaster and emotional elation which once again creates an opportunity for spiritual growth either way.

As incoming freshman and second year sophomores, the ability to face the big game is a mixed bag. Some of the better players have faced big games, and they have experienced the joy and the heartbreak that such big stage competition can bring. The thrill and joy of playing hard and coming out on top in the big game is a feeling that some never get a chance to feel. But for those who have experienced the unique high of victory and success, the continual desire for that joy becomes strong. Other kids have never felt the tingle that only a big victory can bring. Some are players from average teams who never won anything, or worse, came from a program that simply rewarded the child for participation. Even the kids who lost the big game know the feeling of being there and being a part of the big game. Although a big-game loss can be devastating, the desire to want the big smile and happy dog-pile of victory will burn strong afterwards.

Another factor which makes the high school level so unique is the maturation of the body. The bodies of the kids coming into high school are beginning to grow, fill out, and get strong. In this day and age, kids have access to weight training, nutritional supplements, good food, and private coaching. All of these elements, if taken advantage of, can create faster, stronger, more advanced players than we have ever seen before. The player who wants an edge or who has aspirations to go further in the game and play college baseball has at his disposal a myriad of resources to achieve that goal. The development of physical prowess is available to every player; however the trick is to develop the mental skills of the game as well. Too often a player comes along who has every physical advantage working for him, but for one reason or another, the player lacks a piece of the mental makeup needed to be great. Sometimes the player has been the golden child of the youth leagues and has never had to push himself, or worse, never had anyone push him. Other times the player has never accepted the responsibility of his talent and has failed to develop his fundamentals, making him the most troublesome candidate for baseball skills re-education.

The hardest player to coach at the high school level is the player who has been the star and thinks he knows the game and how it is played. At the high school level, the talent jumps in ever greater degrees from year to year. The player who thinks he has it all figured out now faces kids who are every bit as good as he is, however, the difference is that many of those players know they need to continue to work hard to get better. The motivated player of average ability will win out over the complacent phenom more times than not and most assuredly over time.

The game of baseball, as with most any endeavor, will reward the person who has the desire to unlock all that he and the game has to offer. Being involved with the game for over forty years, I continue to be amazed at what the game can teach me in my life, and how much better the game can be played at every level when players allow themselves to be taught both by coaches and by the game.

The high school game is the first real measuring stick for any player who wishes to pursue the game of baseball to a higher level. Most kids' eyes are opened when the tryouts reveal that there are players far better than they are. It can be a shock to see the first baseman from last year who couldn't tie his shoes without falling over and who could barely hit the ball out of the infield is now picking balls out of the dirt with style and crushing baseballs into the gap. It can be a hard pill to swallow when your best friend who you have played baseball with for years and first inspired you to play the game is tabbed to catch for the JV squad while you stay back on the sophomore team.

The sorting of players and the sorting of people by talent becomes all too real at the age of fifteen, and it is a process we will encounter for years to come in the work world. Coming to high school and beginning the march through a sports program will require more than just the ability to play, it requires the ability to become conscious in your own life. I demand full attention be paid to the game you have chosen to play and I demand full awareness of what the game does to you as a person. Being awake for the action happening all around a young man is a large expectation to have. Half the time, a young man walks through his life never seeing the simplest actions or acknowledging the wonders all around. We expect some of that inward self absorption from our youth, however, if you bring that mental fog to the baseball field, you will not have much success, and if you are not careful you may not be aware of the line drive headed toward your melon.

The arrival on campus and on the playing field is an opportunity for the young man to become a smarter student and a greater athlete. Both of these endeavors require more effort than the student athlete realizes because, whether they know it or not, the lessons to be learned extend far beyond the classroom or the baseball diamond. The lessons they learn start in class and at practice but they are actualized and acknowledged at home and in the years ahead. We need to make sure the foundation is laid for the formation of people who we want to have walking around amongst us all.

CHAPTER 12
"A" LEAGUE

As I worked my way through the Little League system I continued to get better and better. Each year I took one step forward in the alphabetical system of the Little League program, changing uniforms and chasing my friend Jonathan up the ladder. Finally at the age of twelve I reached the top of the league, playing for the Heurter Post A team, the top maroon team in the division.

The A league teams played at beautiful Roemer Park, a fully enclosed field with a dark green fence in the outfield, dugouts, and a concession stand...I had finally made it to the big time: hot dogs, popcorn, a PA system and The Star Spangled Banner sung before the first game of the day. Many of my friends had already experienced the thrill of playing at Roemer and were a bit jaded by the time I arrived. Jonathan, due to the fact of our birthdays, had already been playing for a year at the park and was a Roemer veteran. However, bicycling down the little hidden gravel driveway next to Westmoreland Country Club and turning the corner through the entrance to the parking lot and seeing the freshly mown green outfield meant the world to me. It happened every time I came through the gate, that feeling of excitement, nervousness, and joy all rolled into one big smile. I never became jaded; I had worked way too hard to become jaded. I had played at way too many of the crap fields throughout the Wilmette system to take this beautiful site for granted. I never wanted to leave after my game. I usually had a hotdog and bag of popcorn after my game and watched other games for another hour or two because I couldn't tear myself away from the sheer beauty of that green grass and fine dirt. I couldn't wait to get back out there and play the next game, so I would often come to the field early, usually way too early, and watch the game before ours, waiting and then greeting the rest of my team as they trickled to the ball park.

The group of guys I played with and some of the boys I played against were all solid kids, all developing into quality baseball players. Sometimes you see a set of boys who grow up together and seem to mesh well, and they end up doing great things in sports because they have the same desire and love of the game. We were that class, that group who loved to be out playing the games and learning to be better at whatever sport we were presented. At the age of twelve, we were starting to play a brand of baseball that looked like the real thing; hitting homers, turning double plays, throwing curve balls and generally playing the game with style and savvy. The game was not an activity for us, it was a part of us. Baseball was just another piece of our personality, another integral part of our makeup which defined us and made us who we were, young ballplayers... budding young men.

Heurter Post was a solid team and a real powerhouse in the world of twelve-year-old baseball. Our catcher Sam was the biggest most powerful kid I had ever known. His great size coupled with the use of an illegally corked bat made him a potent threat at the plate and a solid force behind it. Bruce Sonen was our ace on the mound, a long haired free spirit who had the first Wilson A2000 baseball glove I had ever seen, a glove I coveted mightily. Bruce also possessed the nastiest curveball around, which went nicely with his sneaky whip-arm fastball. For my part I was an up-and-coming shortstop who had a great set of hands and a consistent bat. Sprinkle in some other solid players around the diamond and we were able to put together a winning record which eventually won us the league championship. The coach of this team was a man by the name of Mort Schachtel and he would be the coach who would set me on the path to baseball enlightenment.

Mort Schachtel was a gravel-voiced commodities broker from the west side of town, the Jewish side of town. Many of my team-mates lived in West Wilmette, an area and way of life which was always a mystery to me. They were an exotic group of people to me, they did things differently, a little more advanced, a little more mature, edgy. The girls were accessible and open and the guys wiser and bawdier than the straight laced East Wilmette crowd.

Coach Schachtel and the west side crowd brought a brand of baseball to the park that was raw, basic, and successful. I guess you could call it old school baseball, however, that term is misleading because successful baseball is simply baseball done well. Coach Schachtel played the game from the ground up. Make the plays in the field by being in position and using good fundamentals. Score runs at the plate by being smart and aggressive. Simply take advantage of the situations that are presented and capitalize on those situations by bunting, stealing, and putting pressure on the opposition. Have your pitchers throw strikes, develop all your pitchers, and be willing to make changes when necessary. All these strategies are simple solid baseball axioms which, when applied, will generally result in good things happening on the field. So what made Coach Schachtel so successful as a coach? What set him apart from the other guys who tried to apply the same baseball formula but came up short? Coach Schachtel had compassion for his players and a love and respect for the game.

Coach Schachtel's voice sounded as though he had smoked a pack of cigarettes while munching a bowl of glass for breakfast. Screaming and yelling every day down on the floor of the commodities board along with that pack of cigarettes had created a voice that was truly unique. I believe at the end of the day, when he arrived at practice, Coach Schachtel had no desire to scream any more, in fact it was all we could do to hear what he had to say when he used his regular voice. The big burly guy with the voice of gravel had us all leaning in listening intently to hear the words coming from his mouth. We didn't want him to have to repeat anything as it sounded like such an effort just to get it out the first time. He was able to explain the game to us in simple straightforward language and with a style that conveyed the importance of the material. When he made a decision on the field we knew he meant what he said and that was that. However, for all his gruff talk, he always had a kind word for strong effort and an encouraging word for effort gone awry.

My strongest memory of Coach Schachtel, outside of the voice which I can still hear in my head, is one particular game in which I was struggling in the field. Coach Schachtel had given me the nickname of "Hoover," in reference to the vacuum cleaner for the way I sucked up any ground ball near me. Well, that day I made an error early in the game, and shortly after that another ball came my way which I also booted. Feeling down and kicking myself for my inability to make the plays, I started to really doubt my ability and to question if I knew how to field a ground ball. Sensing my moment of doubt and weakness, the baseball gods sent a third ball to me and, because I had lost all manner of confidence, I got down on one knee in an attempt to corral the ball into my glove. Letting the ball play you instead of playing the ball is a cardinal sin for any infielder and I was being played like a fiddle. I failed to field the third ball of the inning and looked to the sky for answers. I felt two feet tall and wanted to crawl away and never play this stupid game ever again. Despondent and humiliated I heard Coach Schachtel calling time out. His mammoth frame was heading to the field, probably to tell me to go home. Coach put his arm around me and said, "Smitty, you are my guy, you are the best fielder I have and you will always be Hoover to me. I want you to finish the inning at third base." That was the only game I ever played at third base and it was for only one inning. The next inning, I went back out to shortstop with my head up even though I didn't feel very secure in my abilities. The support Coach Schachtel gave me when I got back to the bench and the lift the rest of the team offered me was enough to at least get me back to my position. I can't say I was hoping for the ball to come my way, and the taunts from the other team about hitting it to the shortstop didn't help, but I did get through the game.

Not only did I make it though the game, but I was able to laugh at myself afterwards and take the good natured ribbing of my team-mates. I don't know what I would have done if I had a coach who yelled and screamed and put me down for what happened in that inning. I wonder how many kids have moved on from the game of baseball because of a coach who put himself before his players and the game. Coach Schachtel would play an even greater role in the growth of my young life when he would be my coach on a team destined to define my baseball and young adult world.

CHAPTER 13
SOPHOMORES

As expected, the March weather changes and the wind and rain sweep into the Rockies forcing us inside. Sometimes we receive a foot of snow late into the spring, and because of it we spend our days inside the school working on conditioning and dreaming of dry dirt. The varsity players use the prime space in the gym while the sophomore squad is relegated to the hallways and tiled floors of the student commons. We are forced to share space with the clubs and peripheral activities of the school which many of the jocks never knew existed. Rolling ground balls to each other and doing drill work next to the "mathletes" and forensic kids puts the bug in us to get out of here. We ache to be outside and we welcome the chance to feel the handful of bees that a miss-hit on a cold day can bring.

However, the time spent inside can be a useful time if used well. Conditioning the body is an important part of our preparation for the season ahead. There are books filled with endless drills on general body development as well as information for baseball-specific activities all of which can be done indoors. We work the drills and I listen to the grunts and complaints and the pining for a ball to throw.

The time inside is a great way to measure the makeup of your team and to get a read on the character of each boy. Coming from the Midwest, you hear talk of the old Midwest work ethic, the nose to the grindstone and all that. This country was built on the stalwart backs of men and women who awoke early each day and headed off to jobs which were neither monetarily nor emotionally rewarding. Yet each day these folks headed out to do the work that was needed so they could advance themselves and their families in the world. The selflessness our parents and their parents demonstrated is a quality not easily duplicated or found in our society today. The desire to work hard and do what is necessary to achieve a goal sounds simple, but for many young people today, hard work and goal setting are foreign concepts.

Looking at the struggling boys as they do the plank drill to work their abs, I can easily see whether or not these boys have the desire to achieve their goals because it is written on their face. Some will do whatever it takes while others wait for me to look away so they can relax and take it easy. The task at hand is to help all the boys discover what their goals are and how they can achieve them.

The motivated high-achieving athlete does not have the problem of wanting to be great; he is already well on his way, he may have other issues, but wanting to be good is generally not one of them. His goal will be to stay committed and to continue to build on the gifts he has. The average athlete also wants to be great but he has to battle the doubts and failures which come with trying to become great. Both of these athletes know they want greatness; the trick is creating the drive and desire to achieve that lofty goal. Working with each motivated athlete is a joy because they don't need the false flogging and hard-sell approach to put in the work. The satisfaction for a coach comes from designing the individual programs for particular players and to help them fill the gaps in their deficiencies and to also pump up their strengths. Being able to watch a talented motivated kid throughout a season of development is one of the real pleasures of working with this particular age group.

One problem with some of today's athletes is how to work with the kid who comes from a family that doesn't value personal commitment, or a family where the word "no" is rarely spoken and life is too easy. Those kids will be shocked by the drive required to achieve even the basic level of success and they will be the ones most likely to give up on themselves. The other problem I run into is the player with average skills and average grades who drives an average car and has an average social life who doesn't know what it means to be great. The task at hand is to show this group of kids the path to greatness. Whether or not a boy accepts the challenge to be great is up to him, but the trick is to show him the path and give him that taste and for him to realize how sweet it is. The biggest stumbling block for most kids when showing them the path to greatness is that it happens to be very hard and very demanding.

To develop a strong work ethic in the young man is not an easy task. I like to keep it simple and keep it fun, that way the rigors of being industrious happen without anyone getting hurt or walking away. The conditioning always sucks and is hard and painful and nobody ever really enjoys it, but letting the guys know that the girls dig strong abs is a helpful motivator. Using the concept of team in all drill activities reinforces the fact that they are in this together, and when one player gets better they all get better. Once outside we continue to expand the sense of self and team with drills that build confidence in the individual's ability as well as confidence within the team. The average underachiever has to be built up, not torn down. When the play is made or the right base is thrown to or even if he brings his shoes to practice two days in a row, that is progress and it needs to be acknowledged.

To be clear, we are not running Sally's day camp here; when the average continues to be average and fails to push hard and work to improve then his lack of progress needs to be pointed out either by me or by his peers. Complacency of skill is not a part of any sports program, nor is it a way of life that is in any way satisfying. The days of working in a factory for thirty years waiting for your pension no longer exist in this country. Keeping your head down and avoiding the boss is a strategy that may work in the large company and may net you some years of security, but in the long run, you will die inside and the life you want will never come to be. The baseball field is no different. The average player has had his time keeping his head down and showing up to practice and doing the minimum. The youth leagues are full of kids who dutifully hopped into the car, showed up to practice, went through the motions, and became the average guy. Some kids were pushed by coaches and parents to be better and work on their goal-building skills, but far too many were left to make their way through practice, hop back into the car, and throw their gloves into the garage to wait for the next scheduled practice. If you are on the field in high school then something inside you wants to be there, so why not put the effort in to make an impact on the team and on yourself?

CHAPTER 14
WORK ETHIC

David Hitt and I had no idea what work ethic was, but we certainly aspired for greatness. We wanted to be great at everything! David lived to the west of our elementary school and I lived to the east. With both of us living about four blocks from school that meant our houses were about a mile from each other, a considerable distance at the age of ten. David, an average athlete, neither super fast nor exceptionally gifted in the eye-hand department, was a determined lover of sports.

Because of David's general "averageness" at all sports, he loved them equally and pursued them all with great passion. When David and I would get together, it generally meant a decathlon sports kind of a day. Upon arrival at his house, we would head to the basketball court in his driveway for some spirited one-on-one or some bombs away "horse." David was a far better basketball player than I ever was, but I was a terrific shoot-around guy with a fine shot and a will to survive when it came to do or die from downtown. I never was able to dribble in traffic very well but I had always been able to shoot lights out when no one was on me. After basketball, we would move to his yard for some tennis ball golf; whacking a tennis ball with a golf club was about the closest I would ever get to the game of golf, and it was a real challenge which I thoroughly enjoyed.

David would go on to run track in high school as well as play golf and soccer, sports in school that I never would go to see and that I rarely heard about except from David. Continuing the Hitt decathlon, we took a break and went inside to play a baseball card game which was popular in the seventies. You picked yourself a particular team or an all-star team then, through the role of dice and action cards, you were able to play a nine inning baseball game in simulation. What we found out through the playing of this board game, one of the odd bonding elements in our friendship, besides the love of sports, was that we had a mutual love for the Baltimore Orioles baseball team.

Living in the suburbs of Chicago with access to two professional baseball teams you would think our affiliations would be set...either Cubs or White Sox. However, both David and I were drawn to the Orioles for reasons which became clear to me only in hindsight. The Orioles were in the spotlight of the baseball world mainly because they were winners.

Living in the realm of the Chicago Cubs, my first love, losing was a habit which although a bit tiresome was a way of life. I was all too present for the great collapse of the 1969 Cubs team. With weeks to go in the '69 season, the Cubs seemed a shoo-in for the pennant only to see their lead evaporate along with the hopes and World Series dreams of many young dedicated baseball fans. I can still remember the dismay and frustration at my lack of control over the situation. I pleaded with Ernie Banks, our hall of fame first baseman; I begged Don Kessinger, our slick shortstop, to do something to stop the madness. I implored Glenn Beckert, Fergie Jenkins, and Billy Williams to win just a couple more games to make a faithful fan happy. And that was the problem with those guys; I was always begging and pleading with the Cubs to do something. I never had to do that with the Orioles. The Orioles won ballgames, they won championships; they won and they played the game right.

The Orioles had a lineup of players who were a notch above my beloved Cubbies. Brooks Robinson was a man among boys on the ball field. Quick and sure at third base, he never seemed to miss a grounder and always made the impossible play. At the plate, Brooks didn't look like much with his sawed-off helmet brim and paunchy body but he was clutch when the team needed a hit. All around the diamond, the Orioles had players who went about the business of winning, and they got it done with style. Mark Belanger, the Orioles lanky underfed shortstop, was a role model for my baseball aspirations in the way he contributed to his team's victories by playing reliable, consistent defense. Not much of a hitter, Belanger more than made up for that deficiency with solid defensive leadership. On the days when my hitting was not up to snuff, I would work extra hard in the field to lift my teammates with solid defensive plays, spectacular plays, and guidance from my position.

There was a style and class about the Orioles which set them, at least with David and me, above the rest of the league. The fact that they had really cool looking uniforms was a big plus in our book, and David and I would wear our Orioles caps with pride and answer inquiries about our allegiance with gusto. Watching the Orioles when they played the White Sox or when they were the game of the week, or better yet, when they were in the playoffs and World Series, reinforced my love and respect for their game. Watching a classy pitcher like Jim Palmer take the mound and conduct himself like a gentleman made clear to me the beauty of both the game and the playing of the game. The confidence with which the Orioles took the field and played the game came across to me as clear as day and without a doubt was just as clear to their opponents. Looking good and feeling strong was the edge they had and the substance the Cubs lacked, it was that spirit of invincibility which put the Orioles on top and left the Cubs watching the Miracle Mets win the series in September of '69.

The last activity of the David Decathlon was a made up game of baseball home run derby which we played at our elementary school on the weekends. Playing our fantasy baseball board game usually fired us up to put on our Orioles gear and head to the school to emulate the larger-than-life home run-hitting first baseman, Boog Powell. We would gather our gloves, bats, and all the old tennis balls we could muster and head out to the school to challenge each other in tennis ball hit-it-on-the-roof homerun derby.

The school building at Central Elementary was constructed in a "U" formation with a wall in front, to our left, and behind us. The distance from one side of the "U" to the other was a good ten-year-old home run swing away. Add the two story, thirty foot distance to the roof and you had the perfect Fenway Park type green monster elementary school shot for a homer. There was a set of stairs at the home run wall leading down to the basement, affectionately known as the "spit pit." This railed pit was notorious as a spitting venue for those who ventured down the steps to retrieve a ball. In our game, if you hit the ball into the pit, you would receive a triple. Bounce a ball off of the wall on a fly and you had a double;

a line drive past the pitcher was a single. Any ball hit on the ground was an out and anything caught on a fly was also an out. Add all these elements together and you had a recipe for hours of fun and endless opportunities to become a better ballplayer.

We worked on our pitching skills as well as our mental acuity during our hours at the school. We would try to find ways to psych each other out in order to slip the fastball by. As hitters we worked on refining our batting eye so as to swing at only strikes and to wait for that one pitch we knew we could send onto the roof for the game-winning homer. As the game progressed our arms would tire and the homers started to sail with more regularity. Eventually the game was shut down as the last tennis ball sailed into the sky settling onto the roof thirty feet in the air. A quick run around to the other side of the school would confirm that the game was truly over and that we would have to start accumulating more tennis balls in order for our training to continue.

At the end of a summer full of home run derby and an endless stream of tape measure tennis balls shots onto the school roof, David and I eventually could no longer find any more tennis balls; the sources had dried up. It occurred to our ten-year-old minds that the only real source of tennis balls left to us was on the roof of the school. We had visions of what it would be like up there, balls as far as the eye could see; our balls as far as the eye could see. That roof had our tennis balls and we were determined to reclaim what was ours so we could continue the fun.

Braced with this logic we headed to David's house four blocks away to retrieve his aluminum extension ladder. Now, walking down the sidewalk with a twenty foot extension ladder seemed perfectly logical to us even though we knew our mission would not be approved of by either the school or our parents. To our way of thinking we were simply in need of the balls which were ours to begin with. We had not lost them, we knew exactly where they were, and we were simply going to get them back. Toting a gigantic ladder made perfect sense to us, and we found that when you walk with purpose and believe in your objective you will find people kind of leave you alone.

To get to the land of plenty, we needed to climb onto two different levels of the school roof. The first roof got us onto the kindergarten level and even this level netted us several tennis balls and a big red rubber dodge-ball or two. Making several piles of balls on the lower roof we headed to the next level. We had to pull the ladder up onto the kindergarten level, spin it around and lean it against the next wall for the assault to the summit. Bracing the ladder against the wall to the higher roof we made our way up to a land we were sure no other kid had ever ventured to. Peering over the top of the final rung and gazing out over the endless expanse of tar paper, we were met with a sight far grander than anything our ground bound imagination could ever have envisioned...balls, balls, and more balls. Tennis balls, soccer balls, big red balls, small red rubber balls. Every kind of playground orb we had ever encountered lay basking in the sunshine of the Central Elementary roof. Our elementary minds were smart enough to bring a couple of large paper bags with us and we proceeded to gather all the balls like a smash and grab at a jewelry heist. The big balls we kicked over the edge, the tennis balls we culled into our sacks for endless home run derbies to come.

We knew we didn't have a lot of time, so we worked feverishly to net as many balls as possible. However, I did take the time to look over the edge and scan all around, burning the image into my mind much as I am sure Neil Armstrong had done just a year before on the moon, so that I could lock into my memory the time I conquered the roof of Central Elementary. To this day I can still see the stadium where I learned my batter's eye and my pitcher's mind, and I still see that hallowed ground of learning from thirty feet up, looking down.

CHAPTER 15
FUN PRACTICE

As our practice continues, a week from our first high school game, I look at the boys and wonder just how much fun have these guys had in the development of their baseball skills? How much time has been spent creating games of baseball play; how many times have they envisioned themselves as the pitcher in the last inning of the World Series or been the big at-bat with the game on the line? I am sure there are times when buddies come together to create the magic moments of imaginary heroics, but I know the times have changed, and boys have to work harder to find those simple pleasures.

The region in which I coach is an area of open enrollment for the school district, meaning any child can enroll at any school in the district as long as there is room at that particular school. My daughters grew up on a block where the kids down the street went to a different school than they did. The guys on my team come from all areas of the district which includes four different towns. Many of these boys either played against each other on opposing town teams or have never seen their teammate play because their proximity to each other is too great. So where is the unity of play? How does a boy not only develop his skills but develop his sense of fun and shared play?

Kids at an early age are put together in "play dates," forced together because their parents happen to know each other or some chance connection allows a parent to create an interaction for their child, and in turn, time for themselves. What sort of connection can be made when kids are not allowed to develop friendships on their own or they cannot continue a friendship because of geography? The result of these early pseudo-friendships and forced encounters is a child who lacks any deep bonds.

The ability to create and use one's imagination in play comes from many long summer days when two kids find themselves sitting on the front stoop, exchanging the sing-song mantra, "What do you want to do? I don't know what do you want to do? I don't know, I asked you first." On and on this litany would go on a muggy summer afternoon in Wilmette until an idea would pop into our heads, sometimes a good idea, sometimes an idea about climbing onto a school roof. The process would go on every day throughout the summer, and after school, and in the evenings; it was the search for fun.

It feels like the boys I coach haven't really had the same free-form fun that characterized my younger days because of the changing times. Now that they are in high school, the demands to be serious, focused, and directed are even more of a damper on their search for fun. The messages they receive from the world are: be serious, think of your future. When they want to have fun, the options are girls and partying because that is the picture of fun they see on MTV and those are the sound bytes they hear from their music. The wholesome fun which should be so easy to find is now packaged and delivered to the boys via text message and a reminder from their mom.

The kids who arrive at my field come programmed for their "play date." Their expectations is that I am here to entertain them and keep them busy for a few hours. They have spoken with their moms to let them know when the play date will be over so mom can come and reclaim them each day. My expectation is for these guys to come out and entertain me with a desire to learn the game. It is my task, job, and love to show these guys that sliding in the dirt, running around, yelling, spitting, scratching, and giving each other a hard time is ok. Together we will break down the expectations of what it means to be involved and part of an activity. We will learn to be accountable for our fun and for our own success. By giving these boys the tools to be better ball players, they can put in the effort to experience the satisfaction of achievement. By teaching these boys to be better people and teammates, they acquire the tools to be happy and comfortable individuals. There is and always will be time for fun. The search doesn't have to be forced, just let go and let the child take over.

In practice we work to develop our baseball skills in the areas where we are weak, but we also work on developing our play skills. Practice should always have a balance of work, competition, and play. From the very first day, I try to break through the crust of early manhood these boys have built around themselves. Most of the boys, young men of fourteen and fifteen, have a vague notion of what it means to be a man. The messages they receive to create this man persona come from good sources such as their parents but also from bad sources such as the older delinquent down the street or the distorted media of TV and music.

It takes the kids back a bit when I show up and start to speak the language of baseball with such zeal and emotion. For some reason these boys have been led to believe the game of baseball at high school is serious business. They tend to believe that just as their school work is to be done religiously and presented in a timely fashion so too will the school teams be treated: serious, no fun allowed. My task is to get these kids to lighten up so they can tap into the joy of doing something for the fun of it. If you can come to practice and feel free to try hard, feel free to fail, feel free to make fun of yourself and your teammates, then you will start to be free to be comfortable with who you are.

The whole point of becoming a man is to achieve goals, succeed or fail at what you are after, and deal with that success or failure in a positive manner. In order to have a positive feeling at the end of a task, you need to learn to accept that failure will occur in your life and to accept that you are okay even when things don't go as planned.

Baseball is a sport where failure 66% of the time is an acceptable number. The batter who hits .330 is the guy that takes the ten million dollar paycheck home at the end of the year. So baseball is the perfect venue for a young man to learn to accept his limitations as a human being and to build up his tolerance for the pain of failure.

When we speak of failure on the baseball field, it is a softer version of the word than say the failure to yield at a stop sign, or the failure to live up to your responsibilities as a father, or the failure to live up to your potential as a person. No, failure on the baseball field has so many degrees that to think of failure as a hard and fast negative is unfair. When an outfielder fails to make a catch on a ball hit into the gap which lets in the winning run, as the coach, I have to think hard to determine where the failure has occurred. To say the outfielder failed to make the play does an injustice to the game and to that player even though he clearly did not accomplish what needed to be done. The player will come off the field feeling awful, sure that he has failed and let his team down. But was it his failure? Where did that batter hit the ball throughout the game? Did we adjust for his tendencies? Was the player in a ready position and fully engaged when the ball was hit? Did our pitcher put the ball in the location we knew would be the toughest for the hitter to hit? All these variables come into play when a player fails to make a tough play.

How a player deals with the outcome of a play is the toughest part, because no matter how many variables there are on a given play, the player either makes the play or he doesn't. The exceptional player, the one who has placed himself in the right position, who is tuned in and in an athletic position, who sees the pitch is not where we wanted to throw it, and who makes the good break on the ball but still misses the ball, he's the one who should be reasonable with himself. The player who is not prepared in all these areas should take the miss as a failure and blame himself for a situation which he may have been able to avoid with a little more preparation and a little more desire to help his team and himself succeed. The unprepared player needs to acknowledge inside that he failed to do everything within his control to be ready for the play presented to him.

Because baseball is an individual game played within the framework of a team, the individual player will be faced with many opportunities to succeed or fail. When you step into the batter's box, you either have success or you have failure. Again, the deciding factor in a player's sense of failure comes from the preparation he brings to the plate, as well as his realistic understanding of his abilities. The player who finds himself in the batter's box fully engaged in the game and attentive to the pitcher and what the pitcher has done throughout the game has a better chance of success than the average Joe who goes to the plate hoping for a hit.

Realistic expectations also play a role in how a player handles the result of an at-bat. If a pitcher has a wicked curve and you struggle against pitchers with hard breaking balls, then you must be prepared to battle hard to hit that pitch and be prepared if you don't succeed. No batter should set himself up to fail, but if you are fully informed as to what you are about to attempt, the joy of success is sweeter and the acceptance of failure less. With the acceptance of defeat should also come the resolve to face that pitcher again, to turn the tables and become the victor. No hitter has ever had lasting success pouting and fuming over being bested by a good pitcher. The quality player simply waits his turn to try again with the resolve that the next at-bat will bring an opportunity to do something positive for his team.

Whenever there is failure on one side there is success on the other. Missing the ball and allowing the game to end in defeat also creates victory for the other team. The pitcher who strikes out the side creates failure for that team and success for his team. All around the diamond, the pluses and minuses add and diminish throughout the game. All players must be capable of accepting the changes which will occur in the game and to not let the flow effect their game.

The ebb and flow that is baseball can affect the more emotional players on a team. The power of an emotional player can be an asset to a team, their fiery spirit igniting the team to reach for greater things. However, the emotions of a team are intertwined and must be balanced so that when the big play happens, good or bad, the team is able to use the energy released to move forward in a positive way. The emotional players sometimes have a hard time with the inevitable disappointments that occur and they need to be taught to channel their emotional power for good. The maturation of a player occurs over time because he has to experience the various emotions the game will bring to him. The absurdly crushing defeats on freak plays and inevitable bad hops will bring up emotions that have never been felt before. The cruel behavior of opposing players and the mindless stupidity of clueless umpires can cause rage and anger unimagined by the impassioned ballplayer. How we handle these complex feelings and how we learn to use them to our benefit instead of to our detriment is the sign of growth.

The ability to handle the rage and disbelief which will show up on the field is best learned on the field and best placated by coaches and teammates. The raw aspects of our personalities are better suited for the baseball diamond rather than with our spouses, bosses, or the powers that be. Therefore when the VP of sales steps on your toes and takes credit for your hard work, you may feel an emotion similar to the time when you experienced that blown call by the home plate ump. Due to your years of training on the field from bad hops and blown calls, you can smile, shake your head in dismay, and look forward to the next game or the next project for your next chance to do something good for the team or the company.

CHAPTER 16
YOUNG CHARACTER

At the age of twelve, I completed my journeyman's march through the Little League system. My skill as a ballplayer increased steadily with the help of dedicated dads who put in many late summer hours at the ball field. Their tutelage along with endless summer days of imaginary big league experience at Jonathan's house helped me to become one of the premier players in the Wilmette area. I played in my league all-star game each of the three years I was in the system. In addition I was also called up from C league to B league and B league to A league at the end of each season to add depth to the higher level bench when those teams entered the playoffs. My skills as a sure-handed shortstop and heads-up player earned me the respect of my teammates and the attention of the Wilmette baseball community. But at the age of twelve, what had I really learned from the game of baseball besides the ability to turn a quick and efficient double play? At that point the game was still a physical activity which kept me busy and out of the way of my mom and out of the house on sunny days.

I was a quiet one-dimensional sports kid who lived for the flow of high energy movement and physical rather than social interaction. I was the shy kid who preferred running fast to standing around chatting. The reserved awkward manner of a twelve year old jock is nothing new in the sports world. Sports have been the saving grace for socially inept kids for years. Why speak when you can do? Running and being active was my mechanism of choice when feelings and interaction were required. The papers are full of college and even professional players who go through their entire adolescence and youth sports experience without having to address their inability to socialize and interact. In the world of my youth on the 700 block of Washington Street, I was free to roam and run and avoid anything deeper than what pattern to run or whether to play catch or shoot hoops.

Sports are a great outlet for kids to explore their physical nature, but we also need to prepare them for a world which will require them to speak and engage. At the end of my Little League run, I was a fantastic player, but I was a mess when it came to dealing with the confusion of being a kid. The coaches who molded the sports-me were large personalities who demanded strict attention but required very little in the way of rebuttal. I was not required to do anything but listen, absorb, and produce. The thing was I didn't want to do anything but listen, absorb, and produce.

My sanctuary was on the field. The field was the place where I could do what I did best and receive the attention that I was too afraid to find anywhere else. The quiet blissful ignorance was coming to an end because with greatness comes the responsibility to lead and engage. The game of baseball was about to take on an even larger role in my life, greater than I could ever have imagined.

Although the past few years taught me to be diligent in my desire to get better and to be respectful of the coaches who cared enough to teach me, I still needed to learn the larger lessons baseball had to offer. Just showing up and playing because it gave me satisfaction and boosted my ego was not enough for the baseball gods. Once the thrill of the game gets in your blood and you experience the desire and joy of the next great play that's when the baseball gods really go to work molding the character of the player and person you are to become. My time had arrived, and the gods were ready to make the 1975 baseball season the year baseball became the biggest guiding light and hardest teacher in my life.

Chapter 17

First Game

Our first game is an away game and for that I am grateful. Playing on the road, away from the eyes of students and parents allows me the chance to focus on the game and the kids without all the nagging thoughts, second guesses, and pressure to win. At the sophomore level, the focus needs to be on playing the game well rather than on an attitude of win at all cost. I made a personal choice when I started coaching to make sure all players get into the game at some point, so the long bus ride to the games is not in vain and the sometimes even longer ride home is not an embarrassment.

Focusing on playing the game well has so many elements to it that I have to tackle each component in a progressive order so the skills build upon themselves through the course of the season. When done right, the season can be a surging wave of accomplishments which will leave the players astonished at season's end with just how much their skills have improved. Because so much has to be taught and all their skills refined, the glacial approach to development needs to be employed so that at the end of an eon they can see how far they have travelled. For this first game, I am more concerned with calming nerves and controlling the amped-up excitement of a bus ride to a foreign school. Even though these boys have played countless games through their career the larger stage of the high school arena makes nerves and doubts that much bigger. My goals today are to make sure everyone gets on the bus, they are properly equipped and dressed, and we show up on time looking like a ball team.

The excitement of missing class and getting out early to travel to another school is a lot for these young players to handle. The first trip is always problematic, no matter how much prep you do in practice, plus there is always the forgotten sock and misplaced uniform to add to the chaos of getting on the bus. Once again I am treated to the unique sight of fifteen young men in their finest daily school garb overloaded with additional baseball bags and over-flowing backpacks. I feel for the catchers and the kids who have forced their parents to buy extra gloves and additional equipment because now they need a pack mule to help them move all their gear from locker to bus. After the gear is stowed and the boys are settled and strewn about on the twenty-foot bus, the ride begins and the nerves start to show.

As we bounce down the road, I begin to work on my line-up. I can hear the character of my team with the help of the perfect acoustics of the big yellow tube. The boys of talent and bluster talk a little too loud and swagger a bit too much, hiding the fear of the game ahead. The quiet kids stare out the window, enveloped in their own world of fear, not brave enough to show bravado and bluff. The solid well-adjusted kids keep it all in perspective and stay even and true, working on homework or chatting with a player of minimal talent who seems to be along for the ride.

Chatting with my assistant coach, usually a young guy with as-pirations to be a coach or a former player who still wants to be around the game, I outline the plan for the game; what pitchers to consider, substitutions to be made, team make up, and an overall sense of attitude about the day. Yet I know how little this strategy talk means on the first day because the focus for today will be on getting through the game one out at time.

The larger goal for the boys this season is to get them to play the game by instinct; develop baseball intuition. Up to this point in their baseball careers, the guys, even the most talented of the bunch, have been playing the game by remote control. Whenever a ball is struck or a play is to be made there has always been a coach or a parent or a dad standing a little too close to the fence scream-ing instructions to the poor kid as to what needs to be done with the ball. The kids have been programmed to respond to the screamed commands as though the baseball gods were speaking in tongues through their parents and coaches. The goal this year is to develop the confidence to listen to the baseball god inside their own head and to react to the ball rather than think to the ball.

Over-thinking in any sport leads to indecision and wasted time, therefore instinctive reaction must become the guiding force for a player. Too often there is a moment of doubt and indecision which comes over the boys as the process of deciding what to do and where to go flashes across their face. The fear that they may do something wrong or appear foolish is a constant danger for these cool kids. I want to eliminate the fear and doubt from their game and replace it with success and game joy. We will find the comfort and confidence which comes from playing the game well through repetition in practice, positive reinforcement for success, and constructive discussion after confusion.

The instinct of knowing where to go on a ball hit into the gap with runners on first and second with one out and a fast runner at the plate and a weak armed center fielder with great speed who gets a late jump on the ball does not happen overnight. The first step to understanding all the complexities of the game is to break the game down into bite-size pieces and walk through the various scenarios with the boys. Repetition and endless drills where I hit balls to create those various scenarios helps the boys shrink their confusion and compress the vast space between the foul poles. Practicing the individual mechanics of the game is another way to flush out the automaton movements and develop baseball instincts. Breaking the game down into its simplest form allows the mind to see the beauty of the game and unconsciously transforms the body into a reactor rather than an analyzer. Now that the mechanics and as much information about the game as I deem appropriate for the group to absorb is presented, and at least half of it forgotten, the boys really start to play and a real application of principles begins. Although I have presented the material and explained the theories, we still have a long way to go before we reach the smooth execution we hope to achieve by season's end.

For now, the first game gives us a chance to play a real game... this is not a drill. So as the ball heads toward the gap in left-center field, our swift-footed center fielder miss-reads the ball, this leads to the batter ending up on third base instead of second. On the play, our shortstop incorrectly moves to second base instead of to the outfield to set up a double cut in coordination with the second baseman, which leads to an over-throw by the centerfielder, allowing all runners to advance. While all this confusion and running around is taking place, I begin the work of putting together the discussion we will have to help sort out all the miscues which have occurred on one batted ball. I work to squelch the frustration rising up in my gut as I see the Keystone Cop adventures play out on the all-too visible playing field. I recall all the knowing nods of their heads and the looks of understanding after the fiftieth time we ran our double-cut drill and I wonder just what were they nodding about. Now, facing a team with live bodies moving at way too fast a speed with the goal of achieving and winning, we are frantic to stop them. All the information presented by the coach has been stuffed away and the only reaction happening on the field is one of panic and motion for the sake of motion. Unfortunately for them, I have severed the lines of communication from coach and parent to the field and the boys are searching their own frequencies for the answers.

Mercifully we settle down and find three outs and hustle toward the shelter of our dugout away from the glare of all that open space. Before the boys can hide themselves away, I have the opportunity to help or hinder, teach or taunt, belittle or build-up. I want my team to be better and I want the boys to be better and I want the game to be played better, so I take every opportunity presented to help them understand the events that occurred and to help them with the acceptance of those events.

The questions are simple: What happened? What do we need to do? Where do I need to be to contribute? How will I be better next time? The game is complicated, more complicated than these boys ever realized. The consequences of one player's actions can have a devastating impact on the outcome of the game, on the health of another player, and the mental stability of the coach. The mental anguish of a poor decision or a failure to react properly can make a lasting impression on the player both in a positive way and in a negative way. So we discuss and review the situations, and I see the knowing nods and sounds of understanding which I previously saw in practice.

We soldier on until the next inning when new situations will again test our ability to think and react. My hope is that when the last game of the season rolls around we will not be wondering and talking about the mechanics of the double cut, instead our movements in the field will be fluid and our thoughts uncluttered. I am hopeful that at season's end the decisions we are making will flow from experience and intuition and our discussions will have evolved toward the deeper aspects of the game; ruminations that will hone our character into players of substance, ones with drive and the determination to be great.

Chapter 18
Milestones

In the course of a young man's life, there are certain benchmarks or rites of passage that a boy goes through on his way to manhood. In different cultures, these rites of passage vary from acts of courage to physical tests of bravery and all are intended to demonstrate one's honor and proof of manhood. The American culture also has its trials to mark the path of a young man toward manhood. Although the American demonstration of manhood is not as overt as receiving a piercing from a tribal leader, we do have young men who use piercing as a way to demonstrate their independence from their elders.

Sports also play an integral part in this trial process, perhaps replacing some of the more gruesome tests of blood-letting and bravery which were employed by past cultures. In America we are able to display our courage by picking ourselves up after an injury and toughing it out for the team. Bravery is displayed in the form of taking on the biggest of the big in football or keeping a head held high in the face of insurmountable odds and a horrific defeat.

Sports for those involved, and for the fathers who watch, are a holy rite of passage in the development of a young man's character. For those who do not partake of the sacred ritual of going helmet to helmet and sweat to sweat to prove manhood, the more familiar and accepted benchmarks on the path to being an adult are of course the driver's license, the first beer, the first kiss, and the graduation from high school. All of the firsts a young man experiences in his mid-teens contribute to his feelings of becoming his own man. The first time our parents allow us to travel on our own or be away from the house for an extended period of time is a part of the maturation process which helps create the person we come to know as our independent self. My rite of passage came in the summer of 1975 at the age of fourteen. That was the summer my eyes were opened to the world around me and from that point on, the 700 block on Washington Street would no longer be big enough to hold my spirit.

CHAPTER 19
MAKING ADJUSTMENTS

The summer of 1975 started out just like all the other summers that came before it: hot muggy days full of bike riding, baseball, and a block full of adventure. We lived five short bicycle blocks from Lake Michigan which afforded me the opportunity to spend time at Gilson Park, the local lake-front park, where we fished, hung out at the beach, and played on one of the first Frisbee golf courses in the country. With a close proximity to Northwestern University in Evanston, my mother enrolled me in the Wildcat club, a sports club run by the athletes and coaches from the university. The eight week enrollment kept my active body busy and fit while allowing my mother a quiet window in her day.

My world was full of sports, activity, and play, and very little else. The problems of Watergate, Vietnam, and all the other real world experiences rarely pierced the soft haze of my insular sports world. My evenings were spent pedaling miles and miles through the streets of West Wilmette, riding in a syncopated carefree rhythm to make it in time for baseball practice. The summer of 1975 started the same, but as the regular baseball season came to a close, the beginning of my life in baseball was about to begin. My time dabbling on the baseball field was over; the time was right and the gods were ready to reveal the inner dynamics of the game in all its excruciating glory.

Pony League was another step up on the ladder of youth baseball. The distances on the field were greater and the chance to lead off from the bases and steal at will made the game exciting and as close to "real" baseball as it got. To the small yet expanding minds of former Little Leaguers, the longer baselines and greater distance to the plate were huge adjustments. The ever-expanding universe of the baseball diamond seemed to breathe outward, placing the bases just that much farther away. Our stick-figure arms ached to make the adjustment, and the poor first basemen went home with black and blue shins and a longing look toward the outfield. The regular season gave us all a chance to acclimate to the game at the longer distances. The pitchers did their best to throw to the shrinking sight of their catchers, some realizing that the overpowering fastball they had in little league just didn't quite have the same velocity it used to now that the ball had to travel to the tiny glove on the horizon. For some pitchers it meant the end of their budding pitching career as the weakness in their arm became clear to both the coaches and the opposing batters. The pitchers with true desire and ability stuck with it but they were forced to learn the fine art of pitching so that they could become real pitchers and not just throwers.

In baseball anyone can walk out onto the mound, pick up the baseball and hurl it with all their might towards the catcher, however that doesn't make you a pitcher. Standing on high, mimicking the movements of Fergie Jenkins from the Cubs does not make you a pitcher; in fact there should be a new designation for such a player...the thrower. A pitcher is someone who takes the time to know who he is as a pitcher and competitor by working to understand the strengths and weaknesses of his abilities. A thrower who works to understand his abilities and studies the methods required to get batters out can truly be called a pitcher. The thrower is a guy who believes his great fastball, wicked curve, and other magical pitches will never fail him. He is the guy with myriad excuses for his lack of success, the guy who always has a sore arm or a catcher who doesn't understand him.

The pitcher of quality is the guy who acknowledges he is not a flamethrower but realizes he does have the ability to throw his fastball to a specific spot in a tough situation. He is the guy who has been working on his curveball and knows when to throw it and where to throw it for the greatest effect. He is the player who does not throw the same low and away fastball to the big guy in the number three hole who in his previous at-bat bounced the last low and away fastball off the right field fence for a double. The pitcher pitches; the thrower throws. The pitcher thinks and learns and the thrower just keeps throwing.

I left the pitching to the pitchers because I had to concentrate on adjusting my game at shortstop. I needed to account for the longer throws and the added attention required to watch over base runners that could leave at any given moment. I was the same lanky beanpole I had always been, even more so as I continued to grow skyward. My arm strength was average and showed no signs of developing at the same rate as my height. But just as with the pitchers there are two kinds of infielders, those who are smart and smooth and work to become better at their position and those who stand and wait for the ball.

The stand and wait guys patiently wait for the bouncing balls to arrive at their gloves, and then wonder why only half the balls make it to their webbing. Once again the difference in styles comes down to an understanding of one's makeup and the beginning of a self-realization that many players must make if they want their ability to keep up with the changes in the game. Each player needs to constantly measure himself against the opposition, his teammates, and the player he used to be. The player who still sees himself as the dominate player who ruled Little League, hitting home runs and pitching lights out but who has only grown two inches in the last three years may find he is not the same dominating player he used to be. The kid who made all the plays in the hole and threw out runners by three steps last year may find those same plays are now a lot closer, in fact now some of those plays are not being made.

Adjustments need to be made, and internal honesty needs to be reached. Acknowledging one's limitations is not an easy thing to do, but in order to keep up with the changes in the game and the level of competition, every person needs to be realistic about what he is capable of doing given his physical and mental makeup. My little chicken-wing arm was adequate, but my quickness and ability to field and release the ball were exceptional.

I learned during the summer of '75 that the moment the ball hit my glove, I needed to propel the ball toward first base. I worked on my hand quickness and also my mental quickness. I knew what I needed to do, so I sped up my play to stay in tune with the parameters of the field. The plays I made the previous year getting runners out by three steps, turned into throws that arrived before a runner was four steps from the bag. I realized that the increase in distance for my throws was also an increase in the distance the runner had to travel to the base. The hard hit grounder brought the ball to me sooner, allowing for a quicker turn around to first base, which in turn created a futile trip down the line for the runner and a longer walk back to the dugout.

Most of us made the adjustments we needed to and the rest of the kids wallowed in what would most likely be the last year of their youth baseball experience. Every year, the attrition rate increased as more and more kids felt overwhelmed or unable to find the desire to keep up. The boys who remained to fill the positions on the fields of Wilmette were the boys with the greatest drive and the willingness to adapt. We were a tight bunch of dedicated always-wearing-a-baseball-cap group who could easily be spotted in a crowd for our caps, swagger, and bubble gum. By that time, we had all battled each other, played against each other, and bonded with each other. We knew this summer, the summer before our freshmen year in high school, would be the last summer we would be together on the field as teammates.

The division of East Wilmette and West Wilmette was also the division of the two high schools and we knew that once you became a New Trier East Indian, you would forever be a mortal enemy of a New Trier West Cowboy. The tryout for the Pony League All-Star team was the last hurrah for our time together in Wilmette baseball. Although we all knew most of the players who would be on the team, we didn't really know the exact makeup and assignment of the positions. The big question mark was who would be the coach? We all had our disliked and our favorite coaches. Would we get a screamer or a kid's dad? The powers that be would decide, so it was the least of my worries because my focus was on completing the tryout without falling on my face. The day of the tryout was filled with excitement and loads of anxiety. Who would make the team, and most importantly, who would lead us for the last time?

CHAPTER 20
PROGRESS

A bobbled stumbling play by my second baseman who continues to fight his feet and the coaching, gives us the final out of the game. We come up with the requisite twenty one outs which allows us to meekly leave the field of play. The score of our first game is unimportant to me, but humbling to others. To me the completion of the game and the break down of the events is what matters at this point. The boys gather down toward the right field foul territory grass waiting for words of praise in times of victory and admonishment in times of trouble.

I try not to give them what they expect. It is too easy to gush and fawn when we win, and the temptation to chastise and scold is always great when the game goes badly. What is needed is honesty and thoughtful analysis after any game, no matter what the outcome. So what if we win by eight if half the team doesn't come prepared to play and our pitcher doesn't wear socks and we make five mental errors?

A winning score is hollow if we lose in the area of mental preparation and game organization. So what if we get spanked by eight runs? To me it is a victory when our outfield makes a couple of correct mental plays. There is progress when my left fielder turns the right way on a ball to the gap and our double relay sets up perfectly, keeping the opposing team from winning by nine. That is progress for our team play, and victory for our attention to detail and the will to battle at all times. The view of the game is rarely about the scoreboard, even though I have purposely had some of my teams face the scoreboard at the end of a dismal game so we can look at the score inning by inning to determine how we ended up losing by eight. I have them look at the scoreboard and quiz them to see if they really understand that it is the big number six in the error column or the loss of focus in the five-run fifth that created the train wreck on the field.

All in all, it is the game within the game which creates the result on the scoreboard. The preparation on the bus, the interaction on the bench, the clarity of thought on the field, and the execution of fundamentals while playing that determines how we feel at the end of the game. Sure, wins feel good and losses feel bad, but how good or how bad we feel about either a win or a loss is within our control.

The breakdown after the game goes well and those who had their heads down are now lifted up through constructive discussion of the mistakes that were made and the work needed to correct the problems. Progress is our goal for the spring. Every game is an opportunity to get better; every practice an opportunity to get farther. Every time a player steps onto the field, there is the chance for improvement, whether or not a player takes advantage of that opportunity is up to him. There is within every kid the vision of the player they think they are and the player who actually takes the field. The gap between those two players needs to be reasonable so the kid can realistically match the two versions. Whether or not a player is willing to accept the player who is actually on the field is the difference between the player who will succeed and mature as a person, and the player who will grumble and stumble until he finally quits. A player needs to accept his limitations and abilities at present and work hard to go beyond what he thinks possible in the future.

All the imaginary games of pitching in the World Series and hitting the home run in the bottom of the ninth feature a player who has been cultivated in the mind from a very early age. The arrival of that guy in that situation with those spectacular results is rare. What we want is to cultivate the real guy to handle the real situations at hand: showing up, practicing with purpose, being a good teammate, trying their best in the tough situations. We want the real guy to face the situations that are presented and to do their best and to accept the result and take ownership of that result. Too often the results are not what we want them to be, and in a team sport with so many individual components, the honesty of our role in a defeat or failed attempt is hard to accept.

Teaching the upturned faces in foul territory to accept the results of their combined successes and failures and to learn from them is something we will work on all season. I can guarantee to these boys that throughout the season we will win or we will lose. I can also guarantee my message will always be the same: did we take the opportunity to get better today?

The ride home on the bus is not as bad as the boys might have thought when the last out was being made. The swaggering boys from earlier are a little quieter. The nervous quiet boys are a little louder. The well-adjusted boys are doing their homework and chatting away about math tests and video games. I am smashed up front in my bus seat reliving the game and reviewing all the moves I made in order to be sure I gave us the best chance to do well.

I want to win just as badly as anyone on the bus. I want to play all the best players and crush our opponent and dance on their demoralized carcasses, but that is the player in me boiling to the surface. The task at hand is much larger than my fleeting need for good coach verification. The macho dude inside of me is as ugly as any of the many red-faced foot-stomping coaches I have seen from across the diamond. Rarely have I seen a team thrive under the tutelage of a Genghis Khan-coach. My life is too precious for me to allow myself to fret and paw at the inequities of the game being played by these budding young men. The boys who take the field for me are doing the best they can at any given moment; add to that the incredible complexity of a game that on a good day with the best players in the world still creates events which baffle historians and fans to the point of hair-pulling distraction. No, I cannot place any more demands on the game than showing up with the group I have, being prepared to the best of their and my ability, and putting forth a lineup made to benefit all.

The result has to be accepted by me, and it is up to me to do as I preach, which is to learn from the events that take place and take the opportunity to get better as a coach. If I am making the same mistakes and feeling the same frustrations at the end of the season, then my time has been wasted, because then I am the one who has not been paying attention. The life lessons the game is teaching do not end when you master turning a double play. The game continues on and the baseball gods never rest. So with one game down I absorb the material and go home to get some sleep because there is a lot of work to be done if we are to become the players and coaches we aspire to be.

CHAPTER 21
THE CREATION

The Wilmette Pony League All-Star team of 1975 came together in the middle of July of that year's summer. My regular team had a disappointing season, so I looked forward to starting fresh with a new team, a new season. Seeing all the familiar faces and mismatched hats from the season created a blend of excitement and anxiety which brought out the best in all the players.

We had arrived at the Locust Elementary baseball field to strut our stuff and lay claim to the position we believed to be ours. Bruce Sonen, the coolest guy I had ever known and the measuring stick for all that is nonchalant and unaffected, sauntered onto the field. Long hair cascaded down his back, the A2000 that I coveted in hand, Bruce had come to lend his never fully-developed or cared-about talent to the cause.

Ray Mals, a pitcher with incredible stuff on the mound and an all or nothing swing at the plate, also joined the gang. Ray, all of six feet tall with huge feet, which foretold even further growth to come, was one of those pitchers with immense talent, startling velocity and just enough wildness to keep the batter, catcher, and coaches guessing as to where the ball would go.

Sam Levin, a rock behind the plate, rode up on a bike that seemed way too small and spindly to handle the solid mass of baseball backstop which would surely anchor our squad. The face I searched most for on that bright day was that of Howie Pattis, my competition at shortstop. Howie was an exceptional talent who I didn't know very well but who I had seen play and naturally despised. Howie, a smaller version of me, lean, quick, and baseball

95

smart, strolled up to me and introduced himself thus taking away the satisfying hatred I was nursing to help me cut through my tryout anxiety. Howie and I would develop a close relationship during the summer, forming a mutual admiration society of two that would see us through many epic battles. The rest of the candidates streamed in from all points on bicycles and on foot, gloves in tow, cleats in hand. We were all hopped up on baseball and hoping to continue the season deep into the summer.

Upon arrival, I searched the crowd to see just who would be coaching us. I saw several summer coaches from opposing teams milling about but it was the two adults with brand new hats and clipboards that looked to be in charge. One of the men was Mark Frazacca's dad, a peripheral baseball dad at best, the other a portly gentleman who had been around the Wilmette program for years. Mr. Buddy Meyer, a Burlington sock sales rep with no children to speak of and no wife that I ever saw, was the man in charge. A lover of the game, and apparently a successful sock salesman, he was the deep pockets of the program and a man who due to his ample girth would only be administrative not demonstrative. I was a bit disappointed in our prospects for leadership, but my focus was on making the team and not screwing up.

We took to the field and to my delight I was the only one at shortstop. Howie had given me the ultimate compliment for which a fourteen year old ball player could hope …acquiescence of territory. I looked at Howie and he nodded at me from his second base position where he too stood alone. All the anxiety of the day flowed out of my body as I looked around at the incredible infield of which I hoped to be a part. With Howie at second, me at short, Bruce at third, and Ray at first base, we were a formidable group of baseball players. I had never had the opportunity to be a part of such a solid group of baseball athletes.

You considered yourself lucky if there were two quality players in your infield for the regular summer team. Often during the years I heard rumblings of insider trading and political intrigue when one team in our league scored more quality players than another. Now to be a member of such a quality group of players, a part of a unit that was as solid from position to position as I had ever seen, was truly an exciting prospect. Already I envisioned what we could accomplish, the double plays Howie and I could turn, picking off runners at second, actually executing bunt de-fenses, and a catcher like Sam who could throw runners out.

I was beside myself with excitement as I proceeded to boot the first two balls hit to me and wondered if I really belonged with these guys. Things settled down and we started to click. I could see the brain trust on the sidelines taking notes, moving players, and trying different combinations. The one constant in all the ma-neuvering was our infield, locked and loaded, it couldn't be any better. The team and all the players looked solid, however I was still concerned about our leadership. I was having a hard time imagining our team being led by Mr. Meyer or Mark's dad. The practice broke up and as we headed to the dugout, my discomfort faded as I spotted Mr. Mort Schachtel walking to the field with his new cap on, cigarette in hand, and his mile-wide "thank God I'm at the ballpark" smile.

CHAPTER 22
CHARACTER

With our first high school game out of the way we settle into a schedule of two maybe three games a week for the next two months. Never have I had a season go as scheduled. When the weather goes south, as it inevitably does in Colorado, the sophomore team becomes the last in line for the limited indoor space inside the school. While the varsity and JV programs utilize the gyms, we are relegated to the hallways and cafeteria areas to do the best we can to get in shape using the linoleum and our imaginations. Not only are we the last in line for useable space when the weather turns foul but we are also the last in line for the outdoor facilities, reschedules, information, and equipment. Just as the minor leagues of professional sports, we are the step-children of the varsity program. We must pay our dues so that the light of the varsity program will shine on these fair heads that much brighter when their time comes.

For now, the weather holds and we take the experiences and mistakes we had on the field and translate them into bite size bits of information in an effort to avoid the same miscues. Of course the picture I see from the first game is vastly different from what the average player sees. For the majority of players, the first game was just short of organized running around. The event was exciting, confusing, challenging, and a little disappointing all rolled into one big emotional ball of mess. For the rest of the crew, the day is long past and a little bit fuzzy. However, most of the guys take what happened on the field seriously and wish to work on the mistakes and correct the problems, so the time spent losing was not wasted. The boys want to do well. I can see in the eyes of a couple of the kids that they truly dislike looking bad on the field so they are looking to step up and guide this team. Pride is stirring and unity, chemistry, and leadership will soon follow.

Leaders are most often developed and created when a team plays poorly. It is easy to be a stud and leader when the score is in your favor and you are pounding the opposition. Who is willing to step up when the game is not going well and the team is starting to unravel? Too often I have seen the strongest players be the poorest leaders. I have seen players who are friends on the ride to the game turn on each other when the game doesn't go well. I have been witness to friends casting blame on each other for games lost and situations blown; friends will put relationships at risk as a result of the passion in the moment.

Character is created in times of stress and chaos. Rarely is a leader forged from the glow of victory, more often it is from the chaos of a runaway inning or an inopportune error. Who steps up when times are tough? What is the makeup of the kid who is willing to stand up for the guy who made the bad play or costly error? The players that have come through strong in character and tough in mental conditioning are kids from many and varied backgrounds. Some have been the better players that everyone looks up to; others have been the slow, over-weight guy who never stops trying, never stops pulling for the team.

I have had quiet kids and loud kids, talented kids and weak kids, strange kids and stranger kids. However, all of these young men share one common quality which they bring to the park: a grounded and solid perspective on the game and on life. They bring the same attitude of "baseball as life" which we have been talking about; the thought that the game is a little piece of the big picture of life. All the kids who step up to lead realize the game is not always going to go their way, just as life will not always go as planned.

The leaders I have coached most likely had to face something in their life which forced them to add some perspective to their view of things. I don't try to speculate on what event, trauma, book, parent, or mentor may have guided them to the realization of life's inequities, but they have it and it colors everything they do.

I know there are other kids who have the same perspective, but they have not as yet found the courage to trust the thoughts and feelings spinning around in their head. I believe one of the reasons a young man on a baseball team can step up and lead is because there are so many other budding leaders at his side. I have seen frustrated players who rarely talk launch into speeches after tough games. They gave impassioned speeches beseeching their team-mates to dig deep and play with passion and determination; it was a speech rivaling those you see in bad sports movies. The reaction to such speeches is often met by derision from a teammate uncom-fortable with such talk of passion and determination. Yet, I also see the attention and nods of understanding from the quiet leaders of the future. They too will give voice to their own feelings as the season progresses, thanks to the courage of that first outspoken young man who could not restrain his passion and desire to be better.

The young leaders need to be given full rein in order to test their moral compass. What better place to find out what it's like to stick your neck out or to give voice to the fire inside you than the wide open spaces of left field. I let it happen. I give every oppor-tunity to the players to be the team. I am not the one on the field having to suffer the inning that will never end. I am not the team-mate who has to witness the embarrassing meltdown of two close friends tearing each other apart because a ball was misplayed. A coach can only intervene and give counsel, and that speech has already been given numerous times. The moment comes when the boys have to realize that no matter what the coach says it is up to them to decide how best to shut down an inning, repair damaged teammates, come together as a unit, and to take charge of them-selves and their team. The experience is theirs I am only there to supply the balls.

So we go back to work. We play a game every third or fourth day, weather permitting, and we practice on the days in between, weather be damned. For me, the picture is quite large, way bigger than the seven innings we play. The work at hand is an analysis of the effort presented from the minute we gather to get on the bus to the late arrival back at the school. My job starts when the boys straggle to the bus loading area giving me their personality through their greetings for the day.

The makeup of a fifteen year old high school kid is written all over him from the clothes he wears to the greeting he gives an adult. The first kid to arrive will always be the first to arrive, and the last disconnected, had-to-find-my-hat, sorry-I'm-late kid, will always have an excuse both on the field and off. The connection between the daily boy and the on the field boy is a direct one. The attitude I see on the practice field shows up in so many ways on the bus and in our interaction off the field, so much so that one has to address the connection in order to get to the whole boy.

When my pitcher for the day scrambles to the bus at the last minute with no jacket on and a bag of chips and a can of pop in hand I know just how tough a day it's going to be on the field. He will be late getting ready, tire quickly from no real food, and his arm will stiffen because he doesn't know the value of keeping his muscles warm. And because we have had conversations, in fact it is written down on their rules for success hand-out from the first day of practice; there is little point for me to lecture him other than to say, "Nice lunch, where have you been? Did you bring your jacket?" No, the lesson will be taught during the game when I have him next to me after I take him out in the third inning because he is tired, tight, and cold.

We will have our moment to search for answers and understand the chain of events that got us to the moment of frustration. Perhaps it will take a number of special moments for the lights to turn on, for the teenager to give in and try a measure of maturity. All I can hope for is that, at the next start when the snack is a sandwich and a Gatorade and the jacket is in the bag, the result will be a positive one and the lesson will be learned.

Fifteen kids file by, each giving me their unique brand of greeting; fifteen individuals that require fifteen different approaches to draw out the first fantastic bits of their amazing personalities to be. I understand how difficult it is for many of these kids to interact with an adult. The crushing shyness and awkwardness of the unsure teenager is crippling in its weight. My understanding of that weight motivates me to make the baseball experience the avenue for the lightening of that load.

Through sport we can free ourselves of the feeling of being trapped inside looking out. Baseball, the game, being a part of a team, all these things help us get away from the oppressive work of thinking about ourselves ad nauseum. I think of all the times I have greeted a player as he came running off the field after making a fantastic play. The look on a player's face after he made a great play is one of ecstatic disbelief, for he has no idea how he did what he just did. In the moment on the field when the speed of the game reaches fever pace his whole world slows down to just the flight of the ball and his instinct to be with the ball. Everything he worries about, his girlfriend, the math test, the zit on his forehead, the way his pants hang, what to eat next, they all vanish. Making the play strips him bare, and when he arrives at the dugout he is for that moment the guy he wants to be. However, the sad fact of sports is that several minutes later, after all the back-slaps and contact highs, the player is left to himself and within minutes he has no idea how he could possibly have made the great play. Furthermore he thinks he probably couldn't make it again, and by the end of the game he wonders if it really happened at all. By then, the thoughts of tests to come and what to say to the girlfriend have invaded once again and the grunt goodbye is all I get after my congrats on a game well played.

The trick is to create a lasting self-confidence which doesn't require the fantastic play in order for the person to feel alive and in charge. Each unique player will require as much propping up as the baseball gods can send his way, but it will also require the support of his coach, his teammates, his parents, his teachers, and his friends. The path to his confident self is long and winding and some will get there sooner and easier than others. The role of the game is huge in his development as a young man, and the duty of the coach is to illuminate the hero not just on the big plays but on the small plays and in defeat.

CHAPTER 23
EXPECTATION

Coach Schachtel at the helm of our all-star team gave me confidence and allowed me to relax a little. The history we shared allowed me to boom a greeting to our leader that was met with a rather chilly reply. Coach Schachtel turned and glared at me as if seeing me for the first time. With his eyes locked on me he addressed the gathered players, "Guys, we have four days until our first game. Four days in which to come together as a team. I know that some of you know each other, have played with and against each other, but now you will be expected to excel with each other. You have been selected to play on this team because you are the top players in this program; you will be expected to play as though you are the top players in this program. Make no mistake, you are here to play to your potential and beyond." With that said he released me from his eyes and I became a player determined to make my coach proud.

Four days was all we had to blend the schizoid personalities of Schachtel's "all-stars." The grab bag of flakes and divas could not have been any bigger. Combining the huge personalities of Sam, our bigger than life catcher, and Bruce, our land-locked surfer, was only scratching the surface of the impossibility of blending this group. I thought of all the settings on a Hamilton Beach blender and wondered if we could ever stir, chop, or puree our way to a team where we all blended smoothly into a palatable concoction.

Every kid on the field was an awesome talent I had seen succeed in any number of games in a variety of tough and impossible circumstances. The catalog of big strikeouts, long home runs, and deft athletic feats was humbling. The list of unsavory outbursts, tantrums, and unsportsman-like behavior was equally and ingloriously as impressive. I looked forward to the opportunity to play with all these talented athletes, but at the same time I had spent way too many afternoons on the lot near my house arguing with the same kind of over achieving hot-heads to believe this team could ever really come together.

Where did I fit into this talented bunch of knuckleheads? Sure I displayed some talent, at least that's what I kept hearing, and I was on the same field, picked just like everyone else. However, I didn't have the rap sheet of explosive behavior that some of these guys sported. I had always been the quiet kid on the field and on the bench, never venturing too far out from my shell. Joking and joshing around had never been a natural part of my makeup. I loved the games and the practices, and I worked hard at getting better because I was terrified of looking bad or doing anything to call unwanted attention to myself.

When I made the great play or performed well, I was the aw-shucks kind of guy who was as amazed as anyone that I could actually make the play. So hanging with this cast of characters that I admired not just for their abilities but for their audacity of behavior was a real thrill. I marveled at their casual, comfortable manner, secure in their own skin, willing to be large and loud.

The banter on the bench was unlike anything I had ever experienced. No kid was exempt from the verbal and physical attacks that were launched in all directions and with equal force. Most victims of these baseball invectives were proud of the attention thrown their way, proud to be considered worthy of a titty-twister or new nickname. As for myself, I kept my head down and went about my business.

Although I was an easy target, my reputation as a solid player and serious baseball guy gave me a shield against any full-blown assaults. Most of the jokesters realized there was baseball to be played and someone needed to focus on how we did that job when we were on the field. As I generally didn't rise to the bait when the light of their mirth shone on me, mostly because I didn't know how to handle the attention, I was generally left alone and respected as one of the baseball guys who needed to help the team stay the course.

Four days of practice were assigned and four days of work was what we got. The large personalities who showed up on the first day ran head long into the substantial, yet surprisingly nimble frame of one Mort Schachtel. Spending his day on the floor of the commodities exchange in Chicago was more than adequate training to handle a rambunctious group of fourteen year old boys. If anyone on the field thought they were in any way shape or form the equal in thought or action to Coach Schachtel, they were quickly shown differently. Again the message was brought home to us that we were expected to become something beyond what we saw in ourselves but which coach Schachtel most assuredly could.

The four days prior to our first game were filled with more new baseball knowledge than we had absorbed in all our seven years of work with the always well meaning dad coaches. The game blossomed in front of our eyes. The game we had been playing for the last seven years became infinitely more complex, intriguingly more subtle, and exponentially more frustrating. We started to learn about better footwork so that the rare double play became an expected proposition. The ability to steal bases through better lead-offs and better understanding of pitcher mechanics was added as a weapon. We shrunk the game down and learned how to manufacture runs with bunting skills and heady base running. Fundamentals were reinforced; batting eyes honed, glove work refined, cut-offs understood, team dynamics expounded, and leadership established. Coach Schachtel elevated himself as the smartest guy on the field by filling the cup of baseball and letting us sip from its source. In four days we learned what the game of baseball could be and we were anxious to take our new found understanding for a spin.

The Pony League all-star tournament is an event that has been going on since the early 1950s. Allied with the precepts of the Little League baseball program, Pony League is another level up in youth baseball. Pony League is a baseball program for young men ages 13-14 that allows for the further development of their baseball skills. This is the final step of youth baseball before a player advances to the major league distances in high school, American Legion, and if the spirit and fates allowed, college baseball and the pros.

The tournament is structured just like the Little League national program. The first round of the tournament is a district event in which you play teams from your immediate area and surrounding districts. The next step is to play a larger district round in which teams are brought together from the winners of smaller districts. Following the large district round is the regional event in which several large districts come together to determine the best team from say the Midwest region. Finally the winners of the regional divisions meet in a week-long tournament in an effort to crown the Pony League World Series champion.

In 1975 the number of teams involved throughout the United States, including Mexico and Puerto Rico, numbered 8000 teams. The baby boom generation had given the game of baseball unlimited resources in the way of kids to fuel the immense number of teams throughout the country. In the quiet suburban town of Wilmette, Illinois, just such a group had been preparing since the early sixties to come together to see what they could do on the baseball field. The four days of practice were up and it was time to play ball.

The first game of the 1975 Pony League All-Star season took place on the same field we had been practicing on for the last four days. Whoopee, home field advantage. I was sick of this field and felt let down that I was able to ride my bike to an all-star game. The overgrown weeds along the fence, and the shabby cyclone fencing which was dented and curling from overuse left me a bit deflated. The kid from the side yard at Jonathan's house had visions of large crowds with red, white, and blue bunting draped from the temporary bleachers brought in to accommodate the overflow crowds. Instead it looked like any other baseball game, albeit the crowd and the stomach butterflies were a bit larger.

I looked around the stands and saw many familiar faces from past seasons and games. Many of my teammates' parents were in attendance as were the fathers and baseball groupies; adults who loved the game and had followed and watched us play through the years. These were the baseball smitten, the lovers of the game who would watch any game any time no matter the level or the ability. These were the faithful ambassadors of the game who always had time for an inning no matter what busy-ness they may have going on. If they should spy a game in progress while driving by, a U-turn was sure to follow and a moment would be made to enjoy the sounds of the game.

Some of these fans would never say a word; others were calm and soothing in voice, appreciative of plays well done or battles well fought. A gentle congratulations or sympathetic pat on the back was always forthcoming when their paths were crossed. I think back on those appreciative gentlemen and wonder at their devotion to the game. At the time I just thought it odd that they had no kids of their own on the field; what could they possibly be thinking watching us butcher the game of baseball?

Today as I make my own U-turns and find my seat in the back of the stands or down the foul line I know now that these men were the agents of the baseball gods. These men were sent as guardians to look over the struggling youth to give solace and to soothe the dented psyches of boys struggling to be men. The weary baseball men who haunt the fields throughout this land commune with the boys at play and they reconnect with the lessons that were taught on their own path to manhood.

I knew my dad had not arrived yet because he too would be arriving by bicycle. Always a great supporter of my baseball endeavors, I rarely saw him arrive at a game. Most of the time, he would roll in somewhere in the course of the game and magically appear in the stands. He always had an encouraging wave or smile but never a loud word was heard from his lips. My dad was an incredibly well educated man; he was also a thoughtful, pondering man. His tardiness to my games was not from a lack of interest but from the love of bicycling. His route to the field was never a direct one; it was a path that wandered to and fro, affected by parks, large trees, happy children, dogs, birds, and the joy of rolling along.

Once my father arrived he was happy to be in attendance, yet I knew that half his soul was still lost in the clouds. Although he was not completely without athletic ability, he played tennis regularly and was once known as a world class tree climber, baseball was not a game he ever seriously pursued. Which is not to say that he threw like a girl, no, he was always more than willing to go out to the front yard and "have a catch." We would spend a pleasant half hour throwing the ball back and forth, me with my stubborn Jerry Reinholdt model glove, he with his non-glove that was all padding, no web, and all fingers. I marveled at the way he was able to keep up with me, snagging low balls, balls in the dirt and always with two hands.

I wish I had that glove today because nothing spoke more to the character and determination of my dad than the way he worked to catch everything thrown his way. After twenty minutes to half an hour, some kid would come by and ask to join in our game of catch. By that time Dad and I had connected, caught up on all the important matters of the day, and he was ready to find his paper and his reading chair, and I was ready to air out my arm and sting some palms.

CHAPTER 24
YOUNG PERSONALITIES

Having suffered a loss in their first high school baseball game, the freshmen of the squad are more determined than ever to work hard and come up with a win this week. The young freshmen are experiencing high school athletics for the first time while the sophomore kids, many of whom played for me last year, are a bit jaded and seem to think they have things all figured out. While I look toward the older kids to be the leaders and to set good examples for the younger guys, too often the year of experience and the disappointment of not making the JV team leave a bitter youth.

The older boys spent last spring playing baseball with me as their coach, then the summer legion team, and for some, a casual fall league on top of that. To say they are sick of my shtick is a fair assumption. It is my job to keep the game fresh and new, even for the guys who have been around. It is their job to be willing to get better so the goal of making JV and varsity becomes a reality. The lack of patience inherent in the makeup of a fifteen year old boy can create tremors of discontent and frustration which will rear its head and cause disruption among the ranks. As the keeper of all things attitude, it is my job to suppress these outbursts and cancers so that the players have a positive experience and the goals of all are not derailed. For some, the disappointments of life are difficult to take or have not yet been fully experienced. The reality of their situation, their ability, and their need to work hard is flying fast and hard to their face and it is my charge to help them see how best to handle the perceived inequities of the gods.

The first bit of sass comes from a cocky little second baseman who has some skill but not quite enough ability to give him the kind of license he thinks he deserves at practice. In fact, practice is a bit beneath him; "Haven't you seen me play?" he seems to say with every shuffle and half-ass measure. The next piece of disruption comes from the sloth at first who never seems to leave first gear and is always mumbling something under his breath. The levels of desire and the willingness to achieve the goals of a team are not shared evenly within the patchwork of personalities that makeup the group of freshman and sophomore baseball hopefuls. As the players work their way up to the varsity level, motivations will converge as the goals of all become similar and within sight. But now, at the outset of the trail to the varsity level, the focus of each guy is vastly different. Many of these kids will not be able to find the drive and desire needed to finish the hike, but I will make sure they are in step throughout this season.

Not everyone shares the enthusiasm I have for the game, nor do they wish to work as tirelessly on the small aspects of the game. Often the gap between what a player is and what he thinks he can be is vast. Some players are not ready or able to accept the reality of their true ability, nor are they capable of seeing themselves as others see them. As their coach and an agent of the game, it is up to me to help dissolve the fog between their inner perception and reality. Sometimes the revelation is too shocking for the player to accept, but for the truly desirous, the clarity is just the kick they need to engage their will to be better.

The disruptions in our practice have to be dealt with, and the truth for these boys needs to be revealed. The trick to dealing with young boys who are acting out and unsure of themselves is to be firm and to use the personality of the boy as a mirror for him to see himself. Cocky second-baseman-boy is just too cool to have to work on his footwork at second base. Everyone is working hard except cocky boy, and to be honest he is a fine second baseman, but for him to move on he has to work just as hard as the average Joe. Otherwise in two years cocky boy is on the bench and average Joe gets the girl. Cocky boy has no problem talking smack to me, in a respectful playful manner of course, and so I play along, letting him dig his hole.

The too full young man wants the ball hit to him a certain way so he can dazzle us all with his mad skills...I play along. He builds himself up using his rather clumsy footwork to the best of his ability, and with his natural talent he makes do. Once we have all worked the drills and the team comes together that is the time I take to illuminate his need to be more. With my fungo bat in hand, I begin to hit ground balls to the various infield positions and I note how the average Joes are utilizing the footwork we have worked on, and I praise the obvious improvement in their movement. As cocky boy steps up to receive his grounder I hit the ball to his weakness and watch as he stumbles about trying to get his feet in order. "Again," I say, giving him the chance to save face as all eyes are on him. Once more I hit the ball to his soft spot, and we all watch as the frustration mounts and the ego deflates. I give in a bit and give him a ball he can handle, and we progress through the infield, with all those participating demonstrating mastery over their feet, while cocky boy stubbornly refuses to quit on his natural talent and give in to sound coaching and basic mechanics.

Cocky boy will require a lot more coaching than the average Joe. I will talk to him in private about his natural talent and his stubbornness. I will point out to him, and to the others, just how silly it can be to fight against sound baseball concepts and a coach who is willing to help. The natural player who thinks he needs nothing more than raw ability to succeed is the player who will be shaking his head in frustration for years to come when he heads back to the dugout wondering why he has so little consistent success. Our conversations will be one sided with me doing the illustrating and explaining. Many times the lessons a cocky boy learns have a one or two year delay. After my time with a player is over, and he has moved up the ladder to the next level to harder less forgiving coaches, I often see either a player who has been crushed by his inability to accept help, or a player who has finally opened his eyes, shut his mouth, and learned to play the game.

Grumble boy is a different story. A grumble boy can be a cancer to a team; unfortunately, he must be dealt with in a harsher manner. When a boy comes to the team who is used to getting things his way, sometimes he is the class clown or negative kind of guy, quite often he is a grumbler. A grumbler pisses and moans because he has to be at practice or because we have to run or because he is sixth in the lineup or for some unknown reason he is not starting the game even though he grumbles all the time and is late and last on everything! A grumbler is never satisfied, and if you try to mollify the grumbler, you are only doing a disservice to the rest of the guys who behave like men. Because the grumbler will attempt to recruit other players to his negative ways; as a cancer, he must be dealt with swiftly and decisively if the team is to find any harmony or peace.

The grumbler is the player who doesn't yet realize the world he inhabits is a world of his own making. I spend ample time explaining to all, while looking at the grumblers, that the choice to be at practice, on the high school team, in the fresh air, running around with their friends, has been their choice and their decision. I have not forced anyone to be at the field, soaking in the fresh air, running around with their friends, learning the game of baseball. I do require that those who have made the choice to learn and enjoy the game follow certain guidelines such as: be respectful of coaches and teammates, be on time, be prepared, be willing to learn, and to be mindful of those who want all of the above. Some of the young men who show up to practices are entering an era of responsibility that they are not quite prepared to undertake; the responsibility for their own happiness and well being.

Grumble boy often does not know what he wants or what will make him happy. He is not comfortable enough with his ability to determine what is cool or uncool, what is worth his while or not worth his while. His vision down the road is blocked by uncertainty and fear. He is afraid he will make the wrong choice, so he bitches about all choices, covering his bases in case things don't go as planned. By pooh-poohing having to run or having to put in extra effort, he is guarding against the possibility of actually getting better or of failing. If he doesn't have to take responsibility for the success or failure of his time on the field, then he can blame all the obstacles that were in his way. Should he succeed in his endeavors, he is most likely to chalk it up to luck, for it is so much easier to be negative than it is to succeed and want more success. The effort involved in success is so much greater than the energy required to grumble and dismiss.

The grumbler, as infuriating an element on a team as it is, requires more compassion and gentle guidance than most of the problem cases on a team. A kid who works to see the worst in every situation has to be shown a small piece of the goodness in the world before he can accept the value of letting himself be positive. Telling the grumbler that doing abs work will get the girls or extra swings in practice will eliminate the strikeouts, helps him to see the payoff which comes from effort given. Pointing out to the grumbler, and anyone else within earshot, what a beautiful day it is to be playing baseball at the foot of the Rocky Mountains on a glorious day in April helps give him perspective on where he is in his world.

The value of a grumbler's actions has large and small consequences which he must try to work out. The grumbler is struggling with how much he can allow himself to enjoy his world and how much he can enjoy the process of enjoying his world. For the grumbler to change and be a healthy individual, the work involved in being the grumbler has to become harder than the work involved in simply enjoying the day and making the simple be grand. So, by demonstrating the joy of the day or pointing out his small successes and how simply they were achieved, I am able to slowly deflate the large balloon of negativity he has hurt his psyche blowing up.

The discipline and shaping of character which comes up during a season is all part of running a team with fifteen unique and spirited young men. I do not expect all the boys to agree with every tenet of my baseball philosophies, but I do expect them to give me and the rest of the team the respect due to their acceptance of being a part of this program. I make it abundantly clear that I am the boss of this team and that I am the one who writes the checks that determine who plays and who sits. The requirement for payment is a positive attitude, a display of respect for the game, care for their commitment to play, and a love of the game. If you show up and have fun in practice and treat your time on the field as a privilege rather than a punishment, then you will have your time on the field when little Suzie is watching and the game is on the line.

I expect there to be issues and personality conflicts as the season progresses. There is no way to avoid the many pitfalls and disturbances which arise in the course of a season of high school baseball. The pressures these boys feel from school, families, and personal lives inevitably bleeds into their time at the field, making them feel unsure and irritable. The various emotions and personal ticks which cause disruptions are more the result of growing pains and immaturity than of real personality disorders. The baggage the boys bring to the ballpark at the beginning of the year is not who they are or who they will be when the last game is played.

My role as coach is to give these boys an opportunity to disassociate themselves from all the brain turmoil of their lives and to open them up to the other possibilities of life. The baseball field is the place for them to feel the grass under their shoes instead of the Formica of the hallways; to wear the jersey of play instead of the uniform of their peers. And it is a time to focus on who they are under the pressure of play rather than under the pressure of a world wanting their maturity now.

CHAPTER 25
FINALLY GAMES THAT MATTER

The end of July 1975 in suburban Illinois was as muggy and sticky as any place and time in the Midwest...perfect for baseball. Although we didn't have the red, white, and blue bunting and vast crowds of my World Series dreams, the first game of our Pony League All-Star season felt just as grand. We took the field as a team, and my feet flew across the diamond; I felt fast that day. Our brand-new bright-white polyester uniforms with Wilmette in blue lettering across the chest and our red white and blue socks looked great and I felt great inside them.

As the host site, we stood on our home field ready to defend our team and our town because it was expected and because it was written on our chest. The expectations we took on when we put on our uniform had been more than adequately explained to us in the past four days. Coach Schachtel had done a fine job of taking us to the next level or maybe to the next two or three levels of baseball understanding. We took the field as a budding group of players who would play the game of baseball in a way we had never played before. How we fielded the ball was not to get the ball and throw it, now we received the ball and made the play. Pitching was no longer one guy throwing the ball as hard as he could to try to get it past the batter. Now we worked the count, made a pitch to our battery mate and enticed the batter to swing at the pitch we chose for him to swing at. Our approach to hitting was no longer a batter up at the plate swinging at the first pitch that looked good, trying to hit it as far as possible. Now we were hitters looking for a particular pitch in a particular spot trying to produce a result at the plate that would further our cause given the situation of the game at a given time. The game had changed from one of personal achievement to a game of team success based on the strategy and application of sound baseball principles. Armed with our new knowledge, the support of our adoring fans, and our snappy new uniforms, we couldn't have been more prepared...Let's play!

The strength of our team was surely our defense. Every kid on the field was a solid capable fielder, able to make any play presented to him. Every Wilmette All-star was also capable of going well beyond his basic skills to achieve miraculous and outstanding baseball plays which would thrill the crowd, his team, and himself. Given the array of solid defensive players and a solid group of pitchers, we were equipped to keep every game close.

The problem with playing in an all-star format is that the teams you play against tend to bring all of their best players too. All of the opposing players were quite capable of making the simple and extraordinary plays look easy and effortless. Their pitchers were also of the highest caliber and tended to keep the games close. All things being equal on the field, it was up to the hitters to make the difference.

At the ages of thirteen and fourteen, a growing young man could be in any phase of the maturation process. Some kids could be shaving while others are still checking down below to see if anything is sprouting. Looking at my scrawny 125 pound frame there was not a speck of fat on me, and my long limbs were just getting started toward their six foot one final destination. Other players on the team were further along in the muscle department, but over all we were not a team of Tarzans and we would not win many games with walk-off homers. Coach Schachtel had quickly ascertained the makeup of his team so we worked tirelessly on bunting, stealing, and various other offensive strategies that would help us to manufacture runs. Rather than sitting around waiting for the next noodle-armed batter to hit the ball in the gap for a double, we would be stealing, delay-stealing and spraying the ball around with bloop-hits and seeing-eye grounders. We would squeeze out runs every way possible, taking advantage of the other all-star teams who might be taking their all-star status a little too seriously. We intended to make the other teams play the game of baseball as well as we intended to play it. We would force the other teams to make the simple plays and the miraculous plays because if they didn't, we would score. If they made an error, we would score, if they forgot about a runner, we would score, if they left men on and let us up again, we would score. Give us an opening or an opportunity and we would make them pay because we intend to capitalize at every instance... and we would score.

The weapon we intended to use to our advantage to find the run that would crush our opponent was the suicide-squeeze bunt. With a man on third base, we were alert and ready for the possibility, the probability, and the certainty that coach Schachtel would call on us to execute the suicide squeeze. As soon as the pitcher went into his wind-up to throw to the plate, the runner on third base would break for home. Barreling down the third base line, the runner is counting on the batter to one: know that he is supposed to square around and bunt the ball rather than possibly swing away and decapitate the runner, and two: bunt the ball at all cost no matter where the pitch is thrown so the runner doesn't show up at the plate where a grinning catcher would have the ball in hand.

When executed properly the suicide bunt is a guaranteed run in the bank because if the ball is put in play there is no time for any fielder to make a play on the runner coming home. The down side of the play is that it's a guaranteed out at the plate should the batter fail to get a small piece of the ball.

Our four days of practice gave us the chance to hone our bunting skills plus it gave the coaching staff ample opportunity to impress upon us the importance of our role as a bunter and team player. This weapon, and our willingness as a team to put aside our delusions of being home-run hitters, would allow us to dismantle goliaths that were unable to forgo the desire to be heroes with one swing.

As much as the game of baseball is a team game with individual players facing off against each other, the concept of team and sacrifice for the team is still the best way of achieving the goals for all the individuals. We bought into the team concept, and as we took the field, all the cool personalities and mysterious kids from the previous week were now simply the Wilmette All-Stars baseball team coached by Mort Schachtel and we were there to win some ballgames.

The game started and true to form the game was close. Even though we were practiced and prepared, we were still only kids, and the pressure we put on ourselves and the newness of the situation made it difficult for us to play free and loose. Going into the third inning, I came to the plate with a man on second base the score tied at one apiece and one out. Coach Schachtel was well aware of the importance of the first game, aware of the need to set the tone and tempo for our style of play. Before I even entered the box, I knew what was going to be asked of me through the silent telegraph of baseball signals.

I looked down the third base line where Coach Schachtel was standing. His portly yet solid frame had been squeezed into the same tight white polyester suit that all we hummingbird metabolism bodies were sporting. The acreage of uniform he toted was three times what I brought to the plate, so the canvas was quite large for him to portray his instructions through the wipes, touches, and gyrations of our secret language. "Bunt, but make it a bunt for a hit and try for the third base line" was the message as clear as if he had spoken it in my ear. I had demonstrated a real proficiency for the art of bunting and I was confident I could accomplish the task transmitted to me. I tipped my helmet to the coach as silent acknowledgment of our conversation and stepped into the box to stir things up a bit.

The pitcher went into his windup and sent his first delivery to the plate. Because my task was to bunt for a hit, the element of surprise needed to be maintained, so I waited as long as possible before swinging around to present my bat in order to keep the third baseman at his position. So I waited, poised in my best slugger position. As the ball approached, I sprang into action dropping my right leg back, tucking my left hand with the knob of the bat into my waist and sliding my right hand halfway up the barrel of the bat. I bounced off my right leg, angled my bat down the third base line, and directed the ball with my right hand toward the stunned and unprepared third baseman. I left the bat behind as my feet, so swift in taking the field to start the game, once again felt like speed personified. Beating a path toward first base, I knew the bunt was a good one and I felt joy knowing that I had furthered the cause and completed my mission.

As the base approached, the first baseman's eyes became wide as he tracked the ball from the startled third baseman. I watched the first baseman adjust to the erratic throw and cross in front of my path with his knee hitting me squarely in the chest. The collision was violent and I went down hard. The ball got away from the first baseman and the runner from second scored but I was going nowhere. I lay on the ground with Coach Bleisius overhead. I was panicked because I had completely forgotten how to breathe. All the air in my body had been blasted out by the knee to my chest and I had no idea how to replace what had been lost. Coach Schachtel arrived and helped me to remember how to breathe, forever the coach. After some time I was able to get up, but a sharp pain in my side would not subside, stabbing me with every breath. To my horror I was relieved of my duties on the field and told to sit and take it easy. I was mortified. I never sat the bench. I don't know how to sit the bench. I squirmed and fidgeted and felt uneasy looking at my team on the field, a perspective I rarely saw.

The game ended with a victory for our side, thanks in part to my bunt single. The pain in my side would not go away so my bike was thrown in my mother's car and a trip to the hospital followed. As an active boy, emergency rooms were not new to me. My last broken bone was from riding my bike while steering with my feet. The ensuing crash into the parked car broke my thumb and left me with an itchy summer cast which was cool at first but that severely cramped my summer fun. The x-rays that day revealed a cracked rib and some bruising of the sternum. My all-star status seemed in jeopardy and the ride home was a quiet one.

CHAPTER 26
GAME MIND

With our second game slated to be a home game, the high school players look forward to the game being played on the big field in front of their classmates. The butterflies from playing our first game have been replaced with the butterflies of a home game. I feel my own anxiety rise at the thought of bringing our product to the center stage for all to see. No matter how much I want to believe that coaching is about the kids and the influence baseball and my direction can bring to their lives, there is still the fact that games are played and decisions have to be made and the coach is the decider. The scrutiny from the players, other coaches, parents, and me is hard for my brain and my ego to suppress. I am awake early in the days prior to the game trying to work out lineups and to fine tune our practices so we can address the many problems we have discovered since the boys arrived at tryouts.

We work hard in the days leading up to our home debut. The boys are excited and put in the extra effort to shore up the holes in their game. They too realize the importance of the first home game and the need to show up. Their pride is just as strong as mine, so in our own spheres of fear we work to be as prepared as possible for whatever the outcome may be.

The field is in perfect shape for early April. Although the wind is blowing, a regular occurrence for a spring on the Front Range, the sun is out and baseball is in the air. I arrive at the field early because I don't know how to arrive any other way to a ball game. Loaded down with all the gear which will be my constant companion for the next six months, straight through August and perhaps into September and October, I enter the dugout for a few moments of solitude before the kids arrive. I love sitting and looking out at the quiet field, coifed, lined, and ready for an afternoon of baseball.

The thought of what has transpired on this field and what new magic may happen in just a short time fills me with a sports nostalgia that shears away all the previous anxiety and fear which has been accumulating since I started twisting my head around this inaugural game. I should know by now that the entrance through the cyclone fence is as of a shower of antiseptic, eliminating the petty worries of what the world would think, as if it really cared, about what we do on this field. I am as sure of what I do on this day in this arena as of anything I do in my life. I have no fear on this field because my motives are clear and my experience is long.

The peace of my moment with the dirt and grass is interrupted by early arriver and question asker. Both of these boys have an inkling of what mysteries the game may have to offer them but they are not exactly sure what those answers may be. They know they want that something hidden just behind their view of the game, they just don't quite know how to get at it. Each boy has the desire and the determination; they just don't really know for what they are striving.

Early arriver is the first at practice, first at games. To my amazement he is often sitting in the dugout when I arrive…not an easy feat. He is not always the most talkative kid, but I have a feeling he too is talking and listening to the dirt and grass, absorbing the past and anticipating the future. Early in the year, I welcome him and explore his motives and personality, but as the year goes on I leave him to his contemplation and merely acknowledge his arrival and give him the space he needs to seek out and prepare his baseball spirit. The early arriver knows there is more to the game than the glove and his baseball spirit. His belief is that if he spends just a little bit more time in the presence of the field with his glove and ball more will be revealed to him. He doesn't really want additional instruction or conversation about the game; he is more of an osmosis learning kind of guy. He would prefer to learn the nuances of what the gods have to offer in a more organic way, sort of a Bull Durham, Laloush through the eyelids method of baseball absorption. As the rest of the team arrives, he folds right into the flow of the youthful banter and nervous energy to continue his formal training. The early arriver has his moment to touch the spirit of the game and in turn begins his journey as a student of life.

Alone is how we are most of our lives and to be comfortable with that condition requires practice. What better place could there be to practice the dialogue of self-promotion and internal devotion than at the empty ball field. All things are possible before the teams take the field, all plays are made, every swing a home run; all thoughts are positive in a world where you see your movements and know your possibilities. The early arriver is never the last to leave. The early arriver has his time and his moment to prepare and find the connection he needs and seeks. When all the plays have been made and the game has played itself out, the early arriver is ready to go home, secure in the knowledge that he was ready to receive the information and gifts presented to him during the game. However, just like the fade of a great play made, he will have to get to the park early the next game so he can see and replay all over the lessons learned, because they too fade over time and need to be conjured again and again to be sure they are real and still make sense.

The question asker is a high-maintenance player who tests my patience throughout the course of the season. Full of what could only be self-doubt, the question asker keeps up a constant bombardment of questions about everything under the sun. Much practice time is taken up with the never-ending questions about schedules and what uniform to wear and is it ok to wear this sleeve shirt or that hat or when is the bus leaving and what class will we miss and would it be ok if my mom drives me but what if my uniform is dirty and can we stop at McDonald's after the game, huh can we? And I answer the questions to the best of my ability and with as much self-restraint as possible, for I know there is more to the questions than meet the eye.

Question asker is overwhelmed with life and is at once terrified and exhilarated with being in the middle of his life. The questions he asks are the seepage of his too-full brain. Add the excitement of the game and the unknown that being a part of a team brings to his world of high school and classes and girls and walking down the hall in the flow of humanity, as well as the pressure of his parents and a future that looms on the horizon, and it's no wonder his head is going to blow. So I work to focus the young man. I work to set his eyes on the game at hand and allow him to solve the riddle of the double cut and learn to see the spin of the slider as it approaches the plate. Success at answering a few of the questions about baseball gives him the confidence to answer the questions he faces throughout his day. As many questions as he asks me, I ask him back. As tough as the world may seem to him, I present to him a world as tough but just as beautiful in its simplicity. All the complexity he faces every day from the moment the buzzer goes off in the morning until his head hits the pillow at night can be slowed down and enjoyed once the key is found. Confidence is the key to the self-doubt that plagues the question asker.

The dimensions of the baseball field can be daunting or they can be comforting. 330 feet down the line, 400 feet to center field and bowing to 365 feet in the gaps; that's a lot of space to roam around. Put nine guys into that space and the field seems to be a little better covered. Depending on your attitude, you either have the necessary coverage to get most balls hit into the field, or there is just too much space in-between players to ever get anyone out.

The early arriver sees the field as full of players and possibilities where the play is made and there is no way the ball could ever fall into the spaces. The question asker is unsure and afraid therefore the placement of only nine players could not possibly result in an out; there is just too much ground to cover. I have to admit I have played in games where no matter where we played the ball came right to us. I have also been in contests where no matter how we adjusted and moved, the ball found the spaces and the game was a study in frustration.

How big is your field? What are the dimensions in your mind? Each player comes to the field with a certain mind set, a certain ability to shrink or expand the field. Sometimes we bring the too-big field to the ballpark and no matter what we do we are not able to shake ourselves out of the funk of Eyore's world. Those are the times when the baseball is small and the field is enormous. The reasons for the too big field can be that we got up late, Suzie didn't say hello in the hall, and we forgot we had a quiz in math: bad big field. On the other hand, maybe we popped out of bed, Suzie gives us a big smile, and we ace the quiz: good big field. The trick for all is to find our home field and to be comfortable showing up at the park understanding how to play the carom off the wall in right center and to know how the infield plays after the rain and to always feel inside that you have home field advantage.

Home field is ours for today, the first chance for these boys to play on the big field. The excitement is high in the dugout. The boys arrive in twos and threes and begin the process of dressing and morphing into the ballplayers they want to be for the day. I immediately see the difference in the boys from our last outing; we look prepared and determined to represent the school and to atone for the first game loss. Hats are straighter, the banter more subdued, the focus finer.

The beauty of coaching this age group is the chance to see not just huge progress in their physical abilities as they learn the mechanics of the game, but also to witness day to day the stretching of their ability to believe in themselves. I can see the boys willing themselves to be different. The act of standing up for themselves or challenging themselves to be a leader is at times painful to watch but at other times inspiring in its bravery. Today they are determined not to be who and what they were last week. Today they are focused on being a team, respecting each other and relying on each other because they need each other in order to avoid the awful feeling they ended up with last week.

The boys take the field with a little extra zeal and hop, the kind of hop their overzealous coach seems to bring to the field every day and which just puzzles the hell out of them. My words to the guys before they take the field are simple and similar to the Pollyanna spiel they hear every day at practice, what a beautiful day to play baseball (even though it is 45 degrees and windy), make the plays that are presented to you, have fun and play hard for each other. The game is that simple.

The guys are a little revved up to begin the game and we boot a few balls early, but then we settle down as we realize the fans in the stands don't want to harm us but instead do wish us well. The game is not flawless but it is inspired, controlled, and fun. The boys begin to flow to the ball and on occasion feel the game instead of think the game. Our pitcher is making some thoughtful pitches instead of raring back and trying to impress Suzie, and our hitters are executing the plays that I am signaling.

In the fifth inning, I substitute the last of our bench onto the field, switch pitchers, and take a moment to look at the bench and the faces of my players. The usual goofing off is going on with juggling and seed spitting at the top of the list, but there is also a nice level of joy and freedom occurring which is a first for this bench.

Thought is gone, worry is gone, the guys are here and nowhere else. These moments are rare in anyone's life and I take a moment to search my own status to see if I am truly present. As the coach I have a hard time being completely in the moment, what with thoughts of pitcher changes and playing time to worry about. I have learned to activate my awareness chip when I sense the time is at hand. I am able to share certain moments with the boys and I am able to snatch my moments before and after games. During the games I am in a baseball moment that is separate from the outside world but also hyper-aware within the moment of the game; it is not necessarily a relaxing place but it is a place of self-awareness.

So we all share this game time in which the gods are with us and our baseball Chi is in alignment which allows us to flow to our first win.

After the game I speak to the boys of their solid baseball and execution and playing within themselves; all the clichés come flowing out and the boys puff up and feel good. I give the speech the boys have earned. Tomorrow will be another day of waking up and facing a world that doesn't give pep talks in the morning or reward speeches at night, so today we revel in our effort and reward. These boys will have to keep working at showing up every day, taking their lumps and struggling to satisfy the forces outside and within. At least they have this moment and they have their team-mates. They will have practice tomorrow where I will be doling out a whole lot more attaboys and do-it-agains so we can catch some more joy in the games ahead. Today we got a taste of what can happen when we want together. Today we caught a glimpse of the other side of struggle.

CHAPTER 27
STILL AN ALL-STAR

The pain I felt from the two° cracked ribs received from the knee of the opposing first baseman was nothing compared to the anguish I felt from not being on the field with my team. In the short time together as a team, we had created a feeling of unity that I had not felt on any other team. The fact that we were all close in ability had lent itself to putting aside the divides that can occur on teams with mere mortal talent. We didn't need to prove anything to each other because we were selected by far wiser baseball heads than ours. Ordained by the adult world, we could go out and play freely, with no thought given to impressing or showing off because we knew the guy next to us could do just as well and better. We went out to play the game to the best of our ability which was something to see.

The second game of the tournament found me sitting on the bench with an ace bandage wrapped tight around my chest. The act of breathing was painful but the doctor said I could play when the pain subsided. From time to time I took a deep breath in the hope that the subsiding had begun only to find stars swimming in front of my eyes from the pain.

Spending time on the bench was a new experience for me. I cheered as best I could and tried to suppress the desire for Howie, who had moved from second base to shortstop, to mess up so I would be missed. Coach Schachtel was sympathetic and encouraging, but he had a game to win and personnel to rearrange. Team sports are full of people and possibilities. The combinations of players in various spots can be disastrous or it can be genius. It was

129

just this genius aspect that had me so worried at the moment. What if he found a better combination for the field that didn't include me?

Baseball is a sport of chemistry, full of different components that when mixed correctly can be dazzling. Yet, remove one element or add a different component and the mixture can be volatile. How often have we seen a puzzling mishmash of ordinary baseball players come together to raise their game to a level in which they are able to take on and win against the big, bad, couldn't-possibly-lose-on-paper team of super-studs? Coach Schachtel had a nice bench of interesting elements to work with in his chemistry set. The flakes and funky elements of the Wilmette boys didn't look like much on paper, or in person for that matter, but coach Schachtel was able to cobble together the right combination on the field, and at the plate, to punch out a victory even with me wincing on the bench.

Two wins in two days put us in the finals for the local tournament. Being an active kid I had my share of bumps and bruises. I seemed to sport a black eye every other month and bent fingers, cuts, and bops on the head were common. I had not had to visit the hospital for anything serious other than that time I tried to steer my bicycle with my feet. The whole internal type injury had me baffled and angry because I couldn't put a Band-Aid on my ribs or just take an aspirin.

I was restricted and hovered over; squashed from participating. Although banged up I wrapped my ribs and showed up on Sunday working hard to mask the pain of my every step. Coach asked if I was ready to play and I could tell he was looking deep inside me as I answered. I tried to be brave, but his penetrating gaze melted my bravado, and I told the truth which was that I was sore, but I could play the field and my swing was hindered by pain. Coach Schachtel took in this information and let me know he would think about what to do with me at game time.

The final game of the local round of the Pony League All-Star tournament began at 9:00 on another soon to be scorching day at the Locust Elementary baseball field. With two wins under our belts we were feeling pretty good, and the natural swagger we usually brought to the park was starting to reach an uncomfortable level. Guys who were hard enough to be around because of their big heads were now starting to enter the realm of super-jerk.

The personalities I revered just two weeks ago were now starting to come into focus, and I was squirming with the uncomfortable realization that these guys might not be all I made them out to be. My hope was that we could channel our bubbling high spirits and fire the obnoxiousness of our evolving behavior at our opponents. Perhaps we could annoy the other team to the point of distraction. I knew it would take all my effort to maintain my composure; hopefully the other team wouldn't be as tolerant.

Our warm-up routine was unique and had been carefully choreographed by Coach Schachtel. The unusual way in which we took the field for our pre-game warm up had been designed to instill discipline, order, and unity and at the same time address the other team with the statement: we don't know why we are doing this, but our coach thinks it's important. At least that was what was going through our heads as we executed our little dance routine which at the moment seemed silly but in time would be embraced by all as a statement of our team unity and desire.

As we came out of our dugout, we would lay our gloves side by side on the first base foul line. In an orderly jog we circled the infield grass heading toward first base, around to second then to third base, down the third base foul line, turn left at home, head to the pitcher's mound, around the mound, back to home plate and turn left, picking up our gloves as we went by. After this show of team unity and regimentation, we headed to our positions at a sprint and began our infield and outfield warm up. The hokiness of this display was not entirely lost on us when it was presented to us by the coaches. Asking a group of way too cool fourteen year old boys to do something that nobody else does or ever did, and on top of that doing it in front of another team and all the eyes of the fans in the stands was asking a lot. However, Coach Schachtel was the boss and he had a way of presenting baseball ideas in a way that went beyond real world rationality and kid coolness.

Coach Schachtel brought us to the inner workings of baseball giving us a glimpse of the game that we as players making the plays just didn't think about. The psychological game that underlies the mechanical playing of the game was something we as action figures paid no attention to. The coaches realized this group of rag a muffins was going to need all the help it could get to overcome the sheer dominating ability we would face.

Banding us together in our little war dance, forcing us to embrace the ritual of our team, was a way for us to take the field together as one. The psychological warfare Coach Schachtel was playing would go on throughout this campaign, both within our heads and in the heads of our opponents. For now we accepted the embarrassing show as something kooky the coaches had cooked up to be different; later we would embrace the display as our statement, our time to stuff it in our opponents' faces, a statement that said we are here to play.

The final game at Locust Elementary School in West Wilmette was of a magnitude far beyond anything I had been involved with in my short career, and the butterflies were swarming. I had always been anxious as a player, no matter what the size or scope of the game. I didn't know what it was, performance anxiety or self-consciousness, whatever the reason I had always, even to this day, been knotted-up before a game. At the age of fourteen, I was deathly afraid of looking bad or calling undue attention to myself; to me the spotlight was mortifying. I had never been able to flow through life unaffected by events and conditions. I was always over-analyzing every situation and word spoken to me for hidden meaning and possible slights. The bottom line was that at the age of fourteen I was terribly shy, self-conscious, and lacked confidence in my abilities.

Every time I showed up at the ballpark I was puzzled by how the coaches could have seen their way to give me my all-star uniform. No matter how many amazing plays I made or how many base hits I got, I would show up the next day without any real clear understanding as to how I accomplished the things I did the day before or the week before. My awkward awareness of my place in the world made me a mess, but I showed up because when the time came to play and I ran out on to the field the world melted away and I was as close to peace as I could get.

The doctor cleared me to play and to my amazement the coaches and my teammates still wanted me to be a part of the team. I got a lot of careful pats on the back and I was welcomed to the field by Howie who was overjoyed to be back at second base, relieved of the overwhelming task of running things from shortstop. As I waited for the first pitch to be delivered, that amped-up calm came over me once again. The serenity I felt was one of knowing I was right where I was supposed to be, confident in what I needed to do.

On the dirt infield I was aware of who I was and what was expected of me. The rules of the game were boundaries I felt comfortable conforming to, they allowed me to roam in a closed, safe environment, free of a world that was messy and hard to fathom. As chaotic as a game of baseball can be, it was nothing compared to the cacophony of information that a walk down the street could bring to the senses. The butterflies faded as the pitch was delivered. The person I was most comfortable being rose to the surface ready to take on the task of winning this final game. The shy, self-conscious boy who wondered if he was still allowed to wear the all-star uniform transformed into the loud, brash young man who would take no guff from any opponent, who would slide hard to take you out, who had no qualms about letting a slacker teammate know he was letting his team down, and who had to be restrained at times from letting an umpire have a piece of his mind. I could be on the field. No thought was required when the game was played in real time.

Although I was less than 100% I gave it my all, ecstatic to be shoulder to shoulder with the guys. As annoyed as I was at times with some of these knuckleheads, I realized I was as screwy as the next guy and probably just as difficult to be around. I smiled inside and wore my uniform close knowing I did fit in and belonged here with these guys. My stint on the bench gave me an added appreciation for my team and for my health, also for the opportunity to be on the field all the time, every game.

I did what I could to contribute, and on this day, that meant not hurting the team. I executed the plays hit to me and pulled a little harder for the other guys to pick up the load I brought for them to carry. At the plate my struggle to swing the bat with aggression and velocity only allowed me to contribute with a couple of well-placed bunts. Running down the line was the most painful of all and I gladly gave myself up as first base approached, still a little gun shy from my collision. The seventh and final inning approached with us comfortably in the lead, so Coach Schachtel replaced me in the field. The guys were playing really well, in fact it was a sight to see. Every player looked like they were right where they were supposed to be. The coaches had done a great job finding and placing every kid in the spot they were meant to play, and the result was a harmony and chemistry that was hard to beat.

We won the final game of the local tournament 8-3. For most of the guys, the win was nice, but then again most of us had won plenty of games in our careers. What we didn't realize was this was the first step on our quest to see how good we could be. The next step was a district series in Northbrook, Illinois about fifteen miles West of Wilmette, where we would play some of the best teams in the Chicago Metro area.

As happy as we were about our victory I could hear the coaches and the parents discussing the logistics of getting to Northbrook and just how tough the next round would be. But we had a week in which to prepare and the way we played, although not spectacular, was encouraging for the coaches. While the parents sorted out our future, I soaked in the excitement and happy faces of the players and fans. Now that the game was over I was quiet and reserved, too uncomfortable to do more than accept the well wishes of parents and fans I barely knew. My dad gave me a hug and congratulated me on hanging in the game as long as I did, knowing full well just how sore and uncomfortable my ribs were. I gathered my stuff and headed to the car to get away from the aftermath of our victory.

The ride home was soothing and quiet as my dad had said about all he could think of to say about the game. Watching the trees and streets fly by, I was content and happy with the outcome because I knew the baseball season wasn't over yet. At least for the next week, baseball would still be a part of the summer and I would be free to let my spirit soar between the lines.

CHAPTER 28
SMALL SUCCESS

The boys have now experienced one victory and one defeat for their school team. At practice the day after their home field victory, it is obvious which feeling they prefer. Practice is lively and spirited, and I give the boys their head and let them revel in the feeling of being in control of their world.

It's funny how emotions can alter your outlook on the world. The guys swagger and strut and joke and chide each other as if they have been lifelong friends. The camaraderie the guys feel for each other at this moment cannot be duplicated outside of the sports field unless you want to equate it to going to war, and I am sure that must be a whole different level of human connection. The guys have shared a powerful drug…victory. Working and striving to achieve a common goal against forces which are trying just as hard to knock you from your task and to then come up victorious against those forces is a powerful feeling.

At the ages of fifteen and sixteen, there have been few times in which these young men have been so aware of their places in the world. These young men have been exposed in the last year to the future looming ahead, to the responsibility they must shoulder in order to become men. Although these guys may have won some ballgames in the past, they have not been as aware of their role as a player and as a person in achieving those victories. Some of the guys are further along in their understanding of what it takes to reach goals and victories. The many and varied personalities and abilities of these guys both hamper and accelerate each player's understanding of who they are, but the one thing they all know for sure is that it feels damn good to go out, play hard, and pull out a win.

At the end of our animated practice, in which we competed in some hitting drills and fielding competitions, I gather the guys together for a little reality check. Being the wild unharnessed boys that they are, it seems only fair to their parents that I yank them back down to Earth before I send them home. Although we did win a game, playing rather well in the process, the work is not over and the lessons to come will be devastating as well as elating.

It is important to keep all wins and losses in perspective if you are going to be successful in the long run. Every up and down has value against the larger picture of the journey to be a great player and person. So as we prepare for our next opponent, it is important for us to build on our success, correct our failures, and even out our emotions, so that when the next obstacle comes along we are able to navigate smoothly and find a calm spot. Of course the conversation is a little different with the squirmy bunch of knuckleheads in front of me who are more interested in giving the guy next to them a titty-twister or a shove into another teammate. After a couple of discipline runs and a harsh word about focus, I have their attention and give them the speech about looking ahead to our next opponent and forgetting the last game. I emphasize the fact that we need to continue to work hard to get better because the next team will fillet us if we are not prepared.

And the speech goes on, reaching and grasping at these young men to be vigilant against all the elements working against their success both within their heads and in the outside world. I see faces start to glaze over and I know the meter is up for the day. I am given just so much time each day to influence these impressionable young men, so I take the time given and do what I can. The trick to dealing with this audience is to know when to push and just how hard to pound the message. The opportunities are many, from game situations to practice, from light-hearted chats to disciplinary scolding. For now, and until our next game, the message will be about focus and maintaining an even approach to our progress. I see the confidence and joy the boys feel about the way they won the last game, but I also see who and what I am dealing with in talent and emotional makeup, so I fear for our chances on Thursday.

Chapter 29
Goliath

In every high school program, there are a couple of teams within the league that are rivals or in some way have a history which stirs the blood, or for a coach, sends shivers of fear and loathing down the spine. Our game Thursday is just such a team and the shivers are there. My first experience against this team was as a freshman coach; in fact it was my first game as a high school coach...ever. Riding down to Denver, trying to put on a brave face for my team, I was terrified. The team compiled that year was made up of players who really had no business being on the field. By high school most kids have found their sport or they have discarded a sport because they looked around and saw the sport had passed them by. My first team was comprised of a batch of kids who were not able to see as clearly as one might have hoped. Because we only had a limited number of kids to choose from, we were able to continue their delusional baseball fantasy.

I remember the pre-game warm up on a chilly day in April and looking across the field at my first ever opponent to see them all throwing in perfect unison. Every kid looked to be at least six feet tall, muscular, powerful and I wished I had just one of them in my stable. Looking at my group of players, I felt a lump of pity well up in my throat because I was instantly aware of the severe thrashing these poor boys were about to endure. The boys across the field were long-tossing at distances my guys could only dream about. All my players were spending most of their warm up time chasing the balls that were clattering against the screen behind them or tracking down the overthrown balls long distances into the outfield. My fear dissipated as I looked at my hapless group, the pity replaced with a feeling of compassion and a desire to protect these young men so they would come out of this game with something besides a severe whooping.

We received the expected pasting at the hands of the baseball mutants. I kept my cool and coached my gallant young men as if it were the seventh game of the World Series. To the boy's credit, they played hard and took the defeat, and the many that followed, better than I could have ever hoped. The after-game speech I gave following our sound thrashing, in which we had two hits, no runs, and an insurmountable number of mistakes, was about pride. I told them how proud I was of the way they represented themselves on the field and in the dugout. As delusional as they may have been, they were not blind to the fact that their opponent was light years ahead of them in every category. My point to them was that they were light years ahead of that team in character, and I was damn proud to be their coach.

From that day up to the present, I have been a part of many victories and many defeats, and it is my goal as a coach to try and bring the pride and determination of that first team to every field I step on. If we can play a game with class, pride, and determination, we will come out the back side able to hold our head high and we will take home more than just a win or a loss.

I run all the past history through my head as we rumble down the highway. I have less fear and anxiety about the game ahead knowing I have already participated in the most difficult game of my coaching career. That early ignominy put coaching in perspective for me. The game is not about me or my record or how good I look on the field. The game at this level is about the boys. As we pull into the parking lot, I know we will again have our hands full. Our chances of coming away with a victory are slim, so I hope for a spirited game and an attitude of determination from the guys. Although the talent I now have is considerably better than in the past, we are still playing at the sophomore level with a majority of freshmen on our team. For half the team it will be their first time travelling to the home field of the Denver high school powerhouse.

The elation and confidence from our victory of a few days ago is swiftly fading as we watch the other team take their infield/outfield drill. The crisp routine the opposing team runs through in preparation for the game is a sight to see with whirling infielders and crow-hopping outfielders in perfect synchronization. The psych factor is high as their still over-sized and hugely talented players go through their paces. It is obvious these guys are the cream of the crop of high school athletes, and the attitude they bring to the field clearly states they know they are special.

I usually encourage my team to watch the opposing team's warm up so we can spot any weaknesses in arm strength or poor speed or anything which might help our chances in winning. Today I wish I had a shiny object to flash at the boys to distract them from the display of baseball prowess on the field. Instead I talk to the boys about what they are seeing on the field in front of them. I tell them to watch closely and to learn from these guys because they are good, and they worked hard to become so. Learn what it takes to be an athlete others will admire; you must want to be the athlete others admire. I tell the boys the truth; these guys are good and they expect to come out and beat us.

The truth in sports is not spoken often enough, it is an unspoken truth. Players are not stupid or delusional in their understanding of the quality of another team. The minds of players are full of the fear and doubt and truth of what will happen when faced with the superior talent of a better team. What we do with the mixture of emotions is what makes sport interesting and what creates the legendary games that we speak of in the years to come. Given the fact we are up against some tough odds, I confess to the guys that I like our chances in this game. Based on the work we put in this week and the fine play from our last game, I think we can play with these guys. If we come out and play the game the way we know how, do the things we are capable of, make the plays that are presented to us, and work the pitcher the way we have lately, then I think we can give these guys a shock. So who's with me?

The first three innings are beautiful, just the kind of play my speech was talking about, but words can only go so far. Once the other team realizes we are here to play some ball and not just be cannon fodder for their baseball juggernaut, they take things up a notch. They take the game to a little rarer air than we have been exposed to. The game as we play it is a solid brand of workman-like, make the plays, get some hits, stay aware, take advantage type of game which rewards a team for diligence and perseverance.

The game they demonstrate to us to is one of power, speed, and athleticism unmatched by the conglomeration of players we brought on the bus. On top of being quality athletes, these guys bring to the game a level of baseball acumen my boys are just beginning to learn about. We have touched on the mental game in practice, but the world of baseball strategy, deception, intrigue, and winning attitude are aspects of the game some of the kids do understand but that most do not. In order to achieve the very highest success in a sport, the level of devotion to winning must go beyond the physical prowess of your athletes. The individuals involved need to be committed to understanding every nuance of the game so they can draw on the smaller aspects of inspiration and knowledge in order to overcome the obstacles a given game will throw their way. Although the majority of the obstacles will be physical in nature such as a curveball or bunted ball, there will be many mental obstacles as well. The cat and mouse play of a batter stepping out of the batter's box to disrupt a pitcher's timing or the overt heckling of an obnoxious fan or player must be guarded against with a strong mental will.

A coach is able to control the preparation of his team's readiness to play the game, but he is unable to fully prepare his team for the vagaries of the inside game. How do you prepare a kid to handle verbal abuse from an opposing player? What do you say to a kid who has to watch another coach pour on the runs in a lopsided victory? How do you lift up a kid who is playing third base and is repeatedly bunted on because he has demonstrated slowness to the ball or weakness in his position? The pitcher and catcher, who are struggling to find a way to get batters out, search in vain to understand the psychology of what pitch to throw in a given situation to shut down a team that can do no wrong.

All these aspects of the game come into play as you navigate the different teams throughout the league. Every team we face has a personality which can be felt as soon as we enter their field. I can tell from the way a team maintains their field and from the way their coach is dressed as to what kind of team we are about to face. The personality and style of play we can expect from a team oozes from how they go about their business. The game of baseball can be played in so many different ways and at so many different levels of intensity that if you are not tuned into the subtleties of a team's character you may be blindsided.

Many teams thrive on the ability to disrupt and to take advantage of a team's inability to adjust to shock. Unfortunately, many of the tactics used to cause the disruption are questionable and un-scrupulous, all the better to throw the other team off its game. How a team and a player handle the affront of being run into, or spiked, or hit by a pitch can determine the outcome of a game. How a coach responds to the bush play of a team or opposing coach can also spell disaster for a team and furthermore may set a tone which will not be easy to dispel in the games to follow.

Much of a player's ability to handle the off-putting events which arise in a game must be learned through experience. A lot depends on the character and personality of the particular player. A lot depends on the personality the coach has instilled within his players and the team he puts on the field. Teaching a team when to turn the other cheek and when to get mad or get even is a difficult task when dealing with hormonal, gangsta rap, video-game fueled teenagers. Revenge and retribution for being disrespected is a common theme in movies and on television. Reality shows aimed at the teenage audience constantly pit young people against each other in confrontational situations where honor and reputation are challenged. Lashing out and satisfying the urge to get back at a perceived rival is easier and better television than taking the high road and walking away from the confrontation.

The same can occur on the baseball field where emotions run high. The honor of your team and your reputation in the eyes of your teammates can trump common sense and the cause of the game. The best a coach can do when a tough choice presents itself is to hold a firm hand to the reins of his team and monitor the players who have a tendency to play with too much emotion. However, a coach must also be ready to slacken the reins when the emotions displayed are warranted and can be channeled to a just end.

Sports are all about the release of energy and emotion. When these elements are properly controlled and channeled, amazing things can happen. Many teams that were counted out and done have risen from the ashes, fueled by the foolhardy words of an op-posing player or the spark of an impassioned teammate. Games have turned one hundred and eighty degrees on the spirited play of an underdog player or slighted teammate. A coach needs to be vigilant and tuned in to the tone and feel of each game so that he can take advantage of the subtle undercurrents of events as they progress through each inning. He must always pay attention to the little confrontations and interactions between his players and the opposing team. Even the exchanges between teammates can have an effect on the game in both a positive and negative way. The feud that started to boil in practice the other day can blow up into a storm come game time, causing ripples of concern throughout the team which can erupt in a spasm of negative emotion on the field.

The last four innings of our meeting with the goliaths of high school baseball are a study in baseball prowess and finesse. As solid a game as we play we are no match for the sheer athleticism of this baseball powerhouse. The boys play hard and keep the game from being a whitewash, however, once the other team decides to take the game up a notch, we are unable to overcome their speed, power, and precision. The speech after the dust has settled is upbeat and positive.

A lot of good things happened on the field, and the boys know they have represented themselves pretty well today. I can see on the mud- smeared faces of the boys that they are starting to get the message of a game played well is a game to build on. There is a realization here that every game is an event to be fought over and digested for its nutritional value, not just for the quick sweetness of a victory. We break down the meeting with a spirited and unified call of our fight name, "1-2-3, Knights!" As we head back to the dugout to gather gear and collect ourselves for the ride home, the boys are full of questions and rapid talk about the game and the action that took place. Even though we lost, I hear more banter and excitement from the guys than I heard after our victory the other day. I too am full of thoughts and energy over the quality of baseball I just witnessed, and I chatter on with my assistant over decisions made, plays executed, and the joy experienced at having played the game well.

The boys drift off to the bus and to rides from parents who made the trip down to the city. I accept a few well wishes and engage a few parents in baseball banter. The parents behind the fence have had a completely different experience of the game than what the boys and I experienced. Sure the game is the same at face value, same events, same score, but the reality of the game is very different through the veil of the cyclone fence. Being a part of the internal machinery of fifteen teenagers involved in trying to be great is exhausting. Keeping this contraption moving and heading in the right direction, as well as staying on top of overseeing the controlled chaos of a baseball game with all its outward and internal complexities, is a feat the parents cannot fully appreciate. At the same time I am aware that I do not fully appreciate the twisting and squirming emotions of the parents as they struggle to understand the decisions I am making on the field and what role their son plays in those decisions.

The two worlds meet once I pass through the cyclone barrier. Passing through the gate, the world of baseball serenity melts from my body replaced with the confining role of coach and spokesman for the team. I re-enter the real world where who I am to these well-meaning parents is still a bit tenuous. Although the boys know me well through time spent on the practice field and in the heat of the battle, the parents know me only third hand. I do my best to reassure, prop up, and boost the spirits of these people who think the loss on the field is a tragedy. I choose my words carefully so as to illuminate the bright spots from the day and to reassure them that the sun will rise tomorrow and their boys will be just fine.

I do not try to explain the emotion and energy that not twenty minutes ago was pouring from their children's mouths and bodies. How do you tell a win/loss society that an important moment has transpired in defeat? We will be a much better baseball team and their boys will be much better people as a result of their participation in this game today. Every day we grow, but some days we grow by leaps, and today we traversed a great distance. I can't wait to go to practice tomorrow because I know I will have a whole new group of boys waiting for me when I get there.

CHAPTER 30
A TEAMMATE

Moving on in the Pony League tournament gave me the chance to extend my baseball summer and afforded me the opportunity to further understand my teammates and coaches. Although I had been around these guys and these coaches for years, I really hadn't spent much time trying to get to know them. Most of the boys I now called my teammates had always been "those guys" or "that guy." Up until now they had always been those mysterious players I played against or heard stories about.

I never was the kind of player who stuck around after the game to socialize and get to know the other guys. When the last out was recorded, I was not capable of turning the game off and chit-chatting with the guy who just beat me. The game lived on in my head during the bike ride home, through dinner, as I was brushing my teeth, and while I lay in bed trying to shut my brain down for sleep. Getting to know the guys I spent so much time and energy trying to overcome on the field over the years was a little awkward. They talked about games and events I knew I participated in but for the life of me could not remember. I played the game as it was presented to me, an out at a time, a situation at a time, and rarely could I put a face or personality to a particular out or situation. So I faked it. I tried to be one of the guys laughing and agreeing with all the recollections of past glories and games played. I didn't care for all that standing around; let's put our gloves on and go do the game not just talk about it. My fourteen year old social self was a long way from being ready for the chatter of the cocktail party crowd. If I wasn't chasing a ball then I wasn't completely comfortable; my skin just started itchin' when it wasn't movin'.

My social interactions up to this point were limited to my neighborhood friends, my baseball teammates, and my shy awkward attempts to interact with middle school girls. I was envious of the kids who were comfortable in any situation be it a boy situation or a girl interaction. I watched the way the cool kids joked around on the bus and even held hands or smooched the girls. The easy manner in which they flowed through the torturous days of middle school left me angry with myself and my inability to get the hang of being comfortable in my skin bag.

Truthfully I was not exactly the social outcast I felt myself to be. I was one of the most gifted sports figures in the school, a real gym teacher's dream. I was also a "cute" boy as the girls would tell me on the rare occasion of my being within the ten foot zone of their mysterious world. The only thing keeping me from being one of the cool kids I envied so much was my own shyness and lack of self-confidence. Sure I could run the fifty yard dash faster than most kids, throw a ball farther than the gym teachers, leap and catch and spin with a football as well as Baryshnikov, but I couldn't hold a conversation with a girl to save my life. Becoming a Pony League all-star was just another step in my already well known world of sports. What I failed to realize when I became an all-star was that the journey to freedom of self and self-confidence would also come from the world of baseball.

Because I had always been the top dog on any team I was free to say and do pretty much anything I wanted. My fiery on-field persona was accepted as a positive attribute but it also allowed me to release my frustration at being unsure and awkward with my life. Playing with a whole group of top dogs put a damper on my ebullient field personality and forced me to interact and talk with my equals. I learned to be a real team player, and better still, a fellow human who shared the same passion for baseball and the same desire to win. I began to have real conversations with people who I had previously revered and placed judgment on, yet never really knew. What's more, these new social partners weren't about to put up with my attitude of superiority nor were they going to tolerate my quiet off-field demeanor.

I was fully initiated into the fold of full-time teammate and friend by their insistence that I not take myself so damn seriously and furthermore, they showed me how not to take the world so seriously. I became the butt of jokes and tricks just as much as the next guy. To my amazement, my ticks and quirks were exposed to the full light of day and I was accepted in spite of and because of those personal foibles. I came to realize the cool kids were simply the kids who had taken a good look at themselves and said, "OK, so what, I can live with this." The strong personalities on the team were not afraid to hold the mirror up and say, "Lighten up it's only a game," and on top of all this introspection and examination, we got to play baseball.

Coach Schachtel and his assistants were all buzzing at practice. The level of excitement was palpable within the circle of our brain-trust. Coach Schachtel was the eye of the storm, calm and in control, while his assistants swirled around full of excitement and ideas about the new toy they had been given. We were put through our paces during practice. We understood we played well in the games the previous weekend and we were also feeling confident and sure of our team as the week of practice went along. With the added week, we were able to solidify some of our strategies and to build on the strengths revealed in the previous round.

We were beginning to understand that we had to play our roles on this team in order to compete against the teams we faced. When we were called on to bunt or steal we were being asked to fulfill a duty in one small moment within the game. We were not being asked to win the game or be a hero in a crucial situation, we were simply playing a part in a moment which required a particular effort within the larger picture of the game. Constantly being asked to contribute with a focused effort requires awareness and vigilance at every moment of the game. Along with this hyper-awareness comes a focus and baseball acuity we had never experienced before and it allowed us to play in a zone which excluded the world outside of the fence. We were comforted in knowing that when we showed up to play, the coaches and our fellow teammates would also have the same mind set and focus for the task at hand. We knew the driving effort we put forth would be matched and accepted as a noble aspiration, not as merely a game to be played, but as a goal to be achieved and a point to be proven.

We headed off to Northbrook for the next round of games to determine who would go on to Bay City Michigan as a representative of the Midwest regional, and after that the round to determine who would be the Midwest champion. As high as the stakes were in the minds of the coaches, as players we had no clue. Our parents wound us up and pointed us to where we needed to go. The game, the tournament, the site all became a blur. We showed up and re-united as if by magic, drawn to a speck of dirt and grass in the middle of nowhere. All the cars converged and the guys you knew as your teammates emerged from the multitude and we gathered. How odd to look out over a crowd and pick out the guys who were dressed just like you. Scattered kids dressed in goofy ill-fitting knickerbockers intersected at a designated site and went to work as one. As goofy as we looked, all shapes and sizes, elbows and angles, shaggy and short, we walked with pride and power as we gathered one player after another. Striding en mass, our power as a group separated the crowd in front of us, and we opened the gate to the empty field which today only allowed those that were uniform.

CHAPTER 31
BASEBALL JOY

The high school boys have won one, lost a couple, and gained a ton of experience in the first month of the season. Each boy has learned a lot about himself and his teammates in the past few weeks. The confidence and level of comfort the boys have found is remarkable given the fact these same boys were terrified of their own shadow just four weeks ago. Each person on this team has gone through a transformation in the way they interact with each other, with me, and with the sport they are learning to embrace. Even the boys who are not sure of their relationship with baseball have embraced the notion that learning the game and participating at the high school level has given them something they cannot find anywhere else in their life.

Being a part of a team sport is kind of like joining a therapy group. We meet every day and work at fixing problems with our swing or our footwork or that jerk at first base or how to get Suzie to look at them. Through repetition and talking through our problems with the coach and with another human being, we are able to sort out the answers to our issues. Because we spend our time in the safety of our enclosed ballpark, we break through the barriers we have put up to protect ourselves from others seeing our flaws. When we discuss our inability to adjust to the curveball or our failure to position our glove properly when going for a ball in the hole, we open ourselves up and allow a connection of spirit which is hard to establish in the outside world. Listening to players joke around and vent their frustrations to each other about their failures is a therapy that will pay dividends down the road. When was the last time you heard two executives sharing their feelings of inadequacy at the office? Never do you overhear a group of auto mechanics cussing about feeling frustrated with the new Chilton's manual or their lack of form using a ratchet set.

With the middle of the season ahead of us, we are settling into a routine. Showing up to practice is a fun secure place to work on becoming a better baseball player, and in my mind that translates into becoming a better person. Every time these guys show up, they accept the notion that listening and working hard will create positive results in their game and in turn they work at creating a positive character. You cannot put in the time day after day struggling to perfect the quirky mechanical skills of this game unless you build the character and spiritual presence needed to continually fail. Having a whole group of teammates struggling alongside you making the same mistakes and at times achieving great things allows us to continue in our pursuits.

The success these boys are looking for and see when watching the varsity games or the Colorado Rockies baseball team is illusive but accessible. The saying "Even a blind dog finds a bone" is so very appropriate for the game of baseball. I have story after story of the weakest, most awkward player having a moment of such sublime joy on the baseball field that when I think of them I still smile. There is the kid who couldn't hit his weight but just happens to come up at the most crucial time, of course, and drives in the winning run with a shot into the gap. Or the boy who has bugged me all year to give him a chance on the mound and who I finally let pitch only to see him mow down the side and become an ace on the hill and stud for the next three years.

The success stories I have seen and the legends of greatness from the history of the game are the fuel for the efforts being put forth in practice. The search for game-joy is what continues to motivate these guys. Finding that flash of joy when we hit the ball on the nose or make the un-makeable play is what brings us back, and it is what pushes us past the barrier of fatigue and frustration. These guys are hooked on the juice of achievement, success, and joy. Even though they show up in the carcasses of surly disgruntled teenage boys, angry with their parents, teachers, and hair, they usually leave practice satisfied they are a little closer to making the great play and winning the game in the bottom of the ninth.

CHAPTER 32

EXOTIC TOWN

The field at the Village Green Park in Northbrook was alive with activity on that Thursday night in late July. There were five teams in the round and we were slated to play the team from Waukegan, Illinois at six in the evening to get the district tournament under way. The double elimination event would decide which team headed to Bay City, Michigan to compete in the regional tournament.

All of the tournament information had either been kept from us or we just weren't paying attention to the way things were unfolding. All we knew for sure was we had the opportunity to keep playing, people were getting rather worked up, and the teams were becoming more exotic. Gone were the summer games of playing the same teams over and over, the same faces with the same talent and the same outcomes. The teams we faced now had cool new uniforms with snazzy logos spelling out towns down distant roads. The players were all intimidating and larger than life. Pitchers were huge and threw hard, hitters were big and burley and came with legends whispered from teammates who were completely unreliable. The anxiety we created before a single pitch was thrown was palpable and we all swaggered and spit to mask the churning within.

We get our chance to take our infield and outfield warm-up precluded by our war dance around the infield. Running and going through our paces helped to shed the fear that had been building since we pulled into the parking lot. Snapping the ball around the infield and airing out our arms calmed us down. I took a quick glance over at the kids from Waukegan and I could tell they had the same fear we had. As we wrapped up our pre-game drills, we settled into the zone, confident as fourteen year olds could be, willing to put our best on the line against anyone. Waukegan took the field, and with the cobwebs gone, their players don't look nearly as big and their pitcher didn't seem quite as awesome; on closer inspection they looked a lot like us.

We swept the tournament with wins over Waukegan, Glenview, and finally Freeport, Illinois. The games went by fast, blasting through the bracket and championship games in four days. We were never really pushed to the edge of a loss or faced with the re-alization of what that could mean to our chances on a larger scale. We were simply playing ball on a summer night with a fun group of really talented guys. So winning came naturally and Coach Schachtel made all the right moves. We came to the plate, did what he had in mind and trusted that if we executed the plan we would come out on top.

Every kid was tuned into his role and to the limits he brought to the team, the plate, and the field. The team was composed of a set of known elements, and Coach Schachtel was allowed to mix the elements in a way he saw fit given the team we were playing, the pitcher we were facing, and the particular situation at hand. When you become a coach, you dream of having the toolbox Coach Schachtel was given. No matter what situation we found ourselves, the right guy seemed to always come to the plate and if he wasn't the perfect guy for the job then a simple substitution for a role player off the bench would get the job done.

We trusted Coach Schachtel would do what was needed to ac-complish the task of winning the ball game, and for me, the task of extending the season just a little longer. After each win we got the news that we would play again. For a kid who knew no better way to spend quality time than on the field, the message of playing more was music to my ears. Just tell me where and when and I would be there. After the final victory against Freeport on Sunday, the message was once again a happy one, except the stakes were just a bit higher. Because of our victory in the district tournament, we moved on to an even more exotic locale; pack your bags, we're taking a bus to Bay City, Michigan for the regional tournament.

CHAPTER 33
CAPTIVE GREYHOUND
TO BAY CITY

We were only three weeks into the Pony League tournament, but it felts like months, perhaps years. The guy who showed up for the tryouts was a distant memory. I walked differently, talked differently and thought differently. I didn't quite know inside who the kid was that showed up every day for practice and games; he didn't feel right, yet. I knew more about the game and about my team, but the knowledge of who I am was still taking shape, and I was not fully committed to being the guy who was starting to awaken.

I found I was able to say what was on my mind without censoring or picking the safest words. The trust I was developing with myself was reflective of the trust I was feeling for the guys on the team. They allowed me to be who I was and what was amazing to me was the fact that they accept the "me" I was able to be with them. The growth I felt as I extended myself was both liberating and frightening. I was becoming a full-fledged person, but I was also losing the safety of the child I was trying to shuck off.

Being recognized as an independent self, and demanding the recognition of that independent self, I found came with some heavy responsibility. Hiding behind ignorance and innocence was no longer an option and the world that was revealed to this self-aware self could be harsh and unwavering. I felt raw and alive as I packed my bag for the eight hour Greyhound bus ride to Bay City. The world was out there waiting for me. It had been patiently biding its time, waiting for me to awaken. My excitement was no longer just about the baseball we were going to play, but about the world we would see and the experiences to be presented. I felt different as I climbed on the bus and we rolled out of Wilmette. The game was getting bigger and the stakes were getting higher. I knew the baseball guy could handle the stage but the personality inside the uniform was still up in the air.

I had travelled some down through the years; camping trips to Wisconsin, a train trip through Canada, a long road trip to Maine, however, those trips were with my parents and my brother. Travelling to Michigan with a bus full of jacked-up teenagers, a few terrified chaperones, and a way cool bus driver named Gus was a lot different than kumbya and car games with the folks.

Spending time on the baseball field with these guys followed by a little chit chat after the games was a great way to keep a relationship safe and at arm's length. However, now we were all cooped up in a big metal tube for eight hours and not a one of us really knew how we were supposed to behave. Do we sit and read and have pleasant conversations about our favorite things, bonding, and getting to know each other? Not likely. The ride was a rousing affair in which we indeed got to know each other on a whole new level.

The guys I was playing with in the beginning turned out to be nothing like the heroic icons I had originally made them out to be. I began to have my suspicions that some of these great guys I held up as the coolest might not be as great especially when emotions flared during tight baseball situations. The civility we enjoyed during our finest hours sometimes faded to snappy rebukes and surly demeanors when a strikeout or wild pitch occurred. With no baseball to buffer our interactions, I was now faced with the boy, the brat, the unmasked legend. The patina had started to fade as my eyes opened to the fact that these guys were just like me, trying to find their way, trying to become comfortable with who they were. All the cool bravado was too hard to maintain so the real boys started to bleed through. With eight hours ahead of us, we may not sing songs together, but the bonding would be real and the façade would definitely come down.

The ride to Bay City was a real eye opener and for me a bit of a setback in my progress out of my shell. Without the comfort of my glove and spikes, I felt a little exposed, so I dialed back on the new me and once again watched a bit from the sidelines. The large personalities on the team took over the fun, reveling in the captive audience and great acoustics of the Greyhound theater. Rolling down the highway was anything but quiet reading time, it was a chance for every kid to stick his neck out a little and expose another side of his personality...for most that involved a lot of yelling. By the time we entered the city limits we all had a better understanding of who our teammates were, and like it or not, we checked into a little mom-and-pop motel on the edge of town to further explore the new group of kids who showed up for the trip.

Howie and I were roommates, a natural pairing from a coach's point of view. The rest of the guys were also paired up by position not by compatibility. Although we had learned a great deal mingling with each other on the ride to Michigan, the coaches had spent the ride huddled far up front, happy to let us run wild in the back. We had further divided ourselves from just infielders and outfielders, sluggers and bunters; we were now separated by such distinctions as quiet and loud, cool and un-cool, worldly and sheltered. As much as we got along on the field and meshed in talent, we were now a little unsure of each other and a bit shy of the guy we thought we knew. We unpacked our bags in our little home off the highway and waited for the action to begin.

My roommate Howie was nothing like I thought he was. The solid reliable second baseman who always had my back was a total spazzoid who today would probably be diagnosed with ADHD and be heavily medicated. In fact, half the team turned into a roving pack of Tasmanian Devils, swirling and twirling and seeking out any bit of mischief they could find in the middle of nowhere Michigan.

Buddy Meyer, our manager, had taken on the role of team dad and enforcer; a role he was woefully ill-suited to handle. With no boys of his own, he was way over his head in his ability to handle the sheer energy output of fifteen highly charged unsupervised baseball boys. We were no more than an hour into our stay at the Happy Corral Hotel when Buddy was called to the office to mitigate a dispute with several of the guys and a local melon grower who happened to have a field of watermelons behind the motel. It seemed the wild bunch had helped themselves to several melons, it didn't matter that they weren't ripe, and the melon man had tracked them down to our little string of rooms.

While Buddy was going apoplectic with Bruce, Ray, and Larry, I relieved my own hour of boredom by playing Frisbee with the top to the ice bucket from my room. After several tentative tosses, the game got lively and I proceeded to launch a vigorous toss right through the window of our room door. The face of Buddy coming around the corner of the motel was as red as the piping on our fancy new uniforms, and the blue of his popping head veins slightly matched the scripted Wilmette on the front of our jersey.

An hour later, we were all sitting sequestered in our rooms, resting up for our first game that night; Buddy came to my room and had a conversation with me in a more civilized tone than our previous chat. Buddy Meyer took the time to reveal to me his thoughts on my character and his impressions of me as a young man. I can still picture him standing over the bed, arms crossed, shiny bald head bobbing in disappointment with the words about my character and how surprised and disappointed he was to see I had succumbed to the rabble rousing. He expressed his understanding of the excitement of the situation, but he called on me to be an example for the team and to lead both on the field and off with conduct becoming to the spirit of Wilmette baseball. I must have had a hundred similar lectures from my parents over the years for stupid stuff I had done as a kid, but this one went right to my core and I was truly ashamed and rightly inspired by the call to action. Quiet time continued until game time, and for me it was time well spent.

CHAPTER 34
THE GRIND

The boys shuffle into practice with slumped shoulders and the weight of the Flatiron Mountains upon them. The last couple of games have been lackluster at best, and as we have reached the midway point of our season, it is time for a little talk. Many of the boys that signed up for baseball have not played the game at the high school level. Although the season runs only eighteen games and barely fits into the last three months of the school year, the drain and drag of practice and games which fill six days of the week have taken their toll.

The grind and routine of a high school sport is very similar to having a job. You have to go to the work place every day; the only difference between the two is baseball adds Saturday. As much as I try to keep things fun and different each day, the wear and tear of having to show up each day and work hard to correct that incurable hitch in a swing or throw a ball for the umpteen-billionth time is starting to get to even the most devoted players. Baseball is a game of failure and to have to go to practice every day and be reminded of just how far away from perfection they are surely must be a great way to end each day. Or better yet, we get to travel on a bus for an hour to faraway lands for the opportunity of having yet another team demonstrate to us just what success looks like. So as the down-trodden masses silently prepare for another glorious day on the proving grounds, I inform them that today is the day for their mid-season review.

Because the baseball season grind is so similar to a job, I take the opportunity to expose the boys to the performance review they will experience when they enter the working world. I call each player off the field during the course of practice and have him sit down in my office, which for this review is against the stone marker with the name of our practice space, Manwaring Field, etched onto its side. I have my papers and ever present bound folder in front of me with thoughts written down about each player so I can shine a little light on their work up to this point. It's my belief that these kids do not get enough honesty from the adult world and by giving them a performance review I intend to discuss with them in a straight-forward honest way the truth they already know about the person who shows up every day at practice.

First up is cocky-boy. As full of himself as he was in the beginning of the year, the humbling I have given him through the course of the past few weeks of practice and his awakening to his reality when we played some of the better teams has settled him down quite a bit. He sprints off the field and sits down in my office with the wry smile and twinkle in his eye that seems to say I have a secret.

The spirit cocky-boy brings to the park is not necessarily a bad thing, and I have been careful not to completely crush the confident maverick behavior that powers the raw talent he is learning to control. So I ask him, "How do you think you are doing so far?" I am always surprised at how aware the kids can be when it comes to their self-examination. Usually they are a little shy at first but once we start talking they're able to see themselves pretty much as I see them. The problem areas are generally behaviors they have had to deal with in the past or that they have worked to avoid. Cocky-boy is quick to say that maybe he was a little too anxious and out of control at first, wherein I add, "Maybe a bit cocky and full of yourself?" That sly smile returns and he nods his head in agreement. We spend time identifying issues from the field and on the bench, mechanical and behavioral, and I work to translate those actions into character traits that can be adjusted for better performance.

Cocky-boy, although he has improved his relationship with me, continues to demonstrate an aloof attitude with his teammates which in turn causes friction and discord on the field. I offer to him that working within the group and becoming a part of the team will allow him to eliminate the work and effort of always having to feel superior and cooler than everyone else. Feeling superior to everyone and then making an error or striking out disrupts the aura you have built around you. Your teammates cannot feel compassion or sympathy for you when you struggle, only satisfaction and delight when you fail. I cannot have a team in which teammates root for another player's failure. I press on even though the horror and shock on cocky-boy's face is disturbing. Nobody really wants you to fail, but if you continue to set yourself above and apart from the team, then your progress toward becoming the superstar you so desperately want to be will never be actualized. We are all here to become better baseball players, and to do that we share information, encouragement, and respect.

Cocky-boy quietly absorbs the information I give him. I can see this is nothing like the great performance review he thought he was going to receive. I know he thought we would talk about the game winning double he hit in our previous game and that we would back-slap and bond and be tight in our love for everything cocky-boy. Instead he gets a double barrel dose of honesty and reality right between the eyes. Before I let him go back to the field and think about his world, I let him know how much I admire his many positive qualities and how much I look forward to seeing him get out of the way of his attitude so his true character and talent can come through.

We do bond at the end in a more subtle way than the triple handshake cocky-boy had envisioned. We bond with a simple handshake and an understanding that I am watching and waiting and supporting the growth of a strong individual with talent and spirit who will use his gifts for good, not evil.

Performance reviews go on throughout the course of the practice. Each of the reviews is completely different from the previous one and they are all exhausting. Every kid requires a different motivator or boost to send him down the line toward the quality man he can become. Spending time watching these young men in various situations, be it on the field or on the bus, I see flashes of the kind of person they could be. Through the course of the season I also see indicators of another kind of person lurking inside these teenage shells which, given a different kind of motivation, could send them down a more unsavory path.

The discussions start with baseball but they invariably end up with revelations about their character and the connection their character has to their batting average. The person they are and the way they behave has a direct relationship with their batting average and their success on the field. Some of the guys understand this connection while others require a little heavier load between the eyes before the light turns on.

The players are polite in their acceptance of their slice of humble pie; some even thank me with a sincerity that touches my heart. They head back to the field to take up a position while my assistant throws batting practice. As we get to the end of the reviews, I look out onto the field to see how batting practice is progressing. Normally, during a session of hitting, the guys are clumped together talking about the latest video game or the way Suzie filled out her new sweater, but now as I look around, the guys are all spread out, alone in their staked out spot. I close down my office, hopeful that the messages I have sent reach their target. Looking around the diamond, I see the team is quiet and the field is full of thoughtful young men.

CHAPTER 35
BAY CITY REALITY

Game time finally rolled around in beautiful Bay City, Michigan and it couldn't have come soon enough. The energy pent up from our bus ride coupled with the general horseplay and vandalism of our incarceration at the Dew Drop Inn had us primed for a little focused release.

The drive to the park was uneventful and bland. When you are playing in a tournament out of town or in a new location, the surroundings have no value, especially to a fourteen year old. We could be in the most exciting venue imaginable and the only thing we would remember was how well they stocked the concession stand and how cool the dugouts were. So whizzing through the streets of Bay City was a blur, but the arrival at the tight well-manicured field with the cinder block dugouts with places for your helmets and pizza and long licorice ropes for sale was quite vivid.

After all the fanfare and build up for this tournament, finally we were able to take the field to do our stuff. Ever since we won the first two tournaments, the buzz around the team and the excitement within the Wilmette baseball community had been electric. All the guys had been reading the articles in the local papers and kids would come out to watch us work during the week. It was difficult to avoid the thoughts of greatness being foisted on us by the adults orbiting the youth baseball program. The excitement of a Wilmette team advancing this far had old timers talking about the great teams from the past and the ghosts that played to greatness from those teams. The guys and I were starting to get an inkling of what all the hubbub was about, and to say we were walking tall and swaggering just a bit more would not be a lie.

The effect on the team was measurable. The large personalities on the team had gotten larger and the quieter kids, well, even some of them were breaking windows and feeling their oats. The one constant on the team was Coach Schachtel. If he was nervous or cocky or in any way effected by the progress of our team he never showed it. His preparation for each game was the same, his admonitions to players were at the same voice level, or growl, depending on how many smokes he had that day. The unwavering evenness of his demeanor was noticeable even from the perspective of an awe-struck shortstop playing baseball 400 miles from home. As the pitch of our emotions rose with all our nervous energy and unfocused passion, Coach Schachtel's serenity seemed to deepen. He reveled in the moment, absorbing the great ride he was on.

For a coach of young baseball players, Coach Schachtel was in the middle of the coach's dream, a shot at the big one. Gathering us around him before the game he did his best to send his ripples of serenity out to us. He modulated his voice in an effort to refocus our energy and tap into the control we needed to play the game at this next level. Calm and collected, he did his best to harness the fifteen mini-reactors before him, trying his best to avoid the meltdown.

We took the field against Alsip, Illinois in the Pony league regional tournament on Thursday, August 7. Undefeated in all tournament play going into the game, riding high and full of ourselves, we laid an egg on the field, losing 6-2. The baseball gods looked down on us and they did not like what they saw. The big heads, silly personalities, and uppity disrespectful treatment of our chance to do something special as a team was slapped back into our faces.

As the last out was made and the first feeling of losing a game washed over me, I could see on all the faces around me that everyone knew all too well why we lost the game. Coach Schachtel looked at our faces and I could see he too knew and that very little needed to be said to the contrite group of boys who had instantaneously morphed back into the group of kids he met on the first day of tryouts. He broke down the game going over the mechanical issues and baseball stuff we needed to correct, but everyone knew, without it being said, what needed to be corrected.

The group of guys who rode the bus back to the No-Tell Motel was a far cry different from the boisterous band of knuckleheads who rode the route to the field. I was painfully aware of my surroundings on the ride back, noticing the downtown shops and working class makeup of Bay City in the quiet of our diesel drive. Lights out followed a tasteless pizza and bland beverage. The tournament was just getting started and the powerhouse from Wilmette resumed play tomorrow from the losers' bracket.

CHAPTER 36
BAY CITY DREAMING

Friday was a new day and we were set to play the hometown team. Entering the gate at the Bay City municipal park, the crowd was full and boisterous. The tone from the guys was a bit subdued and pensive. We were not the cocky bunch of misfits and degenerates we were yesterday; today was a work day. Although we were a bit downcast, our mood was refreshed when Coach Schachtel entered the dugout and his voice was raised in a glorious salute to the day. "What a great day to play baseball!" he beamed, a Chesterfield dangled from his huge frog wide mouth in full grin.

Never did an admonition or thought about the day before, either about behavior or play, cross his lips. With the past washed away and our coach focused on the task at hand, we set out to reclaim our winning form. Every guy on the field and on the bench was tuned into every moment of the game in front of us. No signal was missed, no play misread, no attitude out of place; we came to play.

The Bay City boys were not too keen on letting us beat them in their home tournament opener. The fans were jazzed, the field was in great shape, and the opening ceremonies dragged on and on, making all of us twitchy to get started. I was back where I needed to be both in mind and body. Standing at shortstop, waiting for the first pitch, I was relieved to be given a second chance to continue this summer of baseball.

My foray into the world of the cool kids and dangerous living had left a sour taste in my mouth, and the chance to redeem myself could only be found on the ball field. I had never had to grapple with such public displeasure before, and the process back to normalcy and favor in the eyes of others was new and one I did not wish to repeat. With my identity so heavily invested in my ability to achieve on the field, I realized my field currency didn't spend well in the world of mortals.

The expectations of a young man away from the field are greater because of the respect he earns on the field. A higher standard is placed on those who demonstrate character on the field because the expectation is that character achieved in battle should carry over to one's personal life. The battle-tested should demonstrate honor among their fellow man. Waiting for the first pitch to be thrown, I planned to live up to the expectations placed on me and I would work hard to believe in myself as much as others did.

Born again, I tear-up the game, collecting three hits and three runs batted in. We had to fight to the end with the tenacious boys from Bay City, but with Big Larry on the mound, we were able to squeeze out a 7-6 victory. The victory continued our journey, saving us from an early bus ride home and ignominious end.

Once again headed in the right direction, we fired up the horses and crushed North Farmington-West Bloomington, Michigan 18-0 on Saturday followed by a thrashing of Alsip, Illinois, the team that beat us Thursday, 12-1. The game against Alsip was especially sweet as they thought they were all that because they beat us pretty easily on Thursday. The problem was they showed up to play a team that had its mojo back. Funny thing momentum, when you lose it you can't figure out how to get it back; when you have it you believe you can never lose it.

Those poor Alsip boys never knew what hit 'em. Ray, our powerful, hard throwing, don't-quite-know-where-it's-going right-hander was on the hill and he was throwing BB's. Not only was he throwing as hard and as determined as I had ever seen him throw, but he seemed to actually know where the ball was going. He had as much control as he was capable of, enough in fact that he was purposely throwing inside and purposely hitting the occasional batter instead of hitting every fourth batter like he usually did. The velocity of the balls that struck the poor Alsip boys was enough to take the fight out of the cocky crew from the plains of Illinois.

On top of the tremendous display of pitching prowess which Ray gave to Alsip, Ray also swung a mean bat. In the fourth inning, with two men on, Ray came to the plate carrying the same determination he had been using to sit opposing batters down. Ray had always had great power in his swing, and at nearly six feet tall he had the size to get the bat going.

Just as with his pitching, Ray was an all- or-nothing kind of guy. If he missed the ball with a swing or hit a batter while pitching, at least he knew he left nothing behind. So with two runners on base, Ray timed the pitch to the plate perfectly and with one of his come-out-of-his-shoes, buttons-go-flying swings, he connected squarely with the ball, producing a sound I had never heard before. The sheer volume of the sound that came out of the meeting of his aluminum bat with the fastball delivered by the pitcher from Alsip turned every head in the ball park to see what could have made such an explosive noise.

The dimensions of the field in Bay City were fairly standard for a Pony League field, with the fences symmetrical at 300 feet to left, center and right. Behind the fences were light towers that stood 75 feet to the bank of lights at their peak. The ball Ray hit rocketed on a line to dead center climbing at such a rapid rate, that the snap of heads in the park was barely able to keep up with the speed of the ball. As the ball reached the fence, it was still climbing and could be clearly seen arcing over the light tower in the distance behind the outfield wall. Officials at the park after the game attested to the fact that no ball had ever been hit as high and as far in the history of play at Bay City Municipal Field.

Alsip was done. The 12-1 elimination of Alsip set up the meeting of our team from the losers' bracket with Joliet, Illinois in the winners' bracket. For us to continue, we would have to beat Joliet twice, a feat that although difficult, seemed like the perfect challenge. After three days at the Rest Easy Inn, we were pent up, amped up, and ready to wrap up Bay City. Sunday couldn't get here soon enough because life on the road just wasn't as glamorous as it once seemed.

CHAPTER 37
PARENT'S PERCEPTION

We have completed half of our season and the mid-season reviews are done. The only thing left to do this spring is put all the pieces together and play some decent baseball. The journey we've been on together has been intense, and whether the boys know it or not, we have been learning a lot about baseball, each other, and how to get along in the world. However, sometimes the messages I put out don't always get received in the same way by all the kids involved. Many times the lessons taught and the methods used don't always arrive intact to the family dinner table. So halfway into the season, I get my first visit from a perplexed and confused parent. I think to myself, halfway through the season, huh, I must be getting better because it used to be the first or second week.

I make sure at the start of the season to gather up as many contact points for each kid as possible. I especially want to get the email addresses of each player as well as all adults who are of influence to the player. Many times the extension of divorced parents and step-families creates a social network which can be difficult to unravel. When a player goes missing from the bus check-in, it can sometimes be three or four phone calls before the answer to an absence is determined.

Creating an email contact list is an important tool for me to connect not just with the boys but with their parents, in order for all to know what we are working on. I use email as a way to break down certain elements of a game which may be a little too raw to talk about directly after a game, such as a bad call by an umpire or a particularly glaring error or miscue. Some of the touchier topics are best left alone for a while so the players can process the events in private.

Speaking by email in words removed from the glare of the coach and the glare of the fans is a way for the boys to absorb information at their own pace. The various topics I discuss through cyberspace are themes of behavior and conduct, esoteric discussions of baseball etiquette, and the power of the baseball gods. All these heady topics are posited in the form of game review and particular game situation breakdown. I take every opportunity to demonstrate and reveal how the games we play and our response to the events within the game, plus our behavior afterward, reflect the character we need to develop. We need to learn to recognize and learn from the troublesome events of a game so that we can do better the next time we are presented with those same set of obstacles.

By allowing the parents into our discussions, they are afforded the opportunity to understand the power and importance of sports in developing a young man's life. Quite often it is the adult who sees through to the heart of the presented material and makes sure the point being made makes it to the dinner table for further discussion. Other times the information is not received by parent or player and the baffled, angry, confused parent wants a word with the coach after practice.

All parents want what is best for their child. We nurture and protect and do whatever we can to keep our kids from harm and to keep them happy. At some point in the development of their child, the umbrella of protection has to be removed because the forces bombarding a young adult are too great for a parent to shield. The sports world before high school has always been an area of great involvement for parents, and it is an area in their child's life where they feel they still have some control. They would like to feel they can shield their child from harm and disappointment even into high school. Unfortunately the parent is often the last to accept the truth about the growth and development of their evolving teen. More often than not, the player is a lot stronger than the parent when it comes to accepting the pain and challenge of growing up.

My role as coach is to present the complex beauty of the game of baseball to the budding young adult. The game can excite and the game can crush. When you sign up to play the game, chances are you will spend more time being crushed and disappointed than you will exulting in wild success. Even though a parent should realize that a sport tears down and builds up, the reality of seeing their child suffering the abuse of the sport that gave him so much joy in Little League is hard for them to take. The reaction of wanting to protect their baby is a natural one, but their boys are more than ready to shoulder the responsibility of being their own man.

I meet with the parents and listen to their distress over little Billy, the 200 pound six foot first baseman who is working sort of hard to find success on his field of ten year old dreams. I am aware of all the trouble and frustration Billy is having because we discussed his problems at our review session. I was upfront with him about his lack of effort and half-assed attempts to do the drills which I had specifically assigned to help him overcome some of his deficiencies. I spoke with him about his repeated tardiness to practice and his failure to contact me when he couldn't make it to practice for whatever reason and how that translated into less playing time.

Yes, we both knew of poor Billy's problems, but my review and the discussions we had to let him know what was expected of him never made it to the dinner table. The message at Billy's dinner table was the coach is mean and doesn't like me for some reason therefore he doesn't play me as much as Dave (the guy who works his ass off, shows up early, helps the other guys, and has only half the talent). Billy's parents love their son, and I tell them how I too wish only the best for their son, but Billy needs to find out how the world works.

Billy's parents leave the meeting a little wiser about the game of baseball and about the reason why Billy is not on my field. I love hearing from the parents because it lets me know they care and that they are involved in their kids' lives. I hope as Billy's parents walk away from our meeting they realize it's not just them raising Billy but also his teachers and a coach who cares enough to have Billy ride the bench for awhile in order to give him the time to look inside.

CHAPTER 38
TWO AND OUT

Sunday in Bay City, Michigan broke bright and shiny. The birds were singing, the air was fresh, the broken window was taped, and the melon farmer was still on guard. We were packed before breakfast because we were done with the Wagon-Ho Inn, done with Bay City, done with this tournament; done with the road and the too close proximity of team life.

Spending every waking and sleeping moment with these guys was a real eye opening experience. I had never real been too keen on sleepovers, what with the stinky feet, bad beds, and foreign family rituals, it was never a good night's sleep and never a real bonding experience. Guy sleepovers are never the happy stay-up-late-talking-about-girls gab fests that girls have. Guy sleepovers are more like stay-up late-get-cranky-and-wrestle-until-you-break-something-get-yelled-at-and-make-each other-bleed night-mares. Bay City was no different except there was no escape during the day and the sleepover lasted for ninety six hours.

On this day we needed to finish our run from the losers' bracket by winning two games against a very tough Joliet, Illinois team or go home after one and be satisfied with what we had accomplished. As I was putting on my now not-so-new Wilmette uniform with the snappy striped socks that could probably stand up in the corner on their own, the thought of getting on the bus and going home as soon as possible flashed through my mind. As much as I loved the game of baseball, my little body had about enough of throwing and running; and my fragile mind was well past sensory overload. I didn't want to talk to anyone, be nice to anyone, or commune as a team any more. Put me on the field and let's get this thing done one way or another. If I had to smile and be nice to one more parent or tell one more coach I was ready to walk through fire to win the next game I think I would scream.

The eerie quiet on Team Greyhound told me the rest of the guys were in the same state of emotional withdrawal and that made me feel a little better knowing these feelings were not so weird. I chatted with Howie a bit and he too was ready to go home, ready for his house and his own bed. David, Andy, and Barney chimed in saying they too couldn't wait to get back home and have a swim in the lake and an ice cream at Baskin Robbins. Big Sammy, all bluster and tough catcher, couldn't wait to see his cats and hug his little sister.

Rolling into the way too familiar Municipal Park in Bay City we knew the trip home was today…either early or late. We looked at each other knowing we all shared the same pain of being away and as tough as we wanted to be it was okay to miss things and need things. As we walked off the bus in our uniforms that just wouldn't quite get clean anymore we figured, hell, we're here we might as well win.

The first game featured our slugger-stud Ray on the mound. In the course of three days, Ray had become a mythical figure around the Municipal Park complex. Wherever Ray went, players pointed and little baseball players-to-be stared in awe as his lanky, now seven foot frame ambled by. The legend of his home run from the previous day, that some said was still rising somewhere over Ontario, Canada, followed him around and gave him just a bit more swagger than usual. His exploits at the plate and his imposing presence on the mound made him an identifiable sight around the ballpark. We knew if we lost the first game we were done, so we gave the ball to our ace and took the field in support.

Once again I was in my happy place between second base and third base. The sad pitiful boy who was missing his mommy was replaced by the guy who couldn't get enough of this silly game. I realized it was okay to have moments of doubt and disgust. I knew my love of the game was solid but my emotions were not. Thoughts and feelings that go against what I know I love will come and go, I had to trust that deep down in my core lives my true heart.

So I'm all in and the negative thoughts and anger over still being in Bay City become directed at the poor slobs from Joliet.

Ray goes into his arms and elbows wind-up to put these guys away and hits the first batter right in the middle of the back with a blazing fastball...we have these guys right where we want 'em. I didn't know if Ray meant to hit the poor guy who was twitching and crying on the ground at the feet of the helpless umpire, but the look on the face of the guy on deck told me these guys were in trouble. Ray was all over the place that day and walked a number of batters, but Joliet was unable to really settle into the batter's box, so the hits were few, and with two more homers from Big Ray, we defeated Joliet 6-4 to take the first game.

The second and final game in Bay City was also our sixth game in four days. Everyone was tired and sore but our pitchers felt especially worn out. Not only did our best pitchers pitch the most innings we could get from their noodle arms, but a majority of them also played in the field. At this point in the tournament, their tanks were running pretty low and their arms were hanging even lower.

Coach Schachtel looked to our resident delinquent Bruce Sonen to pitch us all the way back from the losers' bracket and take this tournament for the good guys. I didn't think any of the coaches really believed after our first loss that we would be playing in this game, so they had used every possible pitcher to win each game. The sixth game brought us back to Bruce who had been used quite a bit recently, and we all hoped his spidery frame would hold up just once more so we could continue on our quest.

Bruce was our hair puller. Whereas Ray was the guy who could go out and intimidate the opposition with power and wildness, Bruce was the guy who threw the junk; a slider, a big breaking curve ball, sneaky fastball, changeup, the kitchen sink, anything that would baffle and frustrate a hitter. Bruce would also be the first kid to have Tommy John surgery and most likely wouldn't be able to lift his arm over his head by the age of twenty-five. But for now we appreciated the fact that he could snap off breaking pitches which made kids step in the bucket, and the second time through the order stomp with anger back to the dugout. More than one Joliet player left the batter's box shaking his head in confusion as he headed back to the dugout with no real helpful tips for his teammates. We never had a clue as to how effective Bruce was going to be when he showed up on the mound or in what condition his space-case brain would be when he toed the rubber. So we all held our breath and waited to see if we get the baffler or the brain dead.

When Bruce's game was on, the infield could expect to see a lot of ground balls. The fun part of playing behind Bruce was that everyone in the infield was alert, on their toes, and ready to make a play. So far in the tournament, Howie and I had established ourselves as an exceptional middle infield combination. At this level you didn't expect to see too many double plays turned on ground balls but Howie and I had already turned an inordinate amount of routine grounders into double plays. Because of our similar physical makeup, we were able to get to balls with our quickness and feed them to the other guy with enough time to get the ball out of his glove and on its way to one of our big stretched-out first basemen, Ray, Mike, or Larry. The number of double plays we were turning became a real source of pride for our infield and it kept us in games as well as helped us to win several close contests. There was nothing more demoralizing to a team than to mount a rally by getting a man on and then having a hitter smash a ball which is speared by Howie or me and spun into a rally-killing, inning-ending, and momentum-swinging double play.

Bruce took to the hill. The stadium was packed to see the culmination of this wild tournament. The route we took to get to this game and the guts we displayed to propel us to the championship captured the interest of all the baseball fans in the area. Looking around I could see whole teams sitting together that had lost to either us or Joliet or both, commiserating and whining about how it should be them out there playing for the glory. I thought back to the time when some of us sat in the stands watching a game after being eliminated from a tournament, knowing that we were better than what we displayed and wondering why it wasn't us out on the field.

Today was our day to be the team that was envied and reviled and it felt damn good. Parents and fans all around the park were happily ensconced in their seats, enjoying a glorious day in August, watching two very good teams who had weeded themselves out of the crowd. We were all there to witness and decide which one of these teams has what it takes to be champion.

Good Bruce showed up and with the help of our defense, that seemed to get better every game, we were unstoppable. The combination of stunning breaking balls and sneaky fastballs, made faster by the puzzling nature of the off-speed pitches, was too much for a Joliet team that came into the day hoping for one and done from Wilmette.

Bruce pitched a gem of a 2-hitter virtually shutting down the entire Joliet lineup, sending them to elimination with a simpering 4-0 loss to the kids from Wilmette. As the last pitch was thrown for another strikeout and the stadium erupted in cheers, I looked around and really enjoyed the moment in Bay City.

Too often a large victory is all jumping and pounding and puffed-up chests, but this one was in perspective. The look of joy on the coaches' faces and the faces of our fans and parents was great to see, they had journeyed long and worked hard to get here and they deserved their share. However, I looked at my teammates and I saw joy, but I also saw contentment. We were learning to put all this in perspective, to discover the real scope of the game and its place in our lives. Sure, winning was great and we earned all the applause, but we were starting to sense that there was more to know and learn from the game than just beating teams and advancing on. Spending time, a lot of time, together on and off the field forced us to go beyond the game. We were starting to use the game as a way to cope and learn about personalities, both others and our own.

The celebration died down rather quickly, and I could see as we packed our gear the pride and joy from our victory written on each player. We all had a little Mona Lisa going on, a little knowledge of events that had occurred in the last four days. Each of us was processing the footage of the past few days, learning and replaying the events to see if the feelings we had, and the emotions we carried, were truly our own. Bay City had it all from great baseball to misdemeanor extracurricular activities. We understood all the events that took place; now we had an eight hour bus ride to help us put the events in perspective.

Each player would have their own take on how the weekend went and they would assign different values to the events that occurred. For me the trip was one big piece. The events on the field were tied in my mind to the events that happened off the field. The emotions of life at Happy Trails influenced the play at Municipal just as the success and failure at Municipal molded the behavior back at The Ranch. At that date in August, my whole life was a revolving interwoven smash-up of baseball-life. My every movement in some way connected and influenced what happened on the baseball field and in my everyday life. I felt as though I had locked into the baseball gods' jet stream and it was propelling me and my team toward an answer or a reckoning of some kind.

Heading down the highway back to the comfort of a town I had taken for granted, I freely gave myself up to the current of the god flow. I relaxed into the wishes of the higher forces at play in my world, trusting that a world governed by the ebb and flow, the order and chaos, the failure and success of baseball would leave me in good stead. The drone of the big bus heading home and the thoughts of the benevolent beings that had been so kind to me and my team lulled me into a deep well earned sleep.

CHAPTER 39
TOLERANCE

Even though we only play an eighteen game schedule in the course of the high school season, the wear and tear of baseball six days a week for two and a half months certainly takes its toll. We have ten games under our belts with one game rained/snowed out. Today we are heading down the road to play our next game in weather that will barely reach thirty degrees with winds at 20 mph and a chance of snow. Who loves the game now!?

I do not like to be cold, so I do everything I can to make sure I am comfortable for the game. I wear long underwear, two shirts, a thick pullover hoodie, and my emblem- emblazoned cool baseball shell which is the least effective item I have on but is a must to make the two inch thick ensemble come together. Looking around the sauna-hot bus I see the boys reclining in their t-shirts and baseball pants, oblivious to the torture they are about to endure at the hands of the Colorado elements.

In the past I talked endlessly about the lessons baseball can teach us about life, and about the effect playing the game can have on how we perceive the world and on how we handle adversity. However, there is nothing so revealing and life bracing as fighting against the elements. Standing in the middle of the outfield freezing to death in a skimpy polyester baseball uniform unable to feel your fingers or toes will bring you closer to knowing your true character than any set of relentless calisthenics. There really is nothing more absurd than someone telling you to stand in gale-force winds with snow flurries flying, knowing that if you complain or walk off the field your reputation and standing as a man-to-be will be forever tarnished in the eyes of your teammates, your coach, your dad, and yourself.

I feel for these guys, but I too am under siege from the manhood club. As the coach it is my duty to lead these poor unsuspecting sheep to the slaughter. Unlike the good-weather battles against tough baseball opponents, today we are pitted against the great outdoors and our own tolerance for discomfort. A tougher foe there is not because Mother Nature has no compassion. There is no mercy rule when it comes to icy wind and frigid limb-crimpling cold. The game will continue until it is over and all have bowed to the real measuring stick of manhood…tolerance.

As we come off the bus, I admonish the entire group to drive their thoughts of suffering and despair deep inside so they can deal with their pain quietly and individually. I emphasize that I do not want to hear one word about how cold it is. The weather is a fact, it is real, you will each have to accept it and deal with it. Do your best and try to stay warm.

My sophomore year in high school, playing on the north shore of Chicago, we played in some bitterly cold games on some concrete-hard frozen fields. One game which took place early in the season changed the way I thought about the cold. On a grey humid cold day with the temperature down in the thirties, our star pitcher, once again Ray of Pony League fame, was throwing a perfect game against our cross-town rivals. A perfect game is as rare as it gets in baseball, a game in which no batter gets a hit or even reaches first base due to a walk or an error. It is even rarer for Ray, a pitcher not exactly known for his control.

I don't know if the reason nobody was getting any hits was because nobody wanted to have a miss-hit and feel the pain of a handful of angry bees from the horrible vibration of the bat or if it was just that Ray was the warmest guy on the field because he was moving the most. What I do know is that by the fourth inning, I was unable to feel my fingers and I was struggling just to close my hand completely to make a fist. Knowing Ray was in the middle of a special game I started to chant a little mantra to myself, "Don't hit it to me, don't hit it to me." I was terrified thinking that if the ball came to me I would reach into my glove and my palsied hand would be unable to close around the ball; or I would grab the ball and throw it straight into the ground. Thankfully Ray was able to do most of the work himself and he achieved his great game, and I didn't have to have any blackened fingers removed by the trainer.

Because of my hellish experience of arctic baseball, I became one of the first kids to not just accept the cold but to do something about relieving my discomfort at the risk of being thought less than tough by my teammates. During bitter days on the practice field, I started wearing a rather thick running-suit top underneath my practice jersey. The thick stretchy material afforded me enough mobility and flexibility to be able to throw and hit with comfort. I further added to my comfort by purchasing a pair of tight-fitting batting gloves which I wore on both hands at all times, including in the field. I used the batting glove on my throwing hand and became quite comfortable and proficient at throwing with the glove, to the point of using the gloves during games. The success I achieved with my little experiment, and my ability to stand up to my shivering teammates, convinced my third base buddy to adopt the same added equipment, and together we enjoyed the rest of the season in comfort, experiencing an epiphany in common sense that would've made any mother proud.

Today's game in the cold is well beyond anything I had ever experienced. The cold of the Midwest pales to the severity of the game at hand. Perhaps my memory is clouded by the relentless biting wind whistling through my sinus cavities. Or maybe the bitter cold is like the pain of childbirth, and we simply forget the agony of what incessant inescapable cold can do to our psyches once it's over.

The boys try to tough it out, but they are so shortly removed from the little men of their mother's care that I can see them crumbling as the innings, nay, the outs crawl by. As I stand in the third base coaches' box looking at the carnage all around me, boys actually huddling like penguins in tight circles for warmth, parents in the stands hiding behind buildings, I too feel the despair of the moment creeping up from underneath the multi-layered high tech fabric of my soul. Knowing I am cold in all my many layers, my heart goes out to the bravery and stupidity of the boys in their inadequate polyester knickerbockers and earless wool caps.

I can't help but smile at these moments of clarity, when the reality and absurdity of this game we strive to play reveals such fundamental struggles with our condition as human beings. It's not that I think the boys are going to learn some basic survival techniques if they are caught out in the cold blizzard. The lesson here is not that cold weather is unpleasant, we know that. I think the lesson is the gratitude which comes about when the other coach and I get together and accept the fact that the elements win and there is no dishonor in stopping the madness. There is a real elemental gratitude and appreciation for being out of the cold and back on the over-heated yellow tube. There is an appreciation for simple comfort and a pride in tolerating the elements far better than we could have expected. I can also see there is an attitude developing among the boys: one of, we-could-have-gone-longer-except-the coach-stopped-the-game, pride of survival. Yes, there is a lot to be said for the lessons learned when being pushed to the edge, surviving, and living to tell the tale. To this day I still hear the pride in the telling of the story of the game in the snow, wind, and cold which Coach made us stop and that they survived.

CHAPTER 40
MATURITY

The heat and humidity of August on the north shore of Chicago is an environment best grown-up in rather than visited and tolerated. A sweaty grimy river of brown runoff heading down the drain of the shower was my normal end-of-day routine. My long white sanitary socks had only one game in which to look major league new and bright. All the Tide commercials in the world couldn't handle the ankle ring sweat marks that Shroud-of-Turined to the fresh white socks which came in a disposable pack of six. Those poor socks would be worn until the fabric rotted under the acidic onslaught of my teenage endocrine system, finally giving way with one mighty pull, leaving me with a handful of upper sock around my thigh.

Back home from Bay City, I was able to reload with fresh socks and let my mom have at the slowly graying white uniform that had seen a year's wear in just a few weeks. It was good to be home, to be in my bed, to shower in my shower, to ride my bike to practice, and to field balls at Logan Elementary. The summer lived on and we were still playing. School was still weeks away and the buzz from our victory in Bay City kept getting louder and louder.

To come home and wake up to the only street I had ever known was slightly odd, things looked different, and smelled different; were they different? I was seeing the world a little clearer and with a little more understanding. The experiences in Bay City; living and breathing with my teammates, playing high-level do or die baseball, interacting with adults, fans, coaches, and hotel managers, had opened my eyes in a way I couldn't quite fathom.

183

I knew the words "maturity" and "responsibility", but up until that point in my life they were merely words, adult buzz words thrown around and sprinkled about on the heads of young people like so much corn feed to the chickens. Today I felt more mature. I felt like I had applied for and received some special membership card to a club that had been talked about for years. My name had finally come up on the waiting list, and after close evaluation and intense scrutiny, I was accepted as a full-fledged member of the Have Grown Up Club---dues pending. I hopped out of bed with the feel of the day as my own new toy, feeling a few inches taller and a few chest hairs sprouting, I bounded down the stairs to start the first day of the rest of my mature life with a heaping bowl of Fruit Loops. Aaah, maturity...does a body good.

CHAPTER 41
GET AWAY TO BASEBALL

The lessons just keep piling on as the season of discovery continues for the boys of Colorado. The vicious snow and cold snap that pounded our psyches is soon replaced with the school spring break and for many, including this coach, a welcome respite and vacation to the warm weather of Phoenix, Arizona. The first dash of the season is coming to an end and for these boys, a welcome week off from baseball and the zealous coach who is sounding more like their therapist than their baseball instructor.

Unfortunately for many of these struggling athletes, a week off means two steps back in their development as ball players. For some, the time off is a chance to evaluate just how little baseball means to them. For the core group of dedicated baseball guys, it is a time to let the body rejuvenate and to feel, half-way through the break, the itch and ache to be back on the field learning the physical and mental lessons the game has to offer.

For me, the chance to disconnect from this group of guys I have gotten attached to and fond of, to the point of lost sleep and anxious moments of doubt, is a welcome one. My plans are to travel to Arizona with my family and watch the big boys play at spring training as well as catch some of our varsity boys playing in a tournament at a local Arizona high school. As much as I am saturated with the game on a daily basis, this time of year my body yearns for more and more. At every moment and opportunity I search out a game or a chance to watch and dissect some baseball action. My thirst for an understanding of hitting mechanics and a way in to

185

the mind of a crafty pitcher leads me to local parks and when possible to the Mecca of baseball joy, spring training.

There is no place on Earth friendlier and more welcoming to the baseball aficionado than the sun baked fields of the Cactus League in Phoenix, Arizona. With innumerable teams in a small geographic area and countless games to choose from, a fan or student of the game can wallow in the glorious red clay mud pot of endless games. Cheap seats and unimpeded access to the field and ball players allow a fan to study, admire, and worship the heroes of his sport.

As a student, the chance to watch a player like Ichiro Suzuki go through his pregame warm-up or watch Barry Bonds in his non pregame warm-up is an opportunity to see the players as human and athlete. I can watch the man inside the athlete as he prepares his body for the amazing feats he is capable of performing. Too often we see only the athlete on the field. We expect the athlete to wind himself up and do what he has been paid to do with never a bobble or display of the man inside. Up close, in the early stage of the season, the man is more visible and accessible to the fan. The pressure to perform and do the tricks the big money has prompted him to do has not yet kicked in and masked his humanity. March in Arizona allows us to feel the sun, smell the fresh cut green grass, yell and crack wise, crack some peanuts and watch some guys run and play, and the fans get to watch them do it.

I grab a seat ridiculously close to the field to watch my home town team, the Colorado Rockies, play a late-season spring game. Most of the players I am familiar with are back in Tucson, exempt from the bus ride down to Phoenix due to age, contract stipulation, or fatigue. Even though the players are a mystery with numbers on their backs matching linebackers and lineman, the boys inside are giving it their all.

The chance to play on the big field in front of management is an opportunity the fringe players will not get in another week's time when they are bussed off to the Podunk towns of the minor league world. The fresh- faced youngsters wander to the plate, their uniforms wearing them, looking all too familiar to my crew back home. I can only imagine the managing that goes into getting these lanky, awkward boys onto buses, to the ballpark, fed, suited up and on the field day after day. Then again I think I know exactly what it would take to make all that happen.

The fact that the business of baseball involves the playing of a game lends itself to boys being boys. There really is no requirement for the players to fully grow up when they are being asked to play a game. How can you expect young men to behave as responsible adults when the only requirement they have is to hit a ball hard, run fast, and not drop the little white thing. As I look out at the cream of the crop of young baseball talent, it is shockingly clear to me that I had better do all I can to prepare my little batch of knuckleheads because if they get here without a little life-lesson eye opener they aren't going to make it very far. On further reflection I realize I had best do what I can for my boys because it doesn't matter where they go or what they do, without a little life tune- up things could get all too real, real fast.

The 73's and 54's slug it out on a beautiful hot sunny day in Tempe. Everyone around me is happy to be here on this day, soaking up rays and watching guys play the game they love. There is no other reason to be at a spring training baseball game other than the pure love of the sport. There is nothing on the line, no trophy to win or award to aspire to, players are just playing, youngsters trying to impress. In the stands I can turn to anyone next to me or beside me and strike up a conversation about the game. Our conversation can be about the game at hand the games that were or the games to be. We can talk about the old days and our youth or the recent past and the effect it had on our happiness or sorrow. The world of baseball, the philosophy of baseball, the Tao of baseball is all open for discussion on a beautiful day in Arizona.

Today my baseball consultants are three gentlemen about my age sitting directly in front of me. These three guys are at the park reconnecting as old friends, sharing a day together as guys and pals from the past. Jovial and familiar with each other their banter is clever, biting, and fun. Learning of my affiliation with the Rockies they quickly turn on me as the boys in black and purple take some early bruising from the Angels of Los Angeles. We easily establish a jocular back and forth about the lack of potential for my homies and the length of the season ahead for me. And as my boys fight back into the game, I am able to sling back and profess my belief in the heart of my team. Within a few innings, the reunion squad takes leave to go drink and dredge up older more sanguine memories to banter about.

My next-to neighbor is a rather put together gentleman, again around my age, with a bonneted wife and an attention to detail. He has purchased the daily program and accompanying pencil and has meticulously filled out his score sheet in the most dainty and precise manner. The scorecard provided is the most minimalist of printings with blank squares and vast Excel-like columns and rows which require the user to define and create the drama that is to unfold on the green, green grass. But this man is up to the task. Religiously, almost reverently, he records everything that occurs on the field. Taking down the action like a stenographer at trial he transposes the play at hand into the cipher of the scorekeeper. Lines and numbers, abbreviations and notations, signifying outs and hits, success and failure, a player replaced, a pitcher done; all recorded in the script of the baseball junkie.

As a kid at Wrigley Field, my father did his best to tutor me in the language of the scorecard. Three or four innings would be a good day for my attention span before my eyes and mind would wander out to the field. I would lock in on the way Don Kessinger prepared himself before a pitch or on how much pine tar Billy Williams was slathering on his bat, or what kept the ivy from falling off the walls in the outfield? The game would go on, the cotton candy would come by and my scorecard would end up behind my seat.

Not so for my next-to neighbor. Turns out he and his wife are here from North Dakota, getting away from the long winter which is a staple of the state. We freely converse about the game at hand, the games he has seen that week, and the lack of games in his state. Throughout the course of our easy conversation and the chaos of a game filled with thirty hits and thirty runs, he records the many moves in minute stubby-pencil detail.

I can't help but wonder, and I never ask, what does he do with the card when he is done and what does it do for him to record it so? I can only inject my own thinking and to surmise that it is the act of the recording not the treasure of the record which holds the attraction for this man. The connection of the action on the field to the card seems to give this scrivener such purpose and joy. The fact that the game devolved into such carnage with multiple moves and endless new players seemed to add to his enjoyment, whereas this game would cause me to let the card slip to an early grave behind my seat.

The game becomes a blur of prospects for the future, no longer a professional league game but more of a really, really, good scrimmage. My family has been gracious enough to indulge me my passion for being in the presence of all this great atmosphere, but now it is time to leave. Taking leave of the happy couple from the Dakotas, we say good bye having shared the same baseball joy in slightly different ways. The small cozy ballpark is filled with the recipients of a shared energy that only those in attendance could possibly understand. Most in attendance do understand the energy at hand in some way. For some it is the game and the joy of watching it being played, for others it is not as tangible or as easy to access. A day in the sun, free from care and worry, free from their connections to their day; all those reasons and more are what keep them coming to the ballparks of the world.

We can have all our baseball experiences and memories in the course of one day at the park. Everything is a trigger to the flood of memories we have stored up from the past to the present. The more you see and the more you experience the greater the desire to visit that next game. Thinking about this on the way out I look at my two teenage girls who have indulged my baseball passion since they were little, and I feel good knowing they will have inside them the ability to go to the park and live their baseball life over. I will be with them some sunny day in the future when just being at the park with their family will somehow feel right, will somehow bring them a joy they can't quite explain, but which they can't live without.

CHAPTER 42
TOUGH EMOTIONS IN
SKOKIE

The next and last step on the way to the final prize of a trip to the Pony League World Series was the divisional tournament at Laramie Park in Skokie, Illinois. Skokie is another Chicago suburb just a short twenty minute drive down Green Bay road out of Wilmette. What a relief it was not to have to go through the excitement and adjustment of traveling to some far-off land full of too many experiences and too much stimulation. In one summer I had become a worldly-wise home-bound old fart. Being able to put my uniform on at my house after a satisfying grilled cheese sandwich from mom's kitchen was an advantage I relished.

The Pontiac Rambler was my mode of transportation and the sights out the window were familiar and comforting. As exciting as the trip to Bay City was, there is truly no place like home, and the team from Lafayette, Indiana was a long way from their comfort zone. I remembered just how scrambled we were in our first game at Bay City, the game we lost, so we intended to make their visit to Skokie a short one.

Arriving in the parking lot of Larimer Park, I took great pride in exiting the car decked out in my Wilmette uniform. Representing my town and being a part of this team meant a great deal to me now. The pride of making the team had been replaced with a pride of duty and honor born from the camaraderie of fighting for victories in faraway lands with teammates I would do anything for...

191

except touch their socks or wear their grody hats. A confidence had been achieved through the tense moments of the games played and the difficult times on the bench dealing with all the stupid antics and personalities which churned and grew there. We had become impervious to the pressure of the games we were playing. On the other hand, the parents and adults swirling around the team were basket cases, full of nervous suggestions and twitchy hands of help. The next game was just that to us, the next game. We knew that whatever came our way, be it a hard-hitting team or a pitcher with great stuff, we, as a team, would be able to hit back and put down the opposition.

Coach Schachtel had prepared us well, coming up with answers for all the problems presented by the different styles of teams we had faced so far. Coach Schachtel understood that when we were stymied by a dominating opposing pitcher, that team was usually backed by a weak defense. The "Blazer Magee" on the hill lulled his defense to sleep with strikeouts and weak ground balls. Coach Schachtel's response to the one-man show was to bunt, steal, and put pressure on the complacent eight defensemen. Make the other team play the game and get us out. Pretty soon, Magee's team is throwing the ball around wildly and Magee is walking every other batter. Next thing you know Fire-baller Magee is on the bench and their second string guy is on the mound which our bats would then feast upon.

When the team was full of stud-boys who wanted to hurt the ball and inflict emotional damage through blistering homers and extra base hits, our coach would turn the tables and inflicts his own emotional damage. The big slugging teams would have to face the likes of Bruce's big curveball or the off-speed mastery of Barney "Bones" Schaefer. Balls floated to the plate big as cantaloupes then they would suddenly dart down and away or dip and dive, avoiding the massive swings of bats scarred from previous long ball success. Heads would shake and frustration would ensue as batter after batter stormed back to the dugout to tell his teammates how easy the pitcher was to hit even though they had just been schooled on the beauty of the twelve to six curveball.

The anger and frustration would mount, and in turn those emotions would be taken into the field to the tune of three of four costly errors, leading to the difference in winning or losing. The bruisers from the farm land would leave the field thinking they were still the better team; they would drive home thinking they were the better team; they would join all the other teams that had been eliminated…still thinking they were the better team.

We brought to Skokie a barrel of confidence and a bundle of strategies which would be hard for others to overcome. I looked at the boys from Lafayette and saw nothing over there that I hadn't seen already. Cool uniforms and freakishly large fourteen year olds no longer intimidated us. We had faced the largest, the smallest, the fastest, and the hardest. We no longer saw the parts of the team; we saw only another opponent, an opponent that would present challenges for which we had solutions.

On a pleasant Thursday night, August 14, we faced the team from Lafayette, Indiana. Lafayette was a group of boys much like ourselves, and the only thing going through my mind as I looked at them was they were lucky we didn't grow melons around here and I bet the ride home will be long. The game was full of offense and our usual solid defense. In the end we were able to out-clout the Indiana boys and come away with a 10-7 victory earning ourselves a day off and a matchup with a tough team from Rapid City, South Dakota on Saturday.

Things were different. Things had changed. The further along on this road we went the more the atmosphere changed. With just a couple games remaining for a possible trip to the Pony League World Series, the feeling around the team, the town, and my gut had blossomed into fever pitch excitement and a whole swarm of butterflies. I thought I had a handle on the emotions of the big games I had played over my "long" career. The excitement and tension of a big game was merely a fun component of the sport, right? Up until now I never really felt effected by the created atmosphere of two teams competing to settle a score, achieving an ultimate goal, or winning a game against a close friend or rival. However, I had never been involved in an experience and journey such as the one I was now experiencing.

The local newspaper was full of stories of the games we had played and the drama that unfolded on the field and the consequences of each victory. Reading the latest articles of our adventure in Bay City I hadn't realized the great scope and magnitude of what we had accomplished. I was glad to be home because I was so shaken by the whole of the experience, the games seemed like such a small part, an insignificant part, of what had transpired in Michigan. Now I was oh too aware of the enormity of what we were doing and what we could accomplish.

Every baseball-minded individual I ran into had an opinion or piece of advice on how to stay calm and focused in order to make it through the big games ahead. I hadn't really been all that concerned about playing the next game until all these adults started freaking me out with their talk of nervousness and composure. It had gotten to the point where I didn't wear my baseball cap around town anymore just so I wouldn't have to suffer all the good intentions. Thank God Saturday was here so I could suit up and get to the field and play the damn game and get the weird feelings out of my stomach. The only time I felt right was at practice with my teammates, out at shortstop in my baseball world, or early in the morning waking up knowing the summer was still rolling out in front of me and we were still in it.

Rapid City, South Dakota was a long way from Skokie, Illinois. The Dakotas conjured up in my head the Wild West, barren landscapes, Mount Rushmore and baseball fields full of rocks and stone arrowheads. Yet when I looked over at the boys from so far north, they too looked just like us, lanky kids of varying sizes and shapes, uniforms equally as stained, and with caps salt encrusted and bleak. It dawned on me that these guys were having the exact same experience we were having. We were identical in the games we had won, the growth we had achieved, and in the hope we had for more.

Watching Rapid City warm up was like looking in a mirror, and I searched deep into their movements to see if I could detect the same emotions I felt scrawled onto their face and form. The recent realization of just how big a deal this tournament was and how close we were to achieving something very special suddenly scared me, and with it I was scared for the boys across the diamond. In a couple of short hours, the emotions of excitement, a simple easy to understand feeling, was going to be replaced with a flood of some very serious, very new emotions. I was more scared now of what I was going to feel like after the game than I was about playing the game. Facing the possibility of having to deal with defeat and all that came with it, from the parents to the coaches to my teammates, filled me with a dread that buckled my knees. At the same time the thought of winning and the overwhelming emotions which accompanied that kind of outpouring was equally collapsing. I sat down and spit into my glove. The field looked great, green and brown

with sparkling white bases punctuating the immaculate smooth-
ness of the dirt. I didn't realize I would have to think so hard to
play a game so simple. The game flowed easily in my head. I knew
what I needed to do and where to go and how to make the game
move. The consequences at the end of the bliss were new to me,
and I can say they were starting to get in the way of the purity of
the game.

CHAPTER 43
SOGGY JOY

The return from my spring break trip finds me full of renewed enthusiasm for the game and a renewed energy for the continuing task of guiding my young saplings upward. The first day back from the balmy wind of Phoenix is a typical Colorado spring day; windy and cold with a chance for rain and snow. The lush green fields of the irrigated south desert fade quickly from my memory as I gaze at the water soaked, snow-caked fields of home.

While in Arizona, Colorado was hit with a March snowstorm that left twelve inches on the ground and with it our season becomes a quagmire of sloppy fields and afternoons in the gym. We are set back a week, cancelling three games and spending time in the gym hitting whiffle balls and doing conditioning drills. The sunny days and dry fields of February have morphed into the typical Colorado spring of up and down temperatures and vacillating rain and snow. The enthusiasm from all our rest and rejuvenation is replaced with the moans and groans of another day in the gym and forlorn glances at fields which just won't dry and a sun that just won't appear. The boys don't like it either.

I do my best to put on a positive face as we go through our second winter workout in preparation for the season to resume. The boys also do their best to stay focused and engaged, and I do what I can to come up with new drills and exercises to keep their interest, and at the same time prepare them for the next part of the season. As the coach, I need to eliminate my disgust for the weather and for being inside. Instead of carrying a sour disposition, I show the guys that when faced with a situation certainly out of our

197

control we need to make the best of it and do what we can to keep at our preparation. I let the guys know there are teams out there in the same boat. Those teams have better facilities than we do and they are doing what they can to gear up for the next stretch so we need to work hard and be ready.

It is up to the individual to come to an agreement with things like the weather or a late bus or an umpire who doesn't show up or a starting pitcher that gets sick. All of the nagging little inconveniences of life can either make you or break you. If allowed to, the smallest disruption from a carefully laid plan can cause a ripple effect within one's head to the point of such off-putting that an individual can no longer be effective. I have seen people and players, me included, get so rattled over things beyond their control that horrible faces have been made and poor judgment followed. Inclement weather is a good place to start working on letting go of forces beyond our control.

Together we work at not shaking our fists at the sky and accepting that sunny days are ahead. In the meantime we do what we can, work our drills, do our strengthening, take a day off, and try not to kill each other with hard balls in an enclosed space. Finally the sun comes out and the melting and drying begins. The fields remain muddy, too squishy to play or walk on, but the grass is accepting of our advances so we head out, happy to breathe some fresh air.

Without the use of a full diamond, once again we must use our make-lemonade approach and accept what we have and not whine about what we don't have. The boys struggle with the concept of partial instead of all. "Why do we even come out if we can't do what we want?" Whereas my thinking is if I have to play an outdoor sport inside one more day I will scream.

So we lace 'em up and head to the outfield of our practice field where the sun is shining, the mountains loom up clear and snow covered, and we can feel the wind as we run. Outside we can throw and move and feel our bodies stretching to reach and bend in all the great ways baseball forces us to move. I challenge the guys to warm up as cleanly as possible, telling them I will be checking the baseballs to see which ball has the least mud after our warm-up. All around the boys there are regions of mud and boundaries of goo waiting to mar and muck the balls they toss. Our island of safety once again creates a challenge for me to come up with drills and activities to help progress our understanding of our bodies and the way they work in the pursuit of baseball consistency.

Throughout the day, my mind plays with thoughts of new ways to teach and new methods to use to help the boys understand the concepts of hitting and the mechanics behind it. My mind races with ways to illustrate the pace, rhythm, and flow of fielding so their mind and body can come together to feel, see, and translate the motions of their disconnected parts.

For the teacher, the excited look in the eye and the evidence of a kid's fluid movements is a satisfying sight which never gets old. When a player puts all the elements together we have been talking about, but which he has never fully translated physically, and he clicks into place, even for one swing or one ground ball, that moment of baseball joy is what will keep him coming back. It is in the smallest bit of success on the smallest bit of grass on a soggy day when he thought the day would be a bust that he may discover the feeling which allows him to want to be here day after day. The home runs and victories are such huge moments of baseball joy, but they are not the reason the player suits up. It is in the smallness of the game where he will find the reason to remain for the big event. It is in the chain of joys found on muddy fields and musty gyms that will link his heart to the game and give him the motivation to put himself in the position to step to the plate with the winning run at second and calmly and with confidence drive the ball deep into the gap to achieve the full helping of joy he has worked for.

CHAPTER 44
NO ORDINARY DAY

The glint of sunlight reflected off the cyclone fence drawing my eye to the backstop and through the backstop to the rush of traffic beyond; to the everyday errands and chores of people somehow disconnected from the baseball drama playing out at Laramie Park. All around the oasis of green and brown, life continued to swirl and move in its everyday bustle of doing and completing. The dad still had to pick up the part he needed at the hardware store, the groceries are shopped for, and somehow kids were doing things besides playing or watching or thinking about baseball.

My world was small but oh so big in scope. The game at hand was the biggest so far in my life, and I looked around to somehow find a symbol or notation of its bigness. Sure there were people watching the events unfold but why did cars careen on by as if nothing huge and momentous was happening? I looked up and saw only sky, no small planes pulling large banners, no police directing traffic into an overflowing parking lot. Why, if you were walking by, you would think that just some ordinary game with ordinary kids was going on instead of the deciding game that would send a team to the Pony League World Series. The last thought I had before my focus came back to Ray striking out another South Dakota boy was what sad dull lives those uninformed errand runners lead.

The score was 2-1 going into the seventh and final inning. Behind for most of the game, we were not too worried as Ray had been right on and was holding the game close, waiting for us to make our move. As the home team, our time had run out. We were down to our last three outs, it was now or never. Standing in the on-deck circle waiting to start the inning, I could see my dad and mom and all the Wilmette faithful clustered in the stands anxious to see if their boys could keep this journey alive.

I was always a little nervous before an at-bat, and right then there were so many complex emotions running through my body. My head was full of chatter, my tummy was flip-flopping the food I stuck into it before the game, my knees were weak, and my hands were shaky. But I didn't worry about all the body-buzz because I knew it would go away when I stepped into the batter's box and looked out at the pitcher. For me the hardest part of playing base-ball was the waiting for the burst of action. Once I started moving and let my auto-pilot take over, I was fine. I don't know how many times I had looked up at the scoreboard to realize five innings had gone by and just couldn't remember how we had gotten to that point let alone whether I had ridden my bike or gotten a ride with my mom.

Down by a run in the biggest game of my life in the bottom of the last inning...cool. How many times had Jonathan and I played out this scenario in his backyard. I couldn't imagine things going any other way than great for our team because I hadn't ever imag-ined it ever going the other way. I was always victorious and we always got carried off the field just like the books and movies and heroes of all sports.

Stepping into the batter's box, the body-buzz faded away and my sinewy tanned spider-muscles twitched with anticipation and readiness. With about forty games under my belt this summer, my face showed no fear, no indecision, no thought whatsoever that I could possibly fail in what I or my team came to accomplish. My only thought was for this shmoe to throw the ball down the middle so I could put a serious lick on it and get this game over and done. Instead, in my head, he wants no part of this holy terror, so he walked me on four pitches. I trotted down to first base and re-ceived instruction from our first base coach Mr. Blesius, a calm soothing figure who always had a good word and presented infor-mation in a manner that never belied the full meaning and gravity of the situation at hand. In tight situations and tough games, Coach Blesius was a welcome voice among the chaos. He leaned into me and let me know that I was an important run but not the winning run so be careful, don't get picked off, and stay tuned for any plays that might be signaled by Coach Schachtel. Allowing the lead-off man on base is never a good thing for a defense and the Wilmette crowd was going crazy over my simple walk, but I earned the walk with my game face, so the praise was mine and I took it.

After a sacrifice bunt, I found myself standing at second base waiting for Rick Treiber to come to the plate. Rick was a good guy to have up in this situation. Rick was without a doubt the fastest guy I had ever seen run the bases, the fastest guy I had ever seen, period. When Rick ran it was just how you wished you could run and just how you would think a super-fast human would accomplish such fastness. Every part of his body was working together to move itself through space. His arms were pumping like pistons and his feet and legs were a blur, matching the rhythm of his pendulum arms. He had that concentrated elongated face which made an "o" shape with his mouth like he was amazed and surprised all at the same time probably because he couldn't believe he was going so fast. And when he got to where he was going, he would throw himself into the dirt for a slide which immediately arrested his forward progress, but at the same time he would pop up from the slide with his foot on the bag looking around as if to say, "I have arrived, but I am thinking of going again, soon." Rick was the guy we wanted at the plate right now.

Being all alone at second base has to be one of the loneliest places on the field. As a runner, you are the only person on the field not wearing the same uniform as all those around you. Your teammates are miles away in the dugout; the coaches are restricted from coming to speak to you and must yell encouragement as though you were a child who has tumbled down a well. I could feel the anger and resentment the shortstop and second baseman were sending right through my thick plastic helmet. I knew exactly how the middle infielders were feeling about me because I had emitted the same aggressive, hurtful vibe toward many a base runner. How dare I come to the region they dwelled in and protected? How dare this foreign invader show his colors so far from his native land and threaten all they held dear? Well, I was there, I earned it, but I didn't intend to stay long.

Rick sized up the pitcher, and in his quick twitchy way he, flicked the bat back and forth like a lizard testing the air for scents of prey. Finally a pitch, a piece of food to his liking, came his way and in an instant his bat shot out and connected with a mighty metallic ping. The ball was driven long and hard into the outfield and the hapless outfielders gave chase as Rick began to accelerate. I was able to leave my perch of exile and trot home easily. After crossing home I looked out at the field to watch Rick in action. Powering around first base, Rick was in full stride chewing up ground at an alarming rate. The importance of the moment and the need for another run on top of mine was not lost on Rick as he somehow found another gear, a superhuman gear, to shift into as he neared second with no thought of slowing down. Flying by the guardians of that nether region, Rick didn't even think to have his passport stamped as his feet were barely touching down on that foreign soil. His sights were set on the third country of this tour, a land and destination so close yet so far from home. Rick exploded through the air and dirt and was arrested by the third base bag, a triple in hand and a trip to the World Series 54 feet away.

Score tied, one out, bottom of the 7th inning, man on third, and striding to the plate was the largest piece of fourteen year old meat we had on the team. The funny thing about the Pony League age group is that there is such a large variation in size and shape found up and down every bench. Whereas I was a buck and a quarter soaking wet, our next hitter, Larry Tabloff was as thick and solid as any adult man in the crowd. However, just because you are big and solid does not make you the best player or even a good player, as we had discovered throughout the course of our time in these tournaments.

The saying "the bigger they are the harder they fall" was quite apropos, especially for this age, because all the boys were maturing and growing at such an alarming rate, quite often their parts were not communicating with the command center. Too many monsters had approached the plate sending quivers of alarm through the villagers only to take the most pathetic of swings, going down with nary a whimper.

Larry was one of those guys who sent alarms, and his swing, at times a bit pathetic, could deliver a shock wave of wind your way and sometimes a ball at subsonic speed. Striding to the plate, his arms rippling under the polyester piping, the boys from Rapid City looked shaken and worried.

Coach Schachtel was coaching the biggest game of his life and he was absorbing the drama as it unfolded. He saw Rick dancing about at third, constricted by the limited amount of distance left to run. He weighed the fact of Larry's arrival at the plate; the power and potential and possibly the fall of a Goliath. Coach Schachtel took all the elements at hand, stirred them around inside his head, and in the course of the minute it took for Larry to lumber to the plate, he made his decision.

The Wilmette boys had gotten to this game by playing sound baseball and executing the game plan of one Mort Schachtel. Every boy on the team had bought into the philosophy of doing whatever it took to win the game whenever they were called upon. Right now was one of those times when a player of such overwhelming magnitude was asked to perform the microscopic. Squeeze-play. Ham-hands Larry was being asked to remove the funny bone with the tweezers without setting off the alarm.

With Rick at third base, there was a good chance Rick would be sitting in Larry's pocket by the time the ball got to the plate, so Larry better have the sign or Rick would end up with a mouth full of bloody Chiclets. The signs were given, just as they had been a thousand times before, and acknowledged. Everyone stayed cool, which was key so the other team wouldn't be tipped off to the sudden movement about to happen. Sitting in the cyclone cage of the dugout we all held our breath in unison as we had seen the sign and waited for the moment to begin.

The second the pitcher tipped back into his windup, Rick launched himself toward his final destination, head down, confident Larry would do his job. In the instant Rick broke for the plate the Rapid City boys sounded the alarm with people yelling, players moving, and panic in the air. The large mass at the plate had fooled Rapid City into thinking home run hitter instead of delicate bunter-boy. The pitcher once into his routine to deliver the ball to the plate was unable to alter his progress toward the fate of this moment. The ball spun out of his hand and headed toward Larry who had pivoted around and presented his bat in an attempt to make contact, to put the ball on the ground, and send us on to Springfield.

As all the principles of ball, fielders, runner, and bat converged onto one single point of focus on this sunny afternoon in Skokie, Illinois, once again the importance and casual indifference of the moment washed over me, perhaps as a defense to the possibility of our failure to execute the moment. My mind and body worked to guard me against the anguish that would come if we failed to meet our goal. The crushing pain that would overcome my fragile mind would be so great that my body had no notion of how it would be able to cope, so I minimized the importance as best I could and thought of an errand I needed to run and the dinner we would have and the days of summer to come.

The ball kissed Larry's bat just so, and the ball trickled onto the grass in two hops, and Rick flashed across the plate, and we all breathed.

The celebration was beyond anything we had experienced before. We were fully and completely aware at that moment of what we were doing and what we had accomplished. We were no longer playing as boys showing up for a game at the ballpark, we were ball players assigned and designed to compete and succeed in our goal to be champs. The belief that we were capable of accomplishing astounding feats on the baseball field had been proven and accepted. Now we needed to finalize the journey by accepting what we were and what we had become and by showing it to the baseball world in Springfield, Illinois.

CHAPTER 45
OH, DOUBT

As the spring continues to unfold, signaling its indifference to our schedule with wildly varying weather, we are finally allowed back onto a dry field. The winter months of January and February in Colorado can be dry, with March and April being our wettest months. The cold dry air of winter has a way of baking the moisture from the soil, so when the wet snow and rains of late winter and early spring arrive, the ground is thirsty to receive the drink. Although we have been pounded with double-digit inches of snow, the ground gratefully absorbs the moisture and the mild temperature keeps the wet from staying white.

Every day the world seems a bit greener and the trees start budding as the ground begins to look healthy and renewed. I never aspired to be a gardener or a farmer in any way, so it is with some surprise that I find myself to be such an enthusiastic inspector of soil conditions and moisture content. I have become either the world's worst gardener or the finest mud pie cook. I constantly push dirt around a small area of land, raking, smoothing, and primping, in the hope that nothing will grow. I inspect the moisture content of mud trying to determine whether or not a shoe can stay firm against its viscosity. My mad scientist dirt skills help me compute the equation: amount of sun multiplied by the quantity of drying compound, plus the length of time until the scheduled game divided by the amount of sweat needed to drag a rake through the soil to get maximum air to the underlying mud. All this adds up to whether or not we can play without a boy turning an ankle and for the game to be played with smooth ball-rolling integrity.

208 Gods, Gloves, Pop-Ups, & Ponies

My computations and efforts go hand in hand with the weather forecast. The daily dance to figure out if we will be able to re-take the field and continue our development occupies my mind throughout the day. For my group of guys, it is imperative we see the light of day if we are to salvage the knowledge and effort we have put into the season thus far.

The structure of the freshman/sophomore baseball season is one of tear-down and build-up. These young men come to the program with raw skills and bad habits which need to be alternately torn apart, built up, and polished. The many years of patchwork skill training learned from dads and watching baseball on TV needs to be reconstructed in a systematic way so the learner can feel the change in his body and, over time, locked into a fluid movement. When the timeline is interrupted by bad weather, the connection between physical repetition and mental acceptance is broken, and the process gets extended and disjointed.

Boys at this age need constant reinforcement of the work they are doing. These guys need to be on the field, and in game situations at regular intervals, so the new information they have been given can be tested and found accurate. Without the reinforcement of the line drive or the pretty backhand in the hole, the biggest enemy in sport and life can rear its ugly head: doubt.

The boys finally take the field after several days of inside practice and a few days of tip-toeing through the mud fields of our practice area. Practice is one thing; games are a whole different animal. As much progress as we have made in practice and in our mechanical abilities, it is the application of those skills when the game is in full motion and the boys are making decisions on the fly that really counts. These boys are superstars in practice, but so far this season, when the boys have had to perform, they tend to doubt what they have been taught and revert back to their old habits and dad skills.

Today is no different. Faced with real people in different uniforms, forced to react and think in a new and strange environment, the boys start to crumble. The doubt in their ability rushes at them full force. After a good first inning in the field, we go down weakly at the plate, swinging feebly at whatever is offered. Back out to the field we go, where a pop-up hit to the infield is stared at by several converging fielders as if it were a UFO preparing to land; which it does without a single glove to interrupt its re-entry to the planet.

And so it goes, snowballing along, drawing every player to it as it rolls and gains momentum down the hill. At the end of the game, the whole team is sticking out of the snowball, all arms and legs swept up into a massive ball of doubt.

Teenagers are so susceptible to the power of doubt. Adults are certainly not without their moments, but teenagers have no reference point from which to battle their fears and doubts. Very rarely do I come across a player who is fearless and confident to the point that they are immune to the crippling effects of doubt. Occasionally a player will come along who just doesn't give a damn what anyone thinks or says; who simply plays hard puts all his ability out on the field and is satisfied with what he can do.

However for the majority of kids, they are walking bags of nerves, fears, and doubts which have to be propped up and pushed forward and guided to the realization that they are okay. Now this is not to say I condone failure or dismal performance. No, I am advocating to the boys that they have the information they need to succeed, they simply need to apply the material as best they can and be confident it will see them through. Doubt can be conquered by confidence, and preparation, so do what is asked and apply liberally.

Watching the terror and frustration wash over these kids who have abandoned all the carefully constructed drills and skills is heartbreaking. Several of the kids come up to me after the game pleading for additional instruction or batting practice, some sort of salve for the pain and frustration their doubt has brought them. But with multiple games on consecutive days ahead, there is no time for me to review for the millionth time all the little skills which have been presented over the last five weeks. Patience, I preach to these guys. Patience and trust the material inside of you just let it out and you will be fine. Trust all the time and effort you have put into the season so far. Believe in the athlete buried inside of you. He is ready to display his talent and skill, just get out of the way.

Doubt is not easily talked away; it requires hard currency to fight its hold on these young minds. I know the next few games will be the proof some will require to rise to the level we have been aspiring to. I also know there are a few kids who will see the end of their baseball careers coming if they don't find a way to overcome their doubts and find some joy and success on the field. The fragile nature of these kids and their willingness to put themselves out here has set them up for this epic battle of character.

The game of baseball, with its requirement for a high level of skill, creates at the high school level, a collision of sport and personal success which can make or break a kid who has always seen himself as a successful athlete. The jump to this skill level will either see the player become the big man on campus or the quiet hallway walker who used to be an athlete. Too many used-to-be, frustrated, high school athletes walk among us and work among us, dragging around their stifled dreams and nagging doubts, making themselves and those around them miserable.

The crisis point has been reached for many of these young guys, so with the season winding down, the next few games are critical for them to find their confidence. The job at hand is to illuminate the best in each player, both from their ability and their personality. I want to help these guys find that place in their head where they can let themselves go, to play loose and easy, relying on each other, pulling for each other, eliminating the doubt by crushing it with confidence and fun.

Baseball is about letting go and being part of a team that trusts enough to allow the other guy to succeed and fail with support and goodwill. These guys are so close to that point, but right now they are all too concerned with their own personal success and failure. Tomorrow is another day, another game. We need to rally and focus on the team element in order to get ourselves away from ourselves; doubt cannot survive against fifteen-to-one odds.

CHAPTER 46
GOOD DOUBT

The fragile wall which separates the cocky, confident athlete from the quivering, unsure boy is very thin and susceptible to the slightest shake. The player who arrives at the park after a particularly difficult math test thinking about failure, can cause a rift in his already shaky confidence that is only a bad hop or called third strike away from bringing his whole house down. I think back to my own playing days and one particular afternoon when a series of ground balls brought me to my knees and to the point of psyche-crushing abject dejection. Were it not for the kind words of a compassionate coach and the support of a group of guys who valued my good days, and who also had the good sense to know my troubles could very easily be theirs, I might have thrown in the spikes.

The developing ego of a young man is a confusing thing to understand and get hold of. Too often we applaud the big ego and build it up as though it will serve us well in this world. I suppose for the businessman struggling to the top on the backs of fallen co-workers, it is advantageous to feel you are the biggest and baddest in the boardroom. And for the budding superstar athlete, a certain elevated opinion of oneself and one's ability is helpful in order to gird the player from the natural ups and downs of the game. However, too much self-importance and grandiosity can make the baseball gods very angry, not to mention the wrath it will inspire from the bench of resentful teammates. The pressure to live up to one's own inflated sense of self-importance and also play at a high level is a heavy load to carry. That kind of sustained burden inevitably will lead the player to a crash of monumental proportion. Even the moderate athlete who uses big talk and the latest gear to make himself feel important finds out very quickly that the game asks for devotion, dedication, and practice above all in order to achieve success.

The athlete who builds himself up and the modest player who has had a history of success walk the thin line of success and failure every day. Once again the athlete who has been honest with himself and who has worked hard to understand the difficulty of succeeding in the game will be the one most prepared to accept the great highs and the stunning lows the game can drop upon his shoulders. The biggest hero runs the risk of allowing the thrill of winning the game in the last inning to become his worst moment in the sport if he doesn't put the large moment into perspective. Our greatest achievements can become a small scrapbook we look at from the distance of a short career if those moments aren't handled correctly. Whereas the steady competitor may not have the newspaper clippings, but he does have the longevity and joy of many games played in fellowship and competitive acknowledgement.

As long as we are steady in our pursuit of our sports goals and keep the scope of the game and our place in it in perspective, we will be as guarded as we can be against the ravages of doubt. We can never be completely shut off from the thoughts of inadequacy in the field but we are capable of creating a healthy frame of mind with which we can work through the errors and strikeouts. Without the complex interplay of doubt, fortitude, and determination, we would never have comeback players of the year, as well as guys who go from goat to hero in the span of one game. Doubt keeps us alive and striving to find the best in our abilities. The player sitting on the bench after the big home run will soon forget the feeling of hitting the home run and within a few innings he will be amazed he could hit the ball that far, and by the time he comes to the plate again he will be doubting and working hard just to place the bat on the ball. We all doubt ourselves at one time or another, but it is what we do about it that separates the winners from the scared.

CHAPTER 47
AWAKENING

As kids we all spend a lot of time dreaming about the fantastic and grandiose. We take on the role of the commander and leader of the rag-tag group of soldiers who has to storm the battlements and rescue and retrieve the prisoners and the secrets. We are the firemen who must scale the ladders, always the big cool telescoping real high ladders, to the top floor windows to rescue the dog from the burning building. And we are the guys who come from out of nowhere to land a spot on the team and who guide the once hapless group to the World Series and of course victory. Never in all this make-believe do we fully understand the dynamics of the heroism behind our fun or really have a clue as to what it takes to place ourself in that moment of courage and to act.

The journey my teammates and I were on, through the swamps and shark infested waters to arrive at the towering walls of the citadel called the World Series, was nothing like the experience I had envisioned a million times in my mind at the side yard of Jonathan's house. All the visions that I conjured up when I was on the mound in my baseball fantasy world came from the movies. Those visions were sprinkled with, ironically, Wrigley Field as the backdrop, and were peopled with a weird compilation of past and present players as my teammates and with Jonathan as the catcher. This Escher/Dali composition of baseball past and present, fantasy and celluloid mash-up, was actually quite satisfying and to my in-experienced mind quite plausible. However, the true-to-life experiences and bone-weary march that had been our path to the final series was not as glamorous, not as sepia toned, and definitely not a sure thing. The reality of us preparing to travel to the Pony League World Series, which was still days away and which would require a few more victories for us to get to the final best two out of three series, was still quite surreal to all of us. Unlike my fantasy fueled outings at Jonathan's, the wait was long, the preparation was exhausting, and my biggest enemy at the moment was my racing mind which refused to let me rest.

As children we play out our days, literally, never really having to stretch our minds or to be more serious than deciding on vanilla or chocolate. School was fun, relationships were new and exciting, and coming home was warm, welcoming, and restive. Summers peeled out in a long endless series of play dates and explorations that started at sunrise and meandered to dusk until we heard the ringing of our call-in bell. Life was simple, no cares, just excitement for the day and the worry you might miss the next great fun.

Through the course of my fourteenth summer something had been creeping up on me. In the back of my mind, I had that same feeling I got when I turned the lights out in the basement and I climbed/ran the last ten stairs in the dark knowing that something was right on my heels. I had the sense that things were different this summer; something was changing inside of me or was it outside of me? I felt different, and I was beginning to see things differently. I spent more time in the morning lying awake, staring out the window, running things around in my head. I thought about baseball but also about how loud the birds sang and how green the trees were outside my window. I wondered about what my Dad really did for a living and about what my brother thought of high school and whether or not he got scared. I lay in bed with all my thoughts running around until my stomach rumbled and I would shake the last little twinkle of wonder and awareness out of my brain and let my kid-self move toward food.

That summer was different. I knew high school was on the horizon and the days of roaming free and easy were starting to fade. The past month, playing and travelling with my teammates, had aged me in ways I was still trying to get a handle on. I had never experienced time the way I had the past month. Just looking at the marked up calendar on the kitchen wall gave me pause to think about each square and the events which had occurred on each day. The squares marching across the calendar were such a sad indicator of the expansive events that exploded in my mind.

Three weeks of games popped and crackled in my brain as I looked at the minimalist representation on the wall. It seemed like years to my flowering mind.

Thankfully my stomach lurched again and I shrank my thoughts back to a bowl, a spoon, milk, and Cap'n Crunch. Listening to the satisfying early bowl crunch of my cereal, I could tell the world as I knew it was coming to an end. I had been watching my brother the past year, his freshman year in high school, and I saw how he had changed. His worries seemed to be greater and his attitude more serious. As sad as that seemed to me, he appeared to enjoy the added severity of his life. The responsibility and complexity of his relationships had added something to his character, given him a sense of self that my sibling play-pal never had before. I wondered about the year ahead and what the added dimensions of high school would do to my makeup. Would I become the serious guy my brother was becoming or would I evolve into some other type of teenage life form? The fact of my having these thoughts and musings told me there was no turning back from growth and maturity. I realized my time in the backyard with Jonathan and the endless summer days of wondering what to do next were coming to a close.

I knew what the length of a day and a week were now; time held no mystery or vagueness. Responsibility, duty, and schedule had taken away the haze of a summer day.

I slurped up the orange sugar milk which held no more crunchy nuggets and thought of the things that needed to get done that day. Wash the uniform, buy some new sanitary socks, and get out the suitcase recently stashed away after the trip to Bay City, those were the tasks of my day. The bus was leaving the next morning, bright and early, with a full load and plenty of fanfare. What a great summer, would there ever be another?

CHAPTER 48
LAST STOP, SPRINGFIELD

It was just my luck, the 1974 Pony League World Series was held in Hawaii, but the 1975 World Series was slated to be played in the exotic, far away (all of 400 miles) land of Springfield, Illinois. Rather than taking the charter jet full of reveling lei-bedecked supporters, we hopped on our good old Greyhound bus with our faithful fan and good luck charm, bus driver Gus and headed down the road.

We started our journey from the parking lot of Locust Elementary, within sight of our practice field and the location of our first tournament victory. The three weeks since we came together for the tryouts are full of foggy memories. I could just barely see the guy who came to the field scared and in doubt about whether or not he belonged on the field with the rest of the talented boys. My mind was bursting, full of all the sights and sounds from the various places we had played and all the anxious young players we had faced and vanquished. I sat in my scratchy Greyhound chair and watched as parents kissed their boys good luck sending them down the road while hundreds of other boys had already put away their baseball gear for the summer and turned their thoughts to school and the next sport to come.

We kept playing, we kept going; the final tournament was at hand. I could barely see him and I waved goodbye to that kid on the bike who was just hoping to make the team. He was a distant memory, a vague figure I didn't remember very clearly and now realized I didn't know particularly well. That guy was just floating along in kid summer land, the land of endless days and endless hours, free from care and worry. We are allowed to do that as kids, but then there comes a time... The days snap into focus and demands are made of our time, and before you know it, the world is requiring you to participate. Finally the world starts to make sense and all the whispered talk of growth and responsibility and maturity come to pass.

Yeah, that kid on the bike had it made and maybe he should have just kept on riding past the tryouts, a thought which crossed his mind. Maybe then he would still be floating about the neighborhood enjoying what remains of the summer, lost in the heat of the day and the wonder of what to do next. The day comes for all young men to discover what lies beyond the safety of their neighborhood, for me it came in the summer of '75 via a Greyhound bus.

The thrill of bus travel was long past, so the ride to Springfield was one big nap. As much fun as we had in anticipation of the games in Bay City, we had as much in silence and contemplation journeying to the Illinois state capitol. The large personalities that started this adventure stayed large, but they too had changed some along the way. The proving was over, the need to be large just to be large had been replaced with real personality and charm. The obnoxious fat heads had become good guys to know, solid teammates and people with substance. This is not to say that these guys wouldn't let off a noxious fart in a tight space or give you a noogie when you required it, it's just that they too had been on a journey; there had been growth all around. We were all still trying to wrap our heads around the amazing experience we were having, and being in such close proximity to each other all the time still required some getting used to. And as we pulled into Springfield, we headed to our new place of residence which was not the No Tell Motel but a school dormitory where the learning would continue.

CHAPTER 49
SPRINGFIELD AT LAST

The old red brick dormitory was perfect for housing all the teams which had advanced to the final round of games. The stately buildings sat nestled under a canopy of trees in a park-like setting, quiet and serene…for the time being. The swarms of excited boys from all corners of the country soon broke up the solitude of the pastoral setting. The building once again braced itself for the youthful enthusiasm it had put up with for so long.

Howie and I settled into our sparse accommodations by throwing our bags into the corner and checking out the four walls, two beds, and two dressers. How luxurious the Dew Drop Inn seemed now, with its wrapped soap, and bathroom actually within the space of the room. Here at the Springfield penitentiary, the toilet and shower were down the hall and I was sure the doors locked from the outside. But we were kids and we were loose upon the world, so dingy wood paneling and musty showers were simply atmosphere and science projects. We made the best of it and soon joined the rest of the team to compare notes and feel the safety in numbers. As tough as we sounded, we were all a little put off by the storage facility we found ourselves in.

Coach Meyers had been gracious enough to, I think, volunteer to stay with us on site in the same sparse conditions, a decision I believe he would soon regret. The entire floor was ours, so within the hour we took over the hall and all the rooms, and soon wild games, and general chaos could be found throughout the cell block. Coach Meyers was nowhere to be found and his door remained firmly shut against the pent-up Greyhound howl of his all-stars.

Six teams had survived the long tournament process to end up in Springfield, Illinois this late into the summer. The South was represented by Caycee, South Carolina and Tampa, Florida. The Midwest chimed in with two teams, Decatur, Illinois, the host team, and Wilmette, while the west brought West Covina, California to the table. The final team was a representative from Mexico, which added an international flair to the proceedings.

The locations, distances, and countries sent my head spinning. I had a hard time grasping the magnitude of what we were involved in. Here I thought this was going to be a nice way to end the summer, play a few more games, hit the beach, and then off to high school. All the teams playing in the double elimination event were seasoned tournament-hardened competitors who had to face just as many obstacles as we had. The thought of going against these teams that looked tough just from the name of their town and the distance they had travelled caused me grave doubts. What in the world was a stupid little town like ours doing playing in a tournament as big as this? How could we possibly be playing against exotic wonderful towns that I was sure must be way nicer than ours? All the learned bravado and tough ignorance of opponent size and strength was thrown out the window from just looking at the program and reading about the cool teams from neat places. My mind conjured up perfect Mayberry towns where they had parades every week and the store owners invited kids in for free ice cream; a Utopia where the weather was perfect and kick-the-can was played until midnight.

In my head I was on the bus back to Wilmette without so much as seeing another team throw a ball. My fragile mind conjured up two quick losses to superior teams full of swift agile giants that played the game in ways I couldn't possibly imagine. I went to bed on my stiff institutional sheets talking big to Howie, but inside I was a wreck. By the time my mind wound down, I had convinced myself that I was a fraud and a fake, and there was no possible way I could take the field the next day.

The next day did dawn and I launched myself out of my bunk ready to take on the world, ready to slay giants, ready to show the world what my teammates and I could do. Aah, youth and a good night's sleep; there is nothing like it to dispel demons and brighten ones perspective. The late August haze burned off by noon as was my funk and doubt.

We congregated early and traveled about as one large unit. The safety in numbers felt by all. Our hats united us and gave us identity in and around the campus and about town. We were never far from the site of a Wilmette "W", and we rarely separated except to spend time with our families which for the most part had travelled to see us play. Both of my parents had made the journey to Springfield to see their son in what even my mother acknowledged was a pretty big deal. There was even a rumor my brother would be coming down should we make it to the final best of three. The news of his possible arrival floored me as he and I were not exactly close at the moment. All the attention from the tournament officials, the swooning of the parents, and the possible arrival of my brother started to give me some perspective on how huge things had gotten. Outside of my funeral, I didn't expect my brother to attend anything I did.

Friday, August 22: time to play our first game. We were placed in a three team bracket with Decatur, Illinois and Tampa, Florida. The round was double elimination with the winner taking on the winner of the other bracket, composed of Mexico, Covina, California, and Caycee, South Carolina. The events of the next few days would take place in Springfield, Decatur, and Taylorville, all nearby towns.

Our first game was to be played in the sleepy hamlet of Taylorville against the team from Tampa. Although we had played a bunch of games over the past three weeks, every time we started a new event, the same old butterflies returned, the same old anxieties came flooding back. The mounting stress and anxiety hit me in the face at the start of each new series, and it struck me as seriously unhealthy to my well being. I wondered just how much faster my heart could beat, and how much more pressure I could take before I would go running off the field, out the gate, and into the August afternoon never to be heard from again.

As I looked at my companions who had traversed the same minefield as I to get here and also across at the opposing team, who likewise had endured the same to be here, I thought there must be the same hot internal fusion going on inside their minds and stomachs as in mine. This time I was so aware of where I was and what I was attempting to do that I longed for the ignorance and serenity of those long ago days of just three weeks prior. The game had become serious and my role felt more like a job, yet I knew what I needed to do, and I knew there were so many people counting on me and us…my stomach lurched.

The national anthem played as we stood on the first base line, hats over our hearts, and eyes to the flag. We had done all this before, but today we knew the end was near, for this journey which led us to this town in southern Illinois to play baseball against the best teams in the United States and Mexico would soon be a memory. As scared as I was, and as hyper-aware as I was about the buzz in my body I completely tuned into the fact that this was about the coolest thing that could ever happen to a young excited baseball crazy kid like me. So I soaked it in; every little bit. The stands were full of our families, not just the dads who wouldn't miss an inning, but the moms who beamed with pride because their son looked so handsome and cute in his baseball "suit." These moms who were still trying to figure out the game were simply interested in seeing their boys "out there," on the stage of grass and dirt. To them the game was more like the school play where their son has a juicy part and they don't mind letting everyone around them know the boy swinging the bat or running onto the field is their boy.

Brothers and sisters were running around the bleachers, hanging onto the fence, pointing and waving, letting each other know which number player was connected to them. The little brothers in attendance looked on with awe and envy seeing only the flash and show of the event rather than the work, struggle, and achievement which brought the boys there.

They all wanted to be out there, lots of boys wanted to be out there, but thinking about the road to the field was beyond my understanding because when I looked back there was no way we could duplicate the events that had unfurled. Everyone on hand, spectators, families, and officials were excited for the games, ready to see what it was that made these scraggily groups of boys good enough to have thwarted so many. "Show us," they seemed to say with their eyes. Show us what you got because we want to understand and revel in the chemistry of the game and the beauty of a team who put the pieces together "just so."

The Wilmette All-Stars took to the field. I ran to my position at shortstop using the nuclear energy that had been building in every cell since I woke up that morning. My cleats dug into the perfectly manicured grass and exquisitely primped dirt. The day crackled around me as my muscles fired automatically in response to the ball thrown to me. As expected the heavy lead casing of doubt and gloom dripped off my frame, leaving the sinewy summer-hardened body that had lived between second and third base for the last month.

The view from this spot was mine. I could see this angle toward home plate in my sleep, in my dreams, and for all my days to come. For me baseball was viewed from this perspective, the just off center tilt into the dish with the anticipation of a righty pull hitter and a lefty late swinger. From there I paced and smoothed dirt, walked around, and made adjustments, turned and informed the outfield, barked encouragement, and made plays. What a beautiful day in Taylorville and what a wonderful time and place to be a young shortstop. Play ball!

CHAPTER 50
PUTTING IT ALL
TOGETHER

The late April and early May weather settles down enough for us to start stringing some games together. A nice routine is established with a day or two of practice and then a game. Routine is what we have been searching for, a set established series of events that the guys can count on. The lives of teenagers, although seemingly unstructured and filled with vacant time, are to them quite full. The world in which they live is compressed and saturated with their own thoughts and interpretations which quite often are imbued with way more meaning than we as adults believe they should be.

When a teenager says to his parents they don't understand the world he lives in, he is being pretty accurate. We have forgotten how full of ourselves we were at that age and how the slightest transgression or perceived disrespect could have such huge implications. Being a teenager is complicated and hard, and it's no wonder most adults would never want to experience those times again. Routine and stability are rare to the young mind, and when they find it, they latch on and find comfort in it. Going to baseball practice, having a printed schedule of games, set times in which to be held accountable, are all welcome fences for a scattered teen mind to live inside.

As May approaches I think back on the amount of time the boys and I have spent together and I realize the progress we have made. The boys look at their game schedule and see the multiple games that have been cancelled from cold, snow, and rain and they see the season as a stunted disappointment. But they don't have the perspective I have of seeing them on that first day of tryouts. I remember them as the awkward ballplayers dressed in shiny new gear, budding young people full of hope, piss, and vinegar. Those gangly young men are not the same group that checks in to the dugout for our next game. The batch of boys entering our cozy cocoon on the third base line are organized and excited. These guys like being here with their buddies and teammates on a beautiful day in May. They leave the complicated teenage world behind as they walk down the three steps into the womb of our baseball sanctuary. Watching them gear up for the day's event, I am taken aback at just how much they have evolved in the two months since we first met. Granted, their baseball skills have improved, but it is in the way they carry and conduct themselves that gives me pause for reflection.

The cocky-boy is smiling at the ribbing he receives from what he would have deemed a "lesser" player a month ago. He has had a decent spring season, but the game has given him a few lessons in humility along the way with some help from his teammates who will put up with only so much bluster. And it seems all the once-quiet kids are now the guys I have to tell to pipe down when giving instruction or passing along information. Bus ride conversations are no longer focused on the cool kids, instead the discussions are about the world they all inhabit and what to make of it.

The group has become one, with a common goal. I cannot say the goal is my grandiose one of becoming men and striving for quality play and personal growth on and off the field, but a goal it is, for them. Their goal is more along the lines of feeling comfortable in a world which is getting bigger every day. Being a part of this team is a haven of comfort and security against a world demanding more and more from them. The goal of getting better and being better baseball players and men is hidden amongst the need for something solid and unchanging to hang on to. Baseball is becoming that anchor for these young men. All the feelings of belonging and achievement and betterment are new and undefined for these guys. They don't really understand half the blather that comes out of my mouth...yet. If these guys pay some attention to the life goop that comes out of my mouth, and they digest and understand a portion, then I am happy. I look around and the boys are dressed and ready to play, and I take pride in the fact that no one's underwear is showing.

Today the boys play the game as if the stands are filled with Suzies and baseball scouts line the fences. Today the gods are smiling and generous as all the bounces go our way and we are receiving messages directly from baseball central. Every now and then, in sports, the game gets played as it is meant to be played. It is truly a delight to see when the level of play is higher than you thought possible from the group you thought you knew.

Inning after inning, as the boys come in from the field, a different kid bounces into the dugout with the glow of satisfaction after making a play he still doesn't quite believe. The whole team is buzzing with the energy of a game gone right. No blips or bumps, no head shaking or frustration, just pure unthinking intuition-fueled baseball. Every inning, a play occurs which illustrates a certain aspect of what we have been teaching all year. A line drive double play in which our third baseman knows without thinking what needs to be done with the ball without a moment's hesitation. Our pitcher, working ahead on hitters, knows to use his fastball as a waste pitch on 0-2 so he can set the hitter up to chase a curveball out of the strike zone on the next pitch. Outfielders are making adjustments in their position based on what the hitter did in his first at-bat. Infielders cheating-over based on the same information; placing themselves in the perfect position to make the easy play. Hitters, having a plan when they get to the plate, are working the pitcher for that perfect pitch which we are ready for and drive to the side of the field the pitch was designed for. And through it all, I am cheering and back slapping. The only coaching going on is me excitedly re-hashing the play or hit with whomever I can grab, enthusiastically helping them realize and enjoy what a great thing is happening.

When it all comes together, and it is rare even at the highest level, it is a sight to see and even better to be a part of. The baseball planets don't align for very long, so as a player or coach, it is important to revel in the experience. The moment is fleeting and you don't dare force-duplicate the event. Just enjoy the ride, bask in the faces that come in from the field, share the moment, and feel glad you are there.

CHAPTER 51
LET THE BATTLE BEGIN

Our first opponent in pool play was Tampa, Florida. I had grandparents who lived in Tampa/St. Petersburg, so I was familiar with that area of Florida, which added to the whimsy of playing a team from so far away. The many family vacations I had taken to that exotic chameleon-filled land had me searching my brain for even the hint of baseball down there. I could not recall seeing any kids or baseball fields in all the times I had been to the sandy tourist Mecca. Putt-putt golf, shuffle board, chasing lizards, and feeding seagulls were the only images I could conjure from the humid land down south. Now I was faced with a formidable group of young ballplayers who somehow grew up and played ball in the shadows and back alley parks of a Tampa I knew nothing about.

Naturally we started our ace, Ray Mals, to begin the hopefully week long tournament. Pitching Ray gave us the chance to use him again as quickly as possible should we continue to advance. Ray took the mound with his usual lanky just-born-colt stride, which was both graceful and clumsy at the same time. At six feet tall, with the wing span of an albatross, Ray was part baseball stud and part goony bird. With his impressive statistics both on the mound and at the plate, the team from Tampa had to be anxious to see what this freak superstar had to offer.

Warming up before the first official pitch, all Tampa eyes were on Ray and his impossible throwing mechanics and stride which seemed to allow him to reach out and place the ball in the catcher's glove. Although with Ray, as smooth as he may look throwing the baseball, the exact final destination was always in doubt. So as the wide-eyed Tampa boys looked on with trepidation, Ray hurled a final pitch over the head of Sammy our catcher that struck the backstop screen on a fly with a resounding crash. Seeing and hearing the final toss of his warm up, I knew we were ready to go and that Ray was as warmed up as he would ever be.

The whole team was as ready as we would ever be. After all the baseball we had gone through to get there, one more game and one more tournament was just that, one more time on the field. We were all as loose and matter of fact as Ray in some respects. We had all found a way to keep the size of the game in our own personal perspective. Granted, for me, I still got the butterflies, but I knew they would go away quickly once I got into the flow of the first inning and could distract my ever-racing mind from the business of being me.

All the guys had their little ticks and twitches to help them cope with a situation that given too much reflection could cause pre-teen cardiac arrest. Howie, for instance, talked and talked and bounced around and generally created such a nuisance and annoyance with his incessant chatter that it was a relief when the first pitch was thrown just so his energy could be redirected. Our catcher Sammy came to the park with such an intense game face plastered on his mug that nobody wanted to have anything to do with him. However, once the game was over, Sammy always had the most infectious smile on his face which never failed to sweep you in to his happy world. Each guy found the mechanism he needed to help his personality cope with the multiple elements of close long term team association and high-pressure baseball. Were we hanging around for the rest of the summer, like the majority of our buddies in Wilmette, we would have required many more years before we would have been as close as we had gotten, discovering the strengths and deficiencies of each other's personalities. We were the "lucky ones" who had skipped ahead of the class and discovered our character defects and personality quirks early. We would be battling these new found personality characteristics for the rest of our lives, forming the basis of who we were to become in the years ahead.

Ray was solid on that day in Taylorville. Given a two-run lead on a massive blast by Larry Tabloff in the first inning, Ray went on to pitch a six-hit, 3-2 complete game victory. Although we didn't exactly dominate the boys from Tampa, we did enough to win the game. We came to realize, or rather Coach Schachtel realized, the games played at that high level were going to be real close tough baseball games. There would not be a clearly superior team in any of the games from here on. The two teams that squared off on the fields that week would be extremely competent and equal. The team that came away the victor was going to be the team that executed the plays, made the fewest mistakes, and whose coach made all the right moves at all the right times. We were confident in our coach's ability, confident that he had the edge when it came to game strategy and pulling the proper strings when the time was right.

Coach Schachtel had been waiting his whole life for this kind of baseball. Back when we first put the team together, Coach Schachtel laid the foundation for just these kinds of games. His focus on solid defense and the intricacies of bunting and running was in preparation for the games where both teams are equal in pitching and hitting. All things being equal talent-wise, he prepared us to do battle at a higher level of baseball, the level we caught a glimpse of during our initial week of practice. The unselfish role of baseball purist which he created in each one of us was now being called upon to do the pure clear baseball act of listening to the coach and executing the oldest and deepest baseball moves. Play the game as it was designed and only another pure baseball team would be able to stop us. So far we had not run into our equal and Tampa goes down.

CHAPTER 52
WHY DECATUR?

Saturday we played in Decatur, Illinois against the hometown host Decatur. It seemed suspicious to us that Decatur was allowed to have a home game in this tournament; a tournament we had worked so hard to get to. Talk regarding the automatic bid into the tournament floated around the dugout and we started to think Decatur was a patsy, easy pickings for a team that had played only the best to arrive on site.

We sent Bruce to the mound with his multiple throwing angles and variable speed curveballs to slice and dice the pretenders from Decatur. The problem with rumors and innuendo in sports is that it rarely takes into account the fact, that on any given day, a group of athletes can come together and produce something magical. Decatur may or may not have come the distance geographically or played all the teams we had, but they had every bit the heart and determination we brought to the game. The baseball god spirit that creates historical games and also makes the mediocre team great will float around the field and into each dugout equally. The only difference in its effect is how deeply you drink and how strongly you believe. Decatur came to play and they didn't care what we thought about the path they had taken or the gift given to them.

Baseball is a great equalizer. Because the teams are made up of nine individuals there are nine reasons for the game to go sour, add in the subs and it's a wonder we win at all. If there is a player or two who does not believe in the cause or the effort needed to achieve the cause, then a team it will not be. As a team, we saw the

234 GODS, GLOVES, POP-UPS, & PONIES

end of our journey nearing, so we all had a deep sense of our time together coming to a close. The special time we shared up to this point was days from completion, so we were beginning to relish and cherish every moment. We knew the ride could end so we were that much more present for each event and we quaffed the magic in hearty gulps.

Bruce was spot on with his whole arsenal of offerings. Working in and out, up and down, he was an efficient pitcher who didn't seem to need to relish or cherish his time on the mound because he was on it so little each inning. Every inning, he grabbed the ball and served up strike after strike, daring the Decatur boys to prove they belonged.

Jeff Rivlin doubled for us in the fourth inning, followed by a single from Slammin' Sammy Levin which gave us a 1-0 lead. Ray blasted another bomb in the sixth inning to make the score 2-0 going into the seventh. Bruce took the hill in the final inning looking as fresh as he did in the first inning with hardly a shoulder length hair out of place and not a drop of sweat on his olive-toned skin. He made quick work of the last three Decatur boys, and finished the seven inning contest with his fifty eighth pitch.

Again the game was tight in score, but the gap was still great. We didn't need to be winning by five or six runs to feel comfortable at this stage in our game. The confidence we had in our defense and the trust we felt for our coach to find us a run when needed was sky high. I guess you could say we had matured as ballplayers over the course of the last month. We no longer played with desperation and anxiety. The game was seven innings long, twenty one outs were allotted, bat as many times as you can. Every guy knew that until the last out we would keep playing hard; they allowed us to play seven innings, so we took all seven. When the game was 2-0 in our favor, or not, play would continue, at which time we were allowed to try to score more and to try to give up less. We controlled the playing part of the game, the putting the ball in play part. As long as we kept that element of the game in perspective, what we could control, and didn't go wishing and hoping and "what if-ing," then the game was just that, a game of skill and wills. That day our skill and will won out and the next day, as we found out after the game, we would face Decatur again to see if we could send them packing...probably on the seats of their bicycles.

Chapter 53
Not Perfect Yet

With just a few games left in our season and the school year coming to a close, it is increasingly more difficult to keep the boys focused. As good as our last game was, the practices since then have been sloppy and lackadaisical. The boys go about the drills as though they have achieved what they came here to do, and since they feel they have arrived, they stop growing. They seem to think there is an end-game to this whole baseball learning thing. Now that we put a solid game together and coach is pleased we must have gotten to where we were headed.

The thought runs through my mind that all the flogging and cajoling I have been doing to get the guys to see the game as I see it has only fixed in their mind a vision and goal they feel they have obtained. Because coach is so pleased with our last performance, surely we must have gotten to the spot he keeps talking about. Now that we have reached the spot and absorbed the information, we can relax, mission accomplished. So I wait for the next game to come around.

As good as my boys think they are, and I admit they are definitely reaching the potential I saw in them way back in March, they are a long way from getting to their mythical "spot." The fact these boys fail to realize is, while we were working hard to make the strides in our game we have made, the seven other teams in our league were doing the exact same thing. In my talks with the other coaches in the league, they all mention how they are having the exact same experience as we are. Which means the team we are about to face has had the same time to get better and, depending

235

on the makeup of their character and the desire they have to be better, their baseball progress could be considerably greater than ours. So I wait for the next game.

Our next game comes around and we are at home. We are comfortable, we are relaxed, and we are cocky. The boys saunter in just a bit too casually, and play around a bit too loudly. We warm up and get ready without an edge of fear and desperation and nervousness. I know what is about to happen and there is not a whole lot I can do about it except warn them and do my best to shake them awake to the folly of their ways. But then I remember who I'm dealing with, teenage boys, and I know the best lesson-maker is sitting and waiting in the opposing team's dugout. Without that edge of desperation and desire, the need to be better becomes lost in the haze of past glory. Baseball doesn't care what you did last game, last practice, or last at-bat for that matter. Every time you step on the field, the game will present you with a set of obstacles and challenges you have never seen before. The game will give you a set of emotions which will knock you sideways and then expect you to act rationally and clearly as your brain stumbles to right itself. If you take the field blindly sure and over-confident, then you will be crushed by the severe schooling the gods will give you.

A humble player knows all he can do is be prepared for the game at hand both physically and mentally. Physically he goes through the routines of stretching and warming up his body in preparation for the explosive nature of the game. The violent twisting of hitting and the dynamic exertions of throwing require the body to be supple and loose. The sudden accelerations of running from a dead stop to full speed and then the violent braking of a powerful slide can put muscles and limbs to the test. Mentally, a player needs to brace himself for the increasing variety of variables which accumulate through the course of a single game.

The progression of a game will heap layer upon layer of factors and elements that have to be considered when positioning oneself in the field or when stepping into the batter's box. The focus required to process all the information gathered throughout the course of a game is beyond the capacity of most players, yet we use what we can carry in our heads to be the best for that day. The player who desires to be most prepared and is desperate to be most aware will be the player who comes closest to his best. My boys did it once and the effort was all consuming. To have to do it again and again is not for everyone, but for the driven and desirous, the rewards are worth it.

The first indicator that my boys are just off center comes during our first at-bat. Although the pitcher for the opposition is adequate, he is nothing special. However, my boys are determined to make this guy look like Cy Young. Pitch after pitch comes down the pipe, and pitch after pitch gets looked at as though it were some surprise that came out of thin air. The boys stare out at the pitcher as though he has three arms and a tail. The lack of connection between mind and body is no clearer than when you watch a batter who is completely unprepared try to hit a baseball. In order to have success at the plate at this level, a player must have his mechanical skills, his mental acuity, and his emotional needs all in alignment. Without this holy trinity, the best a player can do is battle to keep from looking foolish. The haphazard swings and on-second-thought movements of the boys demonstrates to me the disconnect going on inside their heads. Several innings go by with little success at the plate and the frustration and puzzlement on the bench continues to mount.

The play in the field also reflects the disregard paid to the desire and desperation needed for success. A failure to pay attention to the workings of the game creates doubt and confusion in the field to the point where players throw to the wrong base, ignore fundamentals, and at one point, all the guys stand on the field after the third out because nobody is sure if the inning has ended. In the glare of all that open space, in front of parents and Suzies, the boys have taken the day off and we are only in the third inning.

I have been witness to many brain-dead ballgames in my day. I have been one of the brain dead on numerous occasions. Mercifully the boys work their way back to slightly conscious; enough brain activity occurs to get us to seven innings and a ticket off the field.

The ebb and flow of our season is normal...at least it seems to happens every year.

Although it is tough for me to suffer through the same experiences year after year, I know these boys do have to have these experiences in order to grow. Life requires us to show up every day. You can take a day off in your life, they call them weekends, but when life requires attention, you need to know how to suit up and be present. Today it was just a humiliating loss, but with the requirements of the life to come: driving, relationships, work, responsibilities, decisions, and the entire make-or-break stuff of a life lived, you will need to know how to show up.

The after-game lecture is simple: be prepared. We have worked on this concept all year. Over and over I have talked about doing all the little things needed to be prepared for whatever pops up. We have worked on minuscule fundamentals in preparation for the larger movements. We have talked ad nauseam about preparing our bodies for the first pitch by doing the latest stretching and warm-up routines. And we have talked about the mental preparation needed to battle tough pitching and to block out the distractions of a busy world. The boys are stunned as I re-hash all the elements which made us successful last week and unsuccessful this week. The lesson has been administered by the opposition, and the words I speak are simply salt in the wound. As the contrite group of boys file out of the dugout, I smile and pat backs and give words of encouragement. The lesson was learned, the lumps were taken, and the chance to be better is still there.

CHAPTER 54
TRAGEDY AT THE
ASYLUM

The weather started to fall apart in the Springfield area, so we were postponed and delayed. Cooped up in our baseball monastery, we were twitching and itching from the lack of movement. The hummingbird metabolisms of our bodies which had no fat and needed competition for fuel were buzzing around the halls of the asylum in want of sustenance. Outside my door a rousing game of hall hockey was in full bloom with crashing bodies and subsonic explosions of glee. Coach Buddy Myers' room down the hall was not quite far enough away and the walls not quite thick enough to repel the waves of noise that echoed off the Formica. Numerous times Buddy popped his bald pate out of his room, a manic jack-in-the-box full of loud suggestions for other more sedate activities. Finally he brought his full upright presence into the hall to shut us down and send us to our respective rooms for time out.

Sending us away to our cubicles to cogitate and fester was not necessarily the wisest idea given our choice of entertainments during our last stay away in Bay City. With all the time we had spent together as a team, the barriers of inhibition and reluctance to interact had long since fallen away. There was no shortage of ring leaders on this team as even the shy had come out of their shells, and they too were a scary lot. Soon a plan was conceived, and all the guys put to work gathering the materials needed to execute the heart attack we planned to present to our beloved Coach Meyer.

Our team was staying on the third floor of the brick retreat. All the rooms had large windows that slid up to the ceiling with many of the windows missing screens. The view was terrific and the breeze pleasant in the evening with the cicadas echoing throughout the tree strewn campus. We had already been admonished to stay away from the window ledges, as if any of the incredibly coordinated kids who had won innumerable games of baseball with dexterity and athletic prowess would have trouble sitting on a window ledge. Using the irrational fear of our oh so concerned coach who was personally responsible for the safety of all fifteen boys, we put our plan into action.

Tying all of our bed sheets together, teamwork, we made a rope of linens that we attached to a bed post and dangled from our third story window. We sent Mark Ferzacca down to the ground below, via the stairs, and had him drape his limp lifeless body over the large air conditioner on the ground. Then we sent our most hysterical player, Howie, down the hall to Coach Meyer's room with the horrifying news of Mark's horrific plummet to the ground after attempting to escape down the ladder of sheets. Poor Buddy raced into the room, scanned the makeshift escape route, leaned over the edge of the window sill, and to his horror, saw Mark splayed and broken on the ground below.

I could see Coach Meyer trying to process the scene at hand and all the repercussions that were to come from this tragedy. The phone calls to the police and to the parents and the blame and the horror of a coach remiss in his duty to protect his players. Then Mark sat up and smiled, letting poor Coach Meyer off the hook as we exploded in a gale of laughter. That's when his face went slack, and then he exploded in red-faced, gonna-strangle-a-player-and-cause-a-real-tragedy anger. Screaming and yelling and stomping around, red in the head with bulging eyes, it was hard to take this loveable gnome seriously.

"That's it. I have had it with you guys. I don't care what the league says, we are going home right now. Pack your bags, I am calling all your parents, we are done."

Buddy Meyer was whirling around looking for someone to blame or grab and to throw out the window. Mark walked into the room beaming with pride at the chaos he and his fine acting skills

had created. Buddy took one look at Mark and stormed out of the
room down the hall and into his sanctuary grumbling and grouch-
ing about snot-nosed ungrateful hellions. Slamming his door
against a world he couldn't control, we heard him stomping and
cursing about the scene he had just witnessed. Quickly we all gathered our empty suitcases, latched them up and march down the
hall to line up in front of his door. We knocked on his door which
flew open to reveal a man completely beside himself. He glared
at us.

"Coach, we are packed and ready to go home. When do we
leave?"

Buddy looked around at all his knuckleheads with our suitcases
in hand and smiles suppressed, and he just shook his head and
burst out laughing. The next game couldn't arrive soon enough.

Chapter 55
Who are these Guys?

Sunday the weather cleared enough for us to get to the field to play the next game in the series. Having lost the first game to us, Decatur was desperate for a victory. We entered the game with a 2-0 record, Decatur was 1-1 and another loss would put them out of the tournament.

After our shenanigans at club monastery, we were loose and free-wheeling. Our relationship with Coach Meyer had developed into one of inclusion and fellowship rather than the stiff adult/child guardianship. Because he was able to weather what we now understood to be a pretty horrific prank, we had a respect and fondness for him that went well beyond the normal coach/player relationship. Buddy was a part of us now and his care and well being meant a great deal to us. At this stage of the game, every single member of the team, coaches included, understood the tight dynamics of the group. Chaos theory comes into play at this point, for when a butterfly flaps its wings, or a player falters, it affects every player on the team. So when the ripple hits, the team and its players react, inspire, and rise up to face the wave, redirecting the energy toward the good. We were one unit now and what happens to one affects us all.

Decatur was desperate for a win while we were anxious to finish them off and move on to the big show, the best of three World Series. The short ride to Decatur reminded us again of just how fortunate these Decatur boys were to be hosting this tournament. Being just a grilled cheese sandwich throw from the ballpark was a real advantage, as we well knew from our experience at the Skokie tournament. All the distractions and "bonding" that we were forced to put up with made for a squirrely group of boys no matter how many times you had gone through the experience.

Early in the game, we jumped on the hometown boys, building a 5-2 lead in the second inning. Sensing the season might be over for good, the boys of Decatur scrambled every inning to put runs on the board, scratching and clawing until they were down by only one in the fifth. On the bench and in the field, I could feel the lack of pop and crackle we usually had during a game.

When people talk about a team being flat, I know just what they are talking about because we were pancake flat. I don't know how it happened or what brought it on, but the guys who were usually there every game were just not there that day. We moved the same, ran onto the field the same, swung the same, said the same things, but today the spark was not the same. Perhaps the time spent cooped up and the energy required to entertain ourselves had done us in. Or maybe the endless victories and effortless magical play had run its course and was in need of a re-start. Whatever the cause, we didn't have anything left after the fifth inning, and when Ray came in for relief, the roof collapsed and the Decatur boys slammed three runs home to shut us down.

Our second loss hit us hard as we believed the Decatur team to be patsies who didn't deserve to be in the tournament. Now we had to face them again in the rubber game to determine who would go on to the big show for all the marbles. The short ride back to our cells took forever and the common nerve we shared was exposed and raw. Again, as in Bay City, the loss was tough, but unlike Bay City, the implication of what was at stake was very clear. The thought of having come so far, and to get oh so close to the final prize only to come up short was too painful to think about, so the thought was pushed far from our collective consciousness. As in Bay City, we welcomed sleep in order to get to the next day, just like on Christmas Eve, so that we could wake up to the presents and tear open Decatur.

CHAPTER 56
PLAY DATE

The end of school is in sight with finals looming and the weather turning towards shorts and spaghetti straps. The boys are full of the excitement of finishing the school year and getting away from what has been a stress-filled year. The freshmen, soon to be sophomores, are in awe of the possibility of surviving the year. The sophomores soon to be juniors are feeling the halfway point of the march to the finish.

Many of these kids have come to this particular high school because it is academically challenging and a great prep for name-brand colleges down the road. Other kids have come because of the challenges the sports programs offer. The high-quality competition of a large school can lead to a look by an interested college and a possible sport scholarship. Whatever the reasons for their attendance, this year has been all they can handle, add to that the rigors of a sport and the nagging of parents and they are toast.

The pulse of the team is starting to fade as the weather turns nice, and with only a couple games left on the schedule, coming to practice is losing its appeal. As much as I love the game, I know none of these guys can match my endless desire to be on the field doing drills and perfecting swings and it shows. I realize the days are numbered so it is important to leave these guys with a sweet rather than bitter taste from their first school sport experience. The upcoming Saturday is supposed to be a nice day, so I tell the guys to wear their shorts and be ready for a different kind of drill. At this point in the season, anything besides coach's fundamentals and endless swing practice is a welcome break, so they are eager and curious for what is in store.

There are many ways to break up the seriousness of the drive to perfection. In fact, without the occasional relaxation of pressure, a new grip cannot be formed. Already this year we have played baseball golf, a game in which teams of two must hit a ball toward a designated "hole" by tossing the ball in the air and whacking the crap out of it…with good fundamentals of course. Alternating hits, each team tries to get their ball in the hole, usually a far away fence, in the fewest hits. This is great to do when a boost is needed or teammates are not working well together.

Another activity for blowing off steam and letting the hair down is backwards- opposite baseball. Two teams face off against each other on the diamond in a game of baseball in which all players must catch and throw with their opposite hand; left hand if a righty and vise versa if a lefty. The game is then played in a backwards sequence; once you hit the ball you start running to third, then second, first and then home. The game is a hoot, giving all the goofy personalities who are usually suppressed by their coach a chance to air them out in the sunshine.

Today we are going to play sponge-ball baseball. Recently I stopped at Wal-Mart and shopped around the toy section. Many of the starter sports toys for young kids can be great fun and great learning tools for "big" kids. I find a 24" sponge bat and some semi-soft sponge balls. The bat is just short enough that the guys will have to use one hand and the balls are just hard enough that if hit squarely will travel far and fast. The satisfaction factor is there and if a fielder is not paying attention the semi of semi-soft will surely catch his attention.

I lay out the field in the corner of our practice field with enough distance in the bases to allow for putouts and plays. I have also pinned the field into the outfield fence which allows for that solid smash to travel deep and gone for a fence-clearing homer. As I lay out the bases for our sponge-ball game, I flash to the endless days of fun with Jonathan in Wilmette. The many side yards of his house and the innumerable games we devised to pass the time, and in turn perfect our athletic abilities, race through my head. What fun it was to create a game using the stuff at hand and then play all afternoon at our creation only to forget the game the next week and come up with a whole new variation on the fly.

Laying out the field, my mind is at work coming up with the rules and parameters of the game. The bat can only be swung with one hand with elbow in to mimic our baseball mechanics. The ball can be thrown at the runner to maximize aggression against team-mates, and the pitcher is the source of the force at first to take away bad hits and bunts. I am sure the boys will modify the rules as the game progresses. I'm not really sure how much free play these guys have been exposed to in their young lives. Lives filled with over-organized sports, structured play dates, indoor fun centers, and confined neighborhoods.

Today the young men will get to play, act goofy, and be boys. The game of baseball is that and more, but at its root it is a game which needs to be treated as just that, play. Sure, play the game well and right, but the spirit to which you pick up the glove and bat needs to be one of childish glee. Hopefully the boys who continue to come to the fields and baseball diamonds everywhere know what glee is and have felt the joy of sport-fun freedom. Today we will be searching down deep to dip into that fun spot where it is okay to romp and play. We will let loose today and wash away the world with a rousing game of sponge-ball.

The boys appear from the various entrance points on the field. I have been around most of these guys since the January indoor workout sessions so I have spent the better part of five months watching them develop as baseball players. I have also witnessed their development as independent young men who can now hold a conversation with their coach and behave more comfortably around an adult than was possible at the start of the new year. Allowing a young adult to have his voice and to speak his thoughts is important at this stage in their lives. Most of the interactions they encounter with adults are either a teacher telling them what to do or a parent nagging them about the latest lack of responsibility. The field of play has a way of stripping the stops and filters away from the young adult with the excitement of the game moment. With the action at hand or the attention of learning a skill, the young man is able to forget the division of age and go right to the discussion of what is happening in the game without the self-consciousness of the adult/youngster relationship.

The attempt to fathom the complexities of the game is a great equalizer and I have told more than one player that I just don't know the answer to their question about the game. I have told them what I think with regard to their question and in turn asked them what they think of what I was saying. I will try to elicit an answer to their question from them. We will work together to think about the game and share our thoughts on when to throw the fastball and when to throw the curve or what to throw as a waste pitch on an 0-2 count. Sharing dialogue about baseball is safe ground for the shy and awkward teenager. It is a chance to begin speaking their mind as an adult to an adult. Rather than always talking at a player, I work to have the player talk to me.

The journey to this game of sponge-ball has had to go through the stiff coach/player relationship. I do not make myself available to be their buddy, I am their coach, I will have to yell, and I will have to make the tough decisions about playing time and discipline. I am the adult and I challenge these boy-men to take those first steps to questioning the decisions of adults and engaging in talks deeper than the latest video game graphics. Some are further along on this path than others, but just as I coach each kid differently, I try to make the comfort of engagement easier for those that struggle.

I welcome the maturing group of players who have arrived. The shorts they have chosen for the day's activities are not exactly what I had expected. Each player is wearing the latest basketball/gagsta attire, silky and long, down to mid-calf on some, they remind me of my daughter's capri pants. As an adult and a coach, I bite my tongue so I don't sound like the parents they are here to escape. I have given them the day to run free and unencumbered, the billowing silk of their shorts is testimony to their rebel call.

I explain the basics of sponge-ball with all its rules and variations. One of the guys' little brother has come to the practice, so I grab him and include him in the fun. The boys quickly take to the spirit of the day and before long everyone is sweating and running and diving and flowing along on the joy of made-up fun. All the tensions and rivalries come to the surface where they are dealt with in fun instead of animosity. Exposed to the light of day, many of the petty resentments from the season can't stand up to the scrutiny of fellow teammates and the fun to be had. The poking and prodding and playful banter wash away the perceived slights along with all remaining traces of the too serious spin that has been made of events long over. I stay on the fringe of the game staying clear of all coaching-type behavior. Today is their day, a kid day. No need to put an adult in the way to try to organize and direct, they already get enough of that.

The game evolves and morphs its way to its eventual conclusion, guys are pooped and all laughed out. We wrap up the day with light talk about the remains of the season and finishing strong. The boys are calm and in a good space as I send them on their way, back to the requirements and condescension of their roles as mutating teens.

CHAPTER 57
ANOTHER GIGANTIC
NIGHT

Things in the sanatorium settled down after the simulated death of our utility player. I think Buddy resigned himself to the fact that a group of confined inmates left to their own devises would gravitate toward mischief and mayhem. Now, just like any inmate, Buddy was marking the wall, counting down the days until his release. With the next gigantic biggest game of the year on the horizon the chance for more notches was in doubt. The rubber game against Decatur was set to determine which team would advance to the best two out of three World Series against the winner of the opposing bracket.

The Formica floor of our hall away from home was eerily quiet as we prepared for our rendezvous with Decatur, a team which we were now way too familiar. Both of the previous games had been close, a 2-0 win and a 7-5 loss, tougher games than we had expected from the local squad. Playing three games in three days against the same opponent had created an awkward alliance between our teams which had broken down the barrier of the "other" team. For myself, a guy who liked the anonymity of just showing up, playing the game, and moving on; getting to know the opposition threw me off a bit. I did like that I had learned some of the tendencies of certain of their players, how fast some of their guys were, and the style of baseball they played. I knew Coach Schachtel and Mr. Blessius were pleased with the amount of information they held going into this final game, for it definitely would shape the way we approached the festivities that night. The part that threw me off was actually knowing the faces of the opposition and understanding the sameness of our situations. One of the teams would be done after the game, no more.

The players from Decatur were every bit as excited, thrilled, and scared to be playing in a game of such magnitude. Nobody had any illusions about what was at stake at this point in the proceedings. You win, you go on to play for the national title. You lose, and you are just another team on the scrap heap of teams who had a good run. I could see the thoughts careening through the heads of the Decatur boys, guys I had seen up close every day for the past three days. I knew their thoughts because they were the exact same thoughts running around in my head, and in all the heads next to me on our bench. To come this far and lose would be far worse than having lost in Bay City or Skokie. I ached for all of us.

The big silver Greyhound was waiting for us outside the dorm. The coaches and parents had pitched in to charter the Greyhound once again for this trip to Springfield, and our good luck charm Gus was at the helm with a positive word and an eager look on his face. Gus had become one of our biggest fans, caught up in the thrill of our pursuit; he had watched our games and felt the joy of our wins and the agony of our losses. Gus was like a third-party participant, not a parent and not a coach, he was a free agent who had surreptitiously been sucked into the odyssey of our summer. More than just the pilot of our adventure, he was now our good luck charm who gave us an objective pat on the back rather than all the canned parental hugs of encouragement or the coach-speak about believing in ourselves. Gus kept the game in perspective and it was nice to hear his voice give a simple "good luck" as we stepped out of the bus into the glare of the lights for the night's showdown.

Bruce Sonen was the guy for us tonight. His composure was in direct opposition to the state of my affairs. I was constantly trying to control the torrent of emotions roiling around in my head so that I could function with some kind of fluidity at my position. I kicked myself for my constant struggle to control my pathetic thoughts. I thought about Bruce and what must be going on in his head. I expected to see Bruce with shaky hands and buggy eyes; instead he was as calm as a breeze-free day at the lake.

Nothing seemed to faze Bruce. I can't remember a time when Bruce was rattled or out of sorts. Sure I remember a few instances when he got a bit bent out of shape due to a bad call or tough decision by an umpire, but that was his competitive nature coming to the surface; as for his stride and composure to the mound on that Monday night in late August, not a ripple.

The game got under way and my nerves faded and were gone before I realized to check them. Looking around the dugout at my teammates, I had such a unique feeling inside but I couldn't put my finger on it. The emotions and feelings at the moment, that moment of such high drama and intense sports energy was something I had never quite felt before. All the colors, smells, and sounds were so vivid and present that my mind felt full and engorged with data. I was so present and so connected to what was going on at that particular moment with that group of guys, a warm glow swept over me. The color of the dirt on the floor of the dugout and the way it clung to my shoes made me feel connected to the dirt. The smell of the collected sweat from fear and exertion bound me to the group effort at hand. There was chatter ebbing and flowing from an excited chorus to a groan of disgust.

Waves of emotion swept from our side to their side, from the dugout to the field, from one side of the stands to the other; filling my ears with a music I had never taken the time to appreciate. One of the guys nudged me to let me know I was on deck interrupting my reverie, sending me to the full stage on which my moment in time was taking place. The brightly lit field on which I stepped to take my warm-up swings was as large a world as I could imagine at that time. There was no other place beyond the darkening edge of the light's reach, no towns, no state, just right there. The crunch of the ground, the feel of the bat, the challenge ahead in the pitcher to be faced, that was my world and it was alive and it was perfect.

We took the lead early in the second inning on a double by Sammy and a triple from Mike Rebarchek. Mike hurried home on a passed ball by the catcher, and we had a solid two-run lead with Bruce dipping deep into his never ending bag of tricks. Decatur knuckled down until the fifth inning when Howie reached second base on a clean single and a stolen base.

Standing at second base was a misnomer for Howie. Howie was rarely if ever standing still, in fact I'm not sure he was still at night because I always fell asleep before him and he was up before me, bouncing around making noise. So I couldn't be completely sure he even slept. There was an upside to Howie's excessive verbosity and manic energy, he was fast. Jittering around on second base, aching to move and, I think, get back to the dugout to annoy me, Howie was jacked up and ready to fly.

Our big bopper Ray was at the plate, so we were ready for a blast of fireworks. Decatur's pitcher made a tough pitch to Ray who took a mighty cut, a cut that had sent balls over light stands. However, instead of the deafening roar of aluminum tested to its limits we heard the thud of a ball barely struck. Nubbed off the end of the bat, the ball trickled out past the pitcher's mound with speed enough to barely reach the infield grass in front of the shortstop. At contact, the entire infield including Howie instantly came alive. The pitcher fell to the side in an effort to interrupt the slowly bouncing ball but failed to intersect its path. The third baseman angled toward the pitcher in an effort to transect the same path, but he too was a fraction too late to get a glove on the seemingly protected orb. The only person with a chance to make a play was the sprinting shortstop who had been momentarily frozen by the vicious swing which produced so little velocity. However, once engaged, he locked onto the target that eluded his pitcher and third baseman. On a dead run, he scooped the ball up and worked to bring glove to hand, hand to ball, ball to shoulder, ball to first base.

During the molasses-slow journey of the ball and the ballet attraction of the whole left side of the infield, Howie had been moving. The second the bat made its minuscule contact with the ball, Howie was in high gear. All the frenetic kinetic energy Howie walked around with now had a place to go and he had the stops tied down. As the fielders worked to corral the lone loose ball on the field, Howie was a blur going around third with no thought of stopping. Rick Trieber was classically fast with pumping arms and beautiful strides with a head that never wavered. Howie was Tasmanian devil fast, arms and legs whirling, wagging head flailing, tongue sticking out, crazy desperation scrunchy face sucking in air, and buggy eyes locked on the prize.

As the throw from the shortstop arrived too late to get Ray at first base it took the Decatur first baseman a beat to realize the spastic little guy from second was barreling to the plate. All the fielders who watched the ball go by and all the coaches from the opposing team were screaming for blood at the audacity of this flea for attempting to score from second on an infield single. The late throw to the plate was nowhere near in time to catch the one-minded speedster who seemed to be ever present on this sparkling clear, pungent night full of the staccato sounds of groans and cheers.

Up 3-1 with Sonen in control, we were feeling good about the possibility of going to the ultimate series. But as the sixth inning arrived so did the fatigue we were afraid might catch up with our over-worked pitchers. There were numerous rules in place to protect young pitchers from pitching too much and hurting their arms. Coach Schachtel was aware of the rules and worked hard to keep the guys healthy and fresh. The toll of playing nineteen base-ball games in three weeks was starting to show on our stable of pitchers. Bruce and Ray received the lion's share of innings, so it was Coach Schachtel's constant worry as to when to pitch a guy and when enough was enough.

The sixth inning was one too many. The Decatur boys put up two runs to tie the game and Bruce was replaced by Ray, our ace, to try and save the game. Although Ray pitched the night before he still had some innings of eligibility left and what the hell, if not now, when?

The back and forth swing of the game along with my emotions had me reeling inside. I was not sure I liked the taut stretch of feelings I had to deal with in this do-or-die type game. I never had to cope with such unprecedented consequences before. The last gigantic, beyond-anything-I-had-experienced type game of just a day past had been eclipsed in the course of twenty-four hours and my poor little brain was having a tough time adjusting. I once again started to dialogue with myself about not caring one way or the other about how the game turned out as a protection from a complete mental breakdown. Although I was playing every bit as hard and doing everything I could to be strong and focused, in-between-pitches doubt crept into my skull to ask whether the agony and turmoil of these games was worth the effort. We worked so hard to arrive at these games only to be placed in grave danger of the most catastrophic emotional punch to the gut, for what? What is the payoff for going through the physical and emotional ordeal of a struggle against 8000 teams? Could it really be worth all this?

I had felt the joy of games won and been the recipient of personal glory. I had exalted in the feeling of making the un-makeable play, the buzz, the rush. I couldn't help but wonder if the feeling of winning the final game would be worth all the effort and anguish we had expelled to get where we were. I looked around at the guys in the field and I could see the focus and the drive and determination in every face. I realized at that moment that I didn't have to shoulder the dread of losing all by myself. I was a part of something way bigger than just my petty insecurities and desires not to be hurt. It was my responsibility to make sure my teammates didn't suffer the feelings I dreaded. So I had to play hard and do what I could to produce a positive outcome…with them. We were there. We were striving together. No one person had to do it or feel it alone. I never felt closer to my team than at that moment, in the sixth inning in Taylorville, Illinois, tied at 3, late in August.

The game shrunk back to a manageable size because I had fourteen other guys to share that special night with, win or lose. I was not the center of the universe and my personal doubt was crushed by my love for my team and the desire to do my part to keep defeat and despair from hurting them.

CHAPTER 58
RIVALS

All week the big talk at practice is about the up-coming game against our cross-town rival. No matter what sport you participate in at high school, the major goal and measuring stick to the success of your season is whether or not you beat the town rival. The boys talk tough even though the majority of the kids are first year students and really have no sense of the history or importance of any game, let alone a rivalry game. I help the cause by explaining some of the history of the rivalry as well as recalling some memorable past games which added fuel to the fire. Most of my explanations are simply to define what a rivalry is and in the process try to understand the importance of the game myself. Attaching such huge consequences and responsibilities to a single game is a heavy load for these guys to carry. I understand the varsity squad hoisting the load for the student body but my wobbly-kneed fellows have a hard enough time carry their baseball bags to practice. The bluster continues and I do my best to both foster a healthy animosity towards our opponent and prepare them for the pressure of a big posture game.

The game is to be played at our opponent's home field which is both a blessing and a curse. We have the pleasure of being the guest in a hostile environment, but we also have the advantage of fewer eyes upon us. Without the looming specter of the student body, with all their pleading eyes and fabricated emotions of blood lust, we can play a little freer. Granted we will be under the watchful eyes of parents and friends some of whom are alumni and who have filled their boy's heads with school honor and events that need avenging. All these factors compound daily and it becomes my duty to dispel and release the anxiety I see building in each boy. I know that across town, the opposing coach has to deal with the same set of circumstances with his crew. We are both working to get to the game with a group of kids who resemble the team we developed up to this week. The slow methodical progress we made to this point of the season has been slightly derailed by the mania of the big game.

I haven't had a whole lot of luck playing at the opposition's home field. For some reason, the gods have seen to it that this is to be my humbling ground. The histories of games I played at this diamond represent a killing field for my aspirations of coaching grandeur. The best and the worst teams of mine from years past have all left this field shaking their heads along with a coach who usually leaves pondering his ability to lead. Vowing to do things differently next time, I do, and once again the gods give me the opportunity to become a better person and a better coach…thanks a lot. Today I know things will be different; I can feel it in the air. The grass is freshly cut, the field perfectly manicured, the boys are excited, and I have my lucky hat on, how could we go wrong?

Things don't go wrong. We jump out to an early lead which the boys continue to build on into the fourth inning where we find ourselves ahead 7-1. The emotional aspect of this game which I have been so concerned about plays a role in the game, but I am proud of the way the boys channeled it into a positive motivating force. We do not voice ill will toward our opponent; instead we pull for each other and work together to overcome the opponent at hand. This opponent is not the enemy who did wrong by their father or who dishonored our school in football; instead they are a tough baseball team that would look good on our mental mantelpiece. We have eliminated the emotions which could deflect and derail us from the focus we need to play a solid game against an emotionally charged opponent. By placing the quality of our demeanor above the emotion of the event, we are able to play sound baseball and leave the mental twisting to the other guy.

Ahead by six with three innings to go, I can almost feel the sweep of the god's hands across the infield grass. Is it the slight breeze across my face, the tingle on the back of my neck, or maybe it's the cannon blast sound of a composite bat making contact with the baseball and watching my center fielder chase the ball deep into the gap that heralds my knowing the fortunes of change are upon us. There comes a point in some games when you realize all the maneuvering in the world is not going to help you win the ball game. As a coach I only have so much power. I make the moves I can and that I feel give us the best chance to win and after that, it's cheerleader time.

The cross-town boys come alive; mastering their own set of emotions they level a powerful beam at us. Whatever obstacle they placed in front of their natural playing selves has been lifted and the current is flowing smoothly to all aspects of their game. I look out at my guys with compassion and concern because the game they thought they were playing has now changed. The result of this game which has suddenly gotten very interesting will define and stamp these boys for some time to come.

The six-run lead starts to shrink and we have no answer for it. The sixth inning brings some miscues on the field, the result of panic and frustration, which in turn brings a tie game into the seventh. The team conversations with the boys as they come off the field worry me as more eyes search the ground for places to hide. I take my cheerleading to newer and greater heights as I too struggle to right the ship and find a course which will lead us away from the looming rocky shore. Again I realize just how helpless and powerless I am at times, faced with the turbulent emotions of downtrodden teens at war. The guys are valiant in their efforts to stem the course of the game, cheering each other, trying to pick up their fallen teammates. We stride to the plate with determination and gusto only to have our manufactured bravado hacked away resulting in a meek walk back to the dugout. I know the lesson at hand and there is nothing I can do to shelter these boys from the pain.

The bottom of the seventh, 7-7, home team at the plate, I have been here a hundred times. Watching from the dugout, my heart goes out to these boys who worked so hard to create their baseball persona. All the hard work put in creating the player they see in their mind and that they want to portray to their team, to their coach, to Suzie, to the other team, and to their parents is in jeopardy. A walk to the first batter starts the test of character. The second batter lays down a bunt which is fielded perfectly, just as we have practiced a hundred times, and is promptly thrown into right field to give the opposition second and third with nobody out. We play the infield in on the grass and the outfield shallow to try to stop the run from scoring. The hometown crowd is going crazy and the opposing bench is screaming for the last run and bragging rights. The next batter hits a smash to cocky-boy who moves his feet just like in the drill he has perfected, and makes the out at first without allowing the run to score. The next batter we intentionally walk to set up the double play and possibly, just maybe, get out of this terrible jam. The boys perk up and I hear more chatter and encouragement than in the last three games combined, but I also hear desperation and pleading…gods do you hear them? The number eight hitter in their lineup shuffles to the plate. I know this young man; we are all this young man at one time. The boys see the chance to escape in the terrified eyes of this young lamb. Our pitcher senses the chance to put this weak player away and grooves the ball in an attempt to get ahead. For a moment, I swear I see this pale young man close his eyes before he swings. The ball leaves his bat late and sends it twisting into the afternoon sun. It arcs down the right field line, weak and wobbly and perfectly placed just inside the foul line for the game-winning, soul-crushing hit.

Once the back slapping and jumping around subsides across the diamond, I prod my guys to line up for the handshakes. As crushed as my soul is right now I make sure to let the other team know what a good job they have done and I make a point of actually shaking their hands, not just a weak hand slap. The game is over and a moment needs to be taken to put aside the personal and recognize the physical playing of the game. Pitchers need to be acknowledged, good play recognized, and coaches congratulated for the product they helped mold. Once the formalities are taken care of, I look to see what can be done to repair the tattered sails of my ship. If body language could be printed into words then the sight of these boys before me would speak volumes.

I send the team to a far corner of the park for an out and back jog, together, as a team, so they can clear their heads. The time away also gives me a chance to clear my head and compose some thoughts I can share to help start the healing. These boys have probably had big losses in their careers, losses that hurt until they got to McDonald's or Dairy Queen. Today they have opened up a whole new scrapbook of pain which will be filled with games and events they will carry with them until they share the emotions and plead with their son to avenge the loss against those villains from their freshman year. The cycle goes on and the hurts are real as I search for the words to soothe the pain of being so close and coming up empty. All I can do is prop them up and send out words uttered a million times by coaches down through the ages. The fire inside each player will determine what is done with the message sent from the baseball gods on this spring day. The competitive spirit each player has inside comes in many shapes and sizes and it won't be the words from me that help change or grow that spirit. The events that took place on the field and each player's ownership of how he played the game will determine who he is to be tomorrow and what kind of player he will be the next time he suits up.

I put the helmets and balls into my car after all the well-meaning chats with disappointed parents. I've been here before and I know I will be here again. The sting fades fairly quickly these days because I know the value of this game. I know the sting will fade for the boys, for some sooner and others later. The sting will fade, but I know this game will be vivid in their minds for years to come. Some games are vivid because of amazing plays or personal heroics, other games because of great victories. The games of epic loss have a special spot in our minds and in our psyches; they are like plutonium with an amazingly long half-life. Some of my biggest losses pop up on a regular basis because the feeling or the lesson learned comes up often. I treasure all the games I've been a part of, but the biggies just seem to live on and become a part of our makeup to the point where we hold tight to the comfort of having survived such a thing.

With the last of the gear stowed, I take a moment to stare down the damn field which continually teaches me how humbling this game can be. I vow to be better and I tip my hat to the gods for giving me the chance to add to my scrapbook. The sting is fading and the scar is starting to form. I know as soon as I get home and fix my own Happy Meal, the tough tissue will have formed and I will be ready to face the next challenge.

Chapter 59
The Seventh Inning

The coaches did their best to both pump us up and calm us down in the top of the seventh inning. The Decatur boys tied the score in the bottom of the sixth but the game was only tied, we were not losing, just in peril. I could tell from the way the guys were walking around that everyone was amped up, but I also sensed a control of emotions which was slightly surprising given what I knew about the manic group of young men at hand. Anyone who had spent the kind of time I had with these banshees would be equally surprised at how composed and focused they were given the intensity of the circumstances. Glancing over at Coach Meyer, I saw the same apprehension and surprise on his face, as though he expected someone to tear their uniform off and go running to mommy. Instead we stayed focused on the task at hand knowing we each had a role to play and a job to accomplish. The possibility of losing this game may have been in our heads, but I saw no sign of it, and I for one was working very hard to squash the thought deep into the corner of my brain.

Howie was our leadoff batter for the inning. Words and sounds were coming from his braces-filled mouth but I had developed the ability to tune out only the important information. I communicated verbally with Howie when we were on the field. From across the diamond we discussed positioning and who was covering the bag in a direct business-like manner. Off the field and in the dugout, I had to put my Howie filter on so my brain didn't fill up with the endless excessive Howie chatter. The thought of being in that rapid-fire brain of his sent a shiver up my spine. However, at this moment in the game, it was reassuring to hear his voice, so I adjusted the knobs on my filter and tuned in to the ebullient bubble of his positive output. "Come on guys, whatyasay!? Just need one, just need one. Did you see the last batter swing, whoo, what a shmoe. I think his shoes were untied as he was running to first. Man the lights are bright. Who's up? Hey, who's up? Oh. Where are the helmets? No, the nice red one. Has anyone seen my batting gloves?"

We were Howie. The energy and flow of the fourteen year old boy was the Wilmette All-Star team. Batting gloves found, red helmet located, feet locked into the batter's box, Howie channeled the energy of his reactive mind to the guy with the ball. As scattered as we all could be, when the man with the ball throws it our way, we become the boy with the magnifying glass and the ball is the ant under the white-hot dot. The unsuspecting Decatur boy does the one wrong thing in that situation; he threw the ball to Howie. All the pent-up nervous energy inside Howie slashed at the pitch and drove the ball 330 feet over the head of the center fielder just missing a home run by a few biscuits for breakfast. Launched out of the batter's box with shoe laces firmly tied, Howie whirled and wind milled his way to third base with a leadoff triple. The chatter and nervous expulsion were deafening.

Dancing around third base, I could see Coach Schachtel trying to settle Howie down so he doesn't spin off into space. Rick Treiber was gliding to the plate with the go-ahead run at third base and our ticket to the final event in Springfield. After twenty-one games it was no secret that the Wilmette team didn't wait around for the big home run or the base clearing double to win baseball games. Our team was built on the premise that we came to play good defense and we manufactured and created scoring opportunities to win. If you were not paying attention, we would make you give us runs by executing plays and putting the ball in play. Make the plays and you would beat us, fail and you would be just another average baseball team on our slag heap.

Nobody out, man on third, super speedster and bat technician at the plate; what's the call? Coach Schachtel had gotten us here by making all the right decisions in all the right situations. He knew how the game had gone and knew we might not be able to bring Howie home based on how well the Decatur boy had been pitching. All the variables whizzed through his brain, and seemingly without hesitation, he put on our tried and true method of ruining opposing team dreams: suicide squeeze. The last big squeeze came in Skokie, executed by Larry to send us to Springfield, now Coach was asking Rick to squeeze us to the World Series. If things went wrong, if Rick doesn't make contact, the leadoff triple would be wasted and the momentum would swing to Decatur since they were home team and had last bats. With nobody out, Coach Schachtel was giving up multiple chances to score Howie, rolling the dice, and placing the pressure on one shot to score.

Once again we read the decision from Coach via the baseball telegraph. Once again we held our breath and made every effort to look relaxed and nonchalant but we were not fooling anyone. We were pressed to the wire mesh of the dugout watching the events play out as if in a dream. The pitcher received his sign, checked Howie at third, and began his wind-up. Howie, who had been abnormally quiet up to this point, sprang off of the bag and started his wind milling swim-run to the plate. The pitcher recognized the situation at once and sped up his delivery to the plate making an effort to change his throw from a perfect pitch to one more difficult for Rick to get his bat on.

As ball, runner, and bat moved to their intersecting point, we on the bench could blink only once in the time for all the elements to come together. The pitch was high, a pitch Rick had to work hard to get his bat on. Contact was made but the ball popped into the air, the last place a bunt was designed to go. Howie, flying down the line, tried to arrest his one minded pursuit to the plate as he saw the ball flying up in the air toward the pitcher's mound. The entire infield staff had shifted toward home plate once the play was set in motion, and they too were trying to stop their frantic flight to the point of contact. The poor Decatur pitcher who had adjusted his throw to create the pop-up and who upon the delivery also flowed toward the plate now watched in horror as the bunted ball glided lazily over his head. All eyes stared and all breath was suspended as the miscued bunt landed just out of reach of the convention of infielders arriving too late to catch the seemingly perfectly placed bunt.

Howie readjusted his flight plan and continued into home plate with the go-ahead run to the astonishment of all who witnessed the best placed, worst executed, suicide squeeze bunt ever. Decatur disgustedly fielded the ball dropped from on high and threw to first base to record the first out of the inning. Rick was shaking his head and kicking himself for the poor execution of his bunt right before we mobbed him with head noogies and back slaps. Howie got his share of high fives and congratulations as we talked, and he talked, over and over about the crazy turn of events. By the time we settled down and caught our breath, three outs were recorded and we headed to the field to try to hold our earned gift.

Ray fed off the energy generated by the contraction and release of all the held breath and constricted orifices. Hopped up on the incredible turn of events, he put just a little more juice on his already dominating fastball. Only his second inning of the game, Ray was at full strength with the added benefit of eight highly aroused fielders behind him and a dugout and bleachers still buzzing with excitement. Decatur was no match for the drama and destiny of this band from Wilmette.

The trajectory of our path was laid out and no team of destiny wanna-be's was going to stand in the way of our shot at the grand prize. Somehow, weeks ago, the baseball gods convened a group of guys on a non-descript field in the middle of Midwest nowhere to combine their many layers of boyish uncertainty into a baseball team which knew no limits. The gods had a way of combining elements which didn't look like much on their own but when combined in the right measure, produced a harmony which could not be consciously duplicated.

The chemistry at hand was beyond understanding on that August night as the last pitch was thrown for a called third strike. I raced to the center of the field where the bubbling pot of boy joy was flowing over. Nobody in that tangled mess understood why or how we were there. We played, we won, and we got to jump around. Simply put, we liked to do that, we like the way it felt, so we kept creating the moments so we could look around and see each other's soul rise to the surface.

The pure clean feeling of accomplishment and success was written all around, and for that instant, we were one feeling, one emotion. Team unified could not be any clearer than on that night in Taylorville, Illinois. Out of 8000 teams in the country, there were now just two left and the group of boys from Wilmette, who were hoping to play for another week a month ago and who all just wanted to make the team to get another cool hat was one of them.

Once the excitement died down, I looked around and saw that the world was no different. The major event had not change the landscape in any way. The field we were at returned to a blank canvas waiting for the next drama to unfold. I didn't know if this field would ever experience the magnitude of excitement it had just been a part of, but I thought the field was probably okay with that. An empty field just waits patiently for whatever level of play comes its way. The two friends who come out to practice pitching, the group of kids coming together to form an all-star team, the pick-up game of unknowns, they all transform the static field into an active living breathing element. Whatever emotion is brought to the field, the field absorbs and syncs up to the participants to create the world of the game. The field is happy to contribute all it can to making the action of the moment all it can be.

That day the little field in Taylorville gave all it had and it was happy to have been witness to the high drama and to be the setting for the event. The next day it would be waiting again for the chance to play host, full of possibilities and bad hops, ready to be a part of more baseball joy.

CHAPTER 60
PERSPECTIVE

The sun came up today, the world did not end, and the boys are back at practice. For some of the guys, the big loss against the school rival is still a raw wound which will require some more healing. Others are able to put it in some kind of perspective or in some kind of mental containment area where they can put off fully examining the pain until later. I am surprised at the mix of coping mechanisms at play and even more surprised at the particular players who are using them. The quality players who get the most playing time are struggling with the outcome of the game. I thought because of their full commitment they would be able to put the events in context and move on. Instead they are doing a lot of self-flagellation; kicking themselves for effort not given or for plays which couldn't have been made.

The fringe players seem to be the guys handling the situation best, and I'm not sure how I feel about their blasé attitude. I'm not sure if they have a healthy attitude about the loss or their lack of feeling is a protective measure; perhaps they just have a coldness for the game. Passion is a hard emotion to control, to direct, and to understand. The feeling I have for the game of baseball can blind me to the reality of what we are really discussing, a game with a stick and ball.

My passion cannot be your passion, at least as I live it or feel it. The feeling any player has about the game or any particular game has no equal to any of the others players around him. Each person defines his reality in his own way and for me to dictate the response to a game or a loss is inappropriate. I do know how I feel about the loss and I do know our team would have liked to win the game, but as to how each player handles the loss that is a personal thing. For this practice the emotions run the gamut, so I leave any discussion about the game until we have sweated a bit, purging some of the toxins we have all carried to practice.

Once the boys have run, jumped, and thrown themselves clean of their personal ghosts, we talk about how to move on and finish the year strong. I nibble around the edges of the previous game, talking in generalities, never biting into the nerve of the game. Although the game was as big a game as many of these young guys has ever played, the bottom line is it was a game like so many others we have played; a game we must learn from and use to our benefit. We talk about some of the mechanical issues that occurred, the ones that helped us and the ones that hurt us. We discuss the arc of the game which lead us to the climactic, unavoidable, uncatchable ball that did us in. And as we talk about the nuts and bolts of the game, the boys start to see that although the game was fraught with high drama and intense emotion, the breakdown of the events show two teams who played hard. Both teams got some breaks, but one team just got the bigger serving of baseball magic. We did what we could at the time. We played with the right amount of energy and desire. We wanted to win every bit as much as our opponent but we were bested and we have to be okay with the result, for that day.

Upon reaching the conclusion of our talk about the path to our loss, we arrive at the same spot we did when the winning run crossed the plate. However, we are a day older and a baseball discussion wiser. We are also together again, working out our feelings about the day's events as a group. Left to our own devices and our kooky sports minds, we can always find some way to take a well-played game, in which we came up a little short, and spin it around to a travesty of justice or a blame-fest with ourselves squarely in the middle. Together we are able to throw some reality onto the events which have taken on mythical proportions in the course of one day. My role as coach is to moderate the proceedings so the crushing defeat becomes a motivating baseball lesson. Sure the game will find a special spot in each players mental baseball scrapbook, but rather than the scarring event of their youth, it may become the motivating event which launches them to be the CEO, or become the better friend, or the guy who avenges the loss the next year instead of the guy who sends his future son to do it for him.

CHAPTER 61
TOO FREE

Two left. Out of all the towns and cities and states in the country there were now only two teams remaining. The next day our team, the Wilmette, Illinois All-Star team would face off against the West Covina, California All-Star team in a best two out of three series to determine which of us was the best 13-14 year old baseball team in the country.

Those thoughts went through my mind and my glove hand went numb. I rushed to keep those thoughts as far from my active mind as possible because any further reflection would cause my gut to do some refluxing. Instead I focused on the off day we had ahead and the great feeling of being free of the pressure of all the critical games we had played. One day to hang out and be a kid, a feeling which seemed to be fading more and more as the days piled up. Somehow I needed to work a little harder to be a no-mind knucklehead, bouncing around stepping in my own befuddlement. Everywhere I looked the images were too sharp and the depth of each vision made it difficult to see the world in a youthful haze. Maybe a few more noogies and a totally unexpected wrestling match around breakable objects would help fuzzy things up a bit.

All the guys made plans to meet up with their parents for a day away from the convent. Most of the people down from Wilmette were staying at the Hilton in Springfield, lush accommodations for those of us doing time in the slammer for the past four days. Entering the lobby of the hotel, I could see Wilmette caps bobbing around the dark paneling, accompanied by howls and shrieks. You would have thought we had never experienced carpeting before at

the way we ran around bouncing off overstuffed chairs and sprinting down and around hallways and maid carts. It felt good to be
away from the reminders of baseball confinement.

Under the slightly watchful eyes of our parents, we could tell
anything goes given the accomplishments of the night before. I
sampled a taste of the rock star life, free and uninhibited by the
rules of ordinary citizens. We had carte blanche to destroy a hotel
room, figuratively speaking. Instead we ran around making a nuisance of ourselves until a group of us decided to rob the cigarette
machine that was standing open being restocked. And once again
the visit back to carefree youth came crashing down and the
journey forward to adulthood smacked us right in the face.

The rest of the day was spent with family, good food, and sedate
activities meant to create calm before the storm of more baseball.
Back at the fortress, we compared restaurants and activities as we
started to ramp up our parent suppressed energy. The guys lived at
high octane levels of energy and activity, so any attempt to squash
or diminish their natural state only increased the speed of their
molecules, creating a very unstable mixture.

Someone had purchased a bag of squirt guns which were dis-
persed to all the troops and a mad scramble was on to be the first
to lock and load their weapon. Mad hysterical laughter reverber-
ated through the linoleum halls which I believe had become a
soothing balm for Coach Meyers. Either that or he knew when the
pitch of laughter was maniac-high he should bar the door and
hunker down. It didn't take long for mayhem to ensue and of
course the next tragedy to occur. Howie's squirt gun had a defec-
tive squirt hole so he used a folding knife to create a hole in the
muzzle of his orange pistol. The knife collapsed on him and gashed
his thumb. Blood and gasps of terror at the thought of the game
tomorrow followed as did a real trip to Buddy's door from the boy
in the village crying about a real wolf. Once Buddy realized our
starting second baseman, and the recent hero of our trip to the
World Series was indeed in peril of not playing the next day, he
sprang into action. Bowling Ball Buddy springing into action was
actually quite impressive. Given the severity of the cut, Buddy did
a great job of bandaging Howie in the midst of hovering boys and
less than sterile surroundings.

An endless string of verbal abuse and disappointment spewed
from Coach Meyer's mouth as he worked to fix our second baseman,

putting an end to our water war and shutting down our free day for good. The game was on, looming just over the horizon, and it was time to refocus our thoughts. Twenty-four hours from now we would be playing for the title and we would have to face one of the two best teams in the country with a second baseman at less than full strength. Twenty-four hours previous to this we couldn't have been any higher; tonight at lights out, we knew we would need our best effort to give the boys from California a run for the title.

CHAPTER 62
GAME ONE, GAME ON!

Bunting. We finally got some bunting. Everywhere we looked in the stadium, we saw red, white, and blue banner bunting the same as what we saw on TV for the big league World Series events. The run to the big show had really paid off as we inspected Lanphier Park in Springfield. We had real dugouts that were actually in the ground...dug out. There was a brick enclosed wall around the backstop, a large scoreboard in left field, and a fully stocked permanent concession stand built into the stadium behind home plate...the big times at last.

The field was a major league-size field which had been modified to the dimensions we played in Pony League. Rather than 90 foot distance to first base and all other bases, we played instead at 80 feet. To accommodate us, the grounds crew had repositioned the bases back toward home plate 10 feet so the field looked slightly off. The cut of the infield grass at the outer edges made for a gigantic dirt area that the infielders would have to adjust to. The outfielders were equally put off by the reconfiguration as it created an optical effect they would have to work out. The awkward field configuration was a small price to pay for the big league feeling of sitting in our expansive dugout on the first base side.

Everywhere we looked we were reminded of just how big this game was. Up to this point we were able to create the size and scope of the games based on the information the adults fed us. Looking at the photographers and important men in suits who were mingling around, I got the feeling some information had been withheld from us or fed to us with a baby spoon. Bunting, fanfare, and hoopla abounded. Word quickly spread that the governor of Illinois, Governor Walker, would be at the game to throw out the first pitch and shake our hands. Since our victory the other night putting us in the finals, telegrams had been coming in from around the state to congratulate us and wish us well. Coach Schachtel shared some of the onionskin letters of support with us before our warm up, including one from Mayor Daley of Chicago, wishing his metro suburb all the best.

In the midst of this sensory overload, we got an eyeful of our opponent as they swaggered in to their third base dugout. Across the battlefield we spied our opponent in their bunker, hunkering down for the tussle ahead. Additional information which had been shared with us and overheard in whispers and parental asides was the fact that these boys from Covina, California could play. Covina had scored 36 runs in their last 3 games, and word had it this group played for the California Little League title as 12 year olds.

These guys played all the time, all year round. While we were shoveling snow and keeping our arms tuned throwing snowballs, these guys were basking in the sun hitting home runs. I could picture the idyllic world in which these kids lived...baseball daily, weekly, forever. I could see myself waking up every sunny day wondering which uniform to wear for the day before heading to the field -my office- for a full day of work. My days would be filled with endless ground balls and batting practice, helping me to get better and better as I made my way to the big show, the major leagues.

The longer I watched the boys from Covina the more doubt built inside my head. I forced myself to look away only to see the other guys on my team snatching sideways glances at the golden boys from the West. Coach Schachtel worked hard to keep us focused. It was easy to see that he too was a bit put off by all the attention from the well-wishers and by the magnitude of the game.

The blinders came on as we took the field for our infield/out-field warm up. Once again we were happy to be engaged in the only activity, outside of hiding in the bathroom, which could deflect our minds from the glare of the over-blown contest. Our movements were a bit stiff and forced. The field was so big at this moment and we could feel the eyes of every person in the stands, including the governor, watching our team.

How did we get here? Was it too late to just leave and say we had enough? My head was swimming with contradictions and conflict. I wanted to be here but I didn't think my heart would hold up. I was not prepared for the kind of pressure being placed on me, but then again, we had worked so hard to get to the big pressure point. Standing there was nothing like the dream world of Jonathan's backyard, and I knew the guys from California didn't know how the script was supposed to play out.

CHAPTER 63
THE BEGINNING

The razzing started early, coming loud and clear from the visitor's dugout. At first I wasn't sure I was hearing what was said clearly as I had never been spoken to by the opposing team in such a direct manner. Sitting on the top steps of the dugout it seemed as though each Covina player had been assigned a particular opposing player to have a one-way conversation with and about.

Every movement and act was scrutinized and commented about out loud. Between innings, we confirmed with each other that we were indeed hearing what we were hearing. Never had we been exposed to a team that was so direct in their personal assault. We were shocked and taken aback that they would attack another team so personally. The things being said by the other team were personal, unkind, and at times, vicious. It was hard not to listen and the effect on our confused minds was clearly unnerving.

We started the game strong. Our coaches advised us not to listen to the flapping mouths from the other team and to focus on the game at hand. We worked hard to cover our rabbit ears and force ourselves to play the most prestigious game of our lives to the best of our ability. I tried my best to put the jerks from Covina out of my head, but my position at shortstop put me as close as anyone to their verbal assault. I felt a bit unclean standing at my position. The game had always been about beating another team with better baseball skill and tactics...not verbal distraction. The thought crossed my mind that maybe the game was more than playing hard and striving to do well. Maybe we were just a stupid bunch of hicks

282 GODS, GLOVES, POP-UPS, & PONIES

who kept the game too small and simple. The real game was about doing whatever you had to do to win no matter what.

Standing at shortstop, listening to the Covina players make insinuations about our players named Levin and Cohen, I thought, this is not right. The uncomfortable feeling in the pit of my stomach told me their behavior was not how the game was meant to be treated. I had so many different levels of anger going on in my heart I started to feel nauseous. Split between my outrage at such a breach of etiquette, and the focus of playing the game, the slimy tactics of the team from Covina created a hostile atmosphere in my head which I was not used to. What was supposed to be the crowning glory of our amazing run to the highest goal was devolving into a war of words and a complete loss of baseball joy.

We held our own into the third inning, bringing a 1-1 game to the top of the frame. My anger at the state of the game was churning around in my belly as I went to the plate. I felt a calm wave settle over my body as I walked around behind the umpire to settle into the batter's box. The buzz of the crowd and the beauty of the ballpark, polished and proud at being the host of this culminating event, brought the joy back to my heart. There is no happier loneliness than standing in the rectangle of the batter's box. Locked into the chalk barrier, the world fades away and the only two people alive are you and the pitcher. I couldn't be more exhilarated and at peace. Alone with the pitcher we can spend some quality quiet time matching wits and doing battle. This was the game I loved.

The beauty of the game for me is in the rolling ground ball and the perfectly thrown pitch. The harmony of the spheres comes together when the un-makeable play is made and the contact between bat and ball is clean and sweet. At that moment I knew the game was still about what happened between the baseball and the baseball player. All the rest just gets in the way of what the game can bring to your soul. The personalities and the bluster can color the game, but at its core, the game will always be pure and it will always demonstrate who knows its heart.

Bruce was on first base in the top of the third as I came to the plate. I batted ninth in the order, a spot I accepted. If you think about it, you only bat ninth once in a game, after that, with all the hits and stuff, you just have a turn at bat. I liked to think of myself as more of a second leadoff man since Howie, the real leadoff hitter, followed me in the order. Being a contact hitter, a scrappy hitter, had always been a source of pride for me. I rarely struck out, and my handling of the bat came in handy on a team that won games with bunts. Although known more for my solid fielding, anything I could contribute at the plate was viewed as a bonus by the coaches. So with a man on base in the third I was looking to the coaches to maybe bunt Bruce along to second so the top of the order could drive him home. Seeing no sign to bunt from Coach Schachtel, I settled into the warm embrace of the batter's box.

The Covina pitcher was a solid kid but nothing we hadn't seen before. A fastball went by for ball one, a pitch I saw clearly, and for my first at-bat of the night, I felt pretty good. The next pitch was another fastball and I got all of my scrawny body moving toward the pitch. My bat whipped toward the spinning baseball and the contact was sweet and pure. I don't know how they build a bat so that the small spot they call the "sweet spot" is able to convey such instant feedback through the hands, into the arms, up to the shoulders, into the neck, and then burst directly into the central baseball cortex of the brain with such instant delight. When I hit that ball I knew instantly it was a solid shot. I was out of the safety of my batter's box headed to the field of play following the clearly marked white line to first. As I approached first base, I knew that was not enough, so I headed hard left toward the next beacon of my journey. I felt I had myself a double so I started to coast into the halfway house only to be told by the umpire the ball my little 125-pound-number-nine-in-the-order body had hit just cleared the fence in left field for a two run home run... ahhh, the joy!

Being greeted at home plate by your entire team in the first game of the World Series after hitting a two run homerun to take a 3-1 lead was a feeling beyond compare. All the make-believe moments on sandlots and backyards didn't do justice to the almost-gonna- cry, hard-to-swallow happiness of getting patted on the back by fourteen of your presently closet relations on the planet. The joy we shared at the moment of my foot touching the plate was all encompassing and immediately fleeting at the same time. We were only in the third inning and as much as we would like the game to end right then, we still had to play all the outs.

I don't think the Covina boys appreciated the group hug we just experienced because the intensity and tone of their verbal assault went up a notch. Everyone on the sidelines for Covina was busy in some way making life miserable for us. The concept of team was a little different on their side of the fence. If you were not in the process of getting ready to hurt the other team with your bat then you needed to be telling the other team what you were going to do when you did get to bat. Or, if you were a bench player, your responsibility was to point out to the other team how inferior they were and how insignificant their skills were compared to their teammate who was about to hurt you with the bat. All in all a complete team effort.

CHAPTER 64
MUCKFEST

Coach Schachtel created a team built to put pressure on the opposition with solid defense, timely hitting, bunting, and guys who put the ball in play. We challenged other teams to make plays or to make us make plays that beat them. Covina was the first team to take us up on the offer. Never had we seen a group of players as fundamentally sound in their approach and swing as the Covina group. Every player looked like a clone of the previous hitter. They popped their hips and took pitches just out of the strike zone. They all worked hard to find the pitch they could hit hard and put in play. All those warm days in the California sun, taking endless swings, definitely showed in the way the boys from the West coast conducted themselves at the plate.

Ray was up for the challenge on that muggy August night. The rain which had plagued the tournament for the past week had left the air saturated with moisture and the field less than firm. With the capacity to cripple any batter who entered the danger zone of the batter's box, Ray was confident and obviously less a target of verbal taunts. His blazing fastball was crackling that night, creating less than California-perfect swings from the golden boys. What we did see was a lot of ground balls and given the field conditions and the entire Covina team rattling around in our heads, our normally solid defense started to unravel.

The first miscue of consequence came on a critical steal of second base. Up 3-1, Ray walked the first batter in the fourth inning and on the next pitch he dashed for second. I was at the bag in plenty of time to receive the perfect throw from Sammy only to have the ball tick off my glove. In the game of baseball, it takes only the slightest lack of attention for the ball to not be where you want it to be. I saw the ball, then for just an instant, I looked away at the runner, and the play I had made a million times during games of no consequence was now un-made in the biggest game of my life. Instead of one out nobody on, we had man on second nobody out.

The next batter did exactly what we would do in that situation, he bunted the ball. Covina was putting the pressure on as we had done to so many teams that were now buying school supplies. And as the teams we squelched did so many times, we mucked it up. Sam pounced on the ball and fell down. Collecting himself from his slip, Sam fired the ball into right field, scoring my muck-up from second and putting Sam's muck-up on first. The next batter laced a hit to right field which went through Larry all the way to the wall, scoring Sam's muck-up and leaving Larry's at second. By the end of the inning, we were down 4-3 and the wheels were nowhere close to being restored to the bus.

Coming in from the field, I was as upset as anyone because I felt I started this muck fest. Ray and I crossed paths in the dugout and I apologized for the play at second only to have him bite my head off and tell me to do better. I was floored by the attack and looked around at the group of guys to see if I was in the right dugout. Everywhere I looked I saw anger, disgust, and confusion. What happened to us? Today was the greatest day of our baseball careers, and the game we loved was a cesspool of hatred and anger. I couldn't believe how completely foreign the game was to me at that moment. I had never experienced the game in such a sordid manner. We were so out of our element and so removed from the innocence of our first all-star win four weeks ago, that I ached for the fields with no banners or bunting. We had made the big time… whoo-hoo.

Time marched on with little joy to be found on that night in Springfield. Ray joined the party by misplaying another Covina bunt, throwing it into right field to score a couple more bad guys. Everywhere we turned we ran into chaos and confusion until finally the night ended. No more outs, no more chances to screw-up. The glorious night for Wilmette baseball turned into a mess.

Nobody was happy; in fact as much as we wanted to get away from the scene of the crime, we didn't have the courage to come out of the dugout to face all the long faces and conciliatory pats on the backs from well meaning parents and fans. The cartoons of ostrich's burying their heads in the sand crystallized in my head. Please bring the bus around so we can run into the safety of our Greyhound coach and be whisked away.

Coach Schachtel was as disturbed as anyone but he kept his cool and talked us down from the ledges we had crawled out to. He had a way of putting things in perspective and looking at the game in a way that never occurred to our little minds. The game was over he said, but we get to play again tomorrow to show those bums from California just what we are capable of. Forget about all the mistakes of today because we know how good we are. How would we have gotten here if we were such an awful team? We had an off day and we have had off days before. Let's just put all that behind us and come out ready to play tomorrow, so we can take this thing to the final day. End of speech, end of guilt, shame, and shock.

The one emotion which still lingered as we held our heads up and took the pity pats from our fans was the anger. The way we were treated by the Covina boys and the way it was allowed and encouraged by the Covina coaches stuck in our heads and boiled in our guts. Thank God we still had another day to play because if that game was the last of the year, my winter would have been unbearable.

CHAPTER 65
GROWN?

May is here and the season's end is at hand. These boys are like your own children in that when you spend a lot of time with them you don't have the perspective to really see them grow. You go to the family gathering or weekend BBQ with your family in tow and the poor kids have to suffer through the endless astonished greetings and gushes about how big they have gotten.

Coaching is the same way. Weeks of practice and drills followed by games of success and failure blur into a closed world where time seems to freeze. Then you play that one game against a team you played earlier in the season and another coach or parent stops by who hasn't seen your squad in a while and the gushing begins just like old Aunt Martha used to do. The little guy you knew way back when has suddenly grown up a bit and upon closer inspection, you realize they are right, he has gotten bigger. The group of misfits that took the field in March has indeed turned into a bona fide baseball team while I was busy making sure their caps were on straight.

The chance to step back and look at the boys and the progress they have made is one I try to put off for as long as possible for fear of what I might see. Finding the right moment is tricky because all I see is what more we can do and how we can improve. But now, as the season's end is close at hand, I allow myself the chance to reflect on where we were then and where we are now.

The gangly group of wide-eyed youngsters that wandered through the gate for that first day of tryouts has filled out some. The rapid pace of their physical maturation is startling. As the parent of two girls, I know I must have saved thousands of dollars on groceries in the course of their childhood based on what I know from my own childhood with a ravenous older brother. I hear stories from the parents of these active boys regarding the massive quantities of food they are able to pack away before during and after a ballgame. I have witnessed the feeding frenzy on the bus when a bag of chips is displayed or a sandwich is offered to the group. Small players who bemoaned their stature early in the year are now stretching their uniforms upward. The taller boys are now filling their uniforms outward as muscle starts to thicken and the weight room effects begin to show. The awkward out-of-sync boys are finding grace and fluidity in bodies which were frustrating to control early on. The shy quiet guys are now speaking up and the messages are being listened to because of the confidence in their tone. The loud demanding voices from those nervous early days have been modulated by humility and pride. On top of all the personal growth, the guys have also learned to play the game of baseball.

The start of the journey to full maturity and the awakening of what it means to be a man has begun. Everywhere these boys turn, there are forces acting upon them, to affect them, motivate them, tempt them, distract them, deflect them, and encourage them in their quest to be who they are meant to be.

This year baseball has been a part of the explosion of information which burst before their eyes. High school baseball is one of the pieces of information playing a part in their creation. The game has given them a crash course in all the powerful emotions we face in the scope of our lives. They are being exposed to the emotions of joy and heartache, success and failure, support and friendship, discipline and reward, commitment and honor; the full spectrum of the human condition illuminated on the field, creating growth. These boys have grown this season and whether or not I can see it or whether they can see it, due to the fact we are so close, I know the world surely can see it.

I receive positive feedback all the time from parents telling me about how their son has enjoyed the season. Dad-coaches support what I am doing with words of praise for the development of their son's abilities and the abilities of the team. Moms get excited about a uniform washed on its own or a boy who speaks up freely at the dinner table about a topic of character or conduct. And I know the work is going well when the player who wouldn't say boo in the beginning of the year is able to have an adult conversation with his coach to ask about his hitting or just to say, "Hey, did you see that Rockies game last night?"

Growth is visible in many and varying ways. As I watch the guys get ready for the practice today, there is an air of familiarity and comfort in the way they talk with each other. There is calmness in the way they go about preparing for the events ahead, yet there is also great energy...you can feel it.

Locked inside each one of these dynamos is greatness. Everyone here has such potential and I like to think the game has given them a little insight into how to achieve that potential. The joy to be had through learning a difficult task, perfecting the skill, and applying it to great effect is a feeling which needs to be repeated. These boys are getting a glimpse of what their world can be. The world is waiting for these amazing young men and I have been privileged to know them when.

CHAPTER 66
TOGETHER

Back at the Benedictine retreat, we huddled together in Sam's cell with a copy of the Covina team picture. We were angry, frustrated, and confused at the way the Covina team treated us personally and at the lack of understanding from our coaching staff and parents who told us to ignore them. How do we block out the insults and derogatory comments hurled at us for seven innings? Our solution was to pass around the Covina team photo and circle the player you wished to beat the crap out of when the big rumble breaks out.

As the Covina photo came around to me I searched to see if their diminutive second baseman had been assigned yet because I think I could take him. We all talked loud and tough in an effort to salve the hurt from a game which was clearly awful and clearly not us. Taking our frustrations out on the black and white faces lined up and smiling from somewhere in perfect California-land provided a little comfort to our wounded pride. Our unified voice was comforting and far better than sitting in my room thinking about the three errors I made that day which erased any joy I might have felt about hitting a home run in the Pony League World Series.

Some of the bigger guys like Larry and Sam picked two guys to pulverize as their appetite was so much larger. My stomach still gurgled from the bite-size choice I made and I went to bed early, full from head to toe. Tomorrow was another day, a call for redemption, and our only chance to stretch this thing to its full three games.

The morning arrived with a fresh bowl of cereal and a tall glass of juice to wash away the bad taste of the day before. Every day was fresh and new and the guys were as upbeat and ready to go as always. I felt the same way. I don't know what it was about this team or this time, but every day broke new and exciting. The possibilities were endless, and the game could go any way on any given day. The beauty of the group was we were so far past where we thought we would end up that every next game was a gift. We showed up, played hard, supported each other, and whatever happened on the field was a thrill either way. Unfortunately, we were thrown off our game last night with the taunts and multiple errors which caused some internal squabbles, but the unifying death list brought us back together.

Coach Schachtel talked to us before the game about what happened the night before. He explained to us that some teams and coaches would do just about anything to win a game. The Covina team was simply a reflection of the coaches on that side, just as we were a reflection of Coach Schachtel. Several times during the game our coaches had to speak with the tournament officials about Covina having too many coaches on the bench during the game, a rule violation. Also, the coaches for Covina would go into the bullpen area when a pitcher was warming up previous to going into the game, another rule violation.

The tournament officials downplayed the infractions and told Mort to relax and not make such a big deal over the slight breaking of the rules. I thought the officials were as taken aback by the aggressive manner in which Covina approached the game as we were by their verbal tactics. The whole tenor and approach of the California squad, although admirable in a warrior win at all cost kind of way, felt a bit unseemly for the attitude the tournament had established and for which Pony League stood. Coach Schachtel pointing out the breaking of protocol was a first warning to perhaps the future of the game, a reality the officials would rather not look at. Without the help of the officials, Coach Schachtel turned to his team and let us know it was up to us to play the game the way we knew how and with the integrity and style which had come to embody the Wilmette All-Stars.

Bruce Sonen was on the mound for us on the 27th day of August, a clear Wednesday night in Springfield. The game, the continuation of our season, and the pride of Wilmette all rested on his hair-draped shoulders. It was up to him to keep the bats and mouths of Covina at bay with some wicked junk and snappy fast-balls. It was up to us to play solid behind him and force a few runs across so we could get this series to the third game. The atmosphere was right, Bruce was relaxed, our hit list was in hand, and we could care less about the world outside the fences of Lanphier Park.

The group of guys around me on the bench at that moment was so familiar. I could tell by looking at every one of them, based on their mannerisms and twitches, whether they were happy or sad, hurt or healthy, mad or glad, ready to win or lose. Today everyone was carrying their winning swagger, their happy heads, their mad-at-the- opposition shoulders, and their glad-to-be-from-Wilmette feet. Everywhere I looked, I saw familiarity and comfort. There was a comfort level now that I had not felt in my body in the first fourteen years of walking around in it. The time spent over the past month provided a better fit for my skin because of the acceptance of my teammates and the chance to prove their loyalty to me with my devotion to them. The polyester whites with the horizontal striped socks were a second skin that clung tight to my body allowing me to awaken to the thrill of moving as one. The boys from Wilmette were ready to go, today was going to be different.

CHAPTER 67
ENOUGH

The guys are just about done. We have one more game in the spring season, a couple more practices, but for the most part, the guys are done. I can tell they have had their fill of me, baseball, school and everything associated with broadening their horizon and improving their minds. I get it. There is only so much the average fifteen year old can take and hold onto in the course of one year and one season. I tell the guys if they can understand and incorporate just half of the information I throw at them in the course of the season they will be in good shape.

The game of baseball today is a complicated technically complex sport to teach and at which to excel. The vast amount of information which has been gathered about the mechanics of hitting alone can keep a coach in business for years. Side-angle video and views of top professionals swinging bats and crushing baseballs are all the rage on the internet and at hitting clinics. Endless discussions about the multiple steps involved in the process of getting bat to ball go on with heat and passion at conferences for hours. Bringing all this data to the practice field is an exciting thing for a coach, one that is not always shared by the less-than-passionate masses. Teaching the secret of success at the plate is never as clinical and clean as the squeaky-clean smiling videos portray. Teaching the game is dirty and frustrating with no rewind button and plenty of mistakes and attitudes with which to deal.

On top of the overload of information about the playing of the game, my dogged attempts to infuse the game with the lessons of life and the benefits of sports in the real world are falling on tired ears. At a certain point, the lessons about life have to be discovered instead of talked about and pointed out. The date with Suzie has to happen, so the crime of showing up wrinkled and rude confirms the point the coach was making. The lab is on the field; the truth is out there among those not in uniform.

Without the confirmation of real world experience, a coach is simply another parent with a matching hat. The other fifty percent of the information which hasn't quite taken hold will bubble to the surface in time. Perhaps the light will come on in a month, maybe a year, or maybe it will take until they have their kids and they are trying to teach their passion for the game. I know for myself that I am still having moments of clarity about things presented to me eons ago by coaches, parents, and well-wishers.

So we keep things simple and basic. No great truths will be illuminated in the last week of the season. We run through our drills and take solid batting practice and hone what we know. These guys have come a long way in the three months of our association.

My job has been to move them forward and increase their knowledge of the game. I am here to buff them up, bring them up to speed, and pass them along to the next level where the guys who have the drive will be thirsty for more. I have done that and more. I know the guys I pass along will be better baseball players because I have taught with passion and with knowledge the aspects of the game they need to know. But these guys will take with them a little bit more than just how to turn a double play or field a bunt or what to do in a first and third situation. These guys will take with them how to handle the emotions of a situation out of control. They will be aware of the beauty of a well- manicured field on a dry sunny day after days spent inside.

The joy of accomplishing a difficult task will have more than a personal connection it will be tied to the well being of the group. Personal happiness will be evident to them when they wake up and feel good about how they played the game and treated those around them. These guys move up the line better players and I believe better people because of the way they treated the game.

And those who chose to ignore the lessons the game and the gods offered to them will be back some day. They will be back some day looking for what they vaguely remember, a hint of something they caught a glimpse of, a feeling suppressed that was a little too real to embrace at the time. We teach them all but it is up to them to choose what to accept. The great will try it all and incorporate what works. The stubborn will take it in, mull it over, file it, deny it, and downplay it. All we can do is present the material, what they do with it is up to them. All we can wish for is that someday they are ready to try the material and take it for a spin to see where it takes them.

We have just one more game to play to wind up the season. I too have had my fill. At some point I too have to let it go and be okay with what I've done. These guys are not the only ones who get tired of hearing me talk. The endless repetition and teaching takes its toll on all the ears and brains on the practice field. It's time to put it to rest until the coming summer season when I will be recharged and refreshed with a new batch of minds to mold. We have one more game in which we can put it all together and hopefully use all the material presented to create baseball joy for all.

CHAPTER 68
GAME 2

The pomp and banners didn't mean anything anymore. Shaking hands with the governor held little appeal. And the thrill of getting to the big dance had worn away after an embarrassing game and an angry night. Today it was about baseball and playing the game with the group of guys who, for all their quirks and bodily noises, I still wanted to hang with for a couple more days. However, as ready as we were for Covina, the boys from Covina were ready for us.

Lined up on the foul line listening to the scratchy Star Spangled Banner over the loudspeaker, hat in hand, all our flowing locks blowing in the tepid August breeze, I knew exactly where I was. Everything was so sharp and clear at that moment. I could see the various types of dirt caked onto my Adidas spikes from the different fields of past days. The cut and edge of the dirt to the grass along the first base line somehow held a sharp fascination as the music droned on.

All the colors and smells and sounds of that moment in Springfield were almost more than I could bear, and I struggled to find the lost filters of my brain to help censor the immediateness of the moment. A couple of deep breaths helped pull my expanding consciousness back to the level of the playing field and the task at hand; anxiety, doubt, sadness, exhilaration…such a cocktail of emotions. Thoughts and feelings were coursing through me at such a rate that I was glad I had my skin-tight polyester to hold my molecules from exploding and spinning into space.

Thankfully, the anthem came to an end so I could mash my hat onto my ever- expanding head of blond curls and redirect my thoughts to more physical ponderings. My momentary journey within had left me shaken but with a slight smile. I liked where I was and what I was doing. I took the field, flying over the recently micro-examined grass and dirt with my secret serenity. My arrival at shortstop for the start of the game found me excited for the game at hand and full of joy at being who I was.

We scored in our half of the first inning. A walk by Rick and then a sacrifice bunt and an overthrow by Covina had Rick blazing around the bases for our first score. It was a good start for us, something we needed, as we all felt a little low from the previous night. The problem with good starts is it tends to spark the opposition into action. As much as we disliked the California boys they made it this far for a reason…they were good. In their at-bat in the bottom of the first, they laid some serious aluminum on the ball and banged out three runs on a home run, a single, and two doubles…so much for our feel good start.

Bruce managed to get us out of the inning and back into our dugout. Nobody wanted to quit, nobody wanted to give these jerks the satisfaction of rolling over our team. We spent too many weeks feeling way too good about ourselves to allow some fancy-nancy golden boys to come into our state and run roughshod over us.

Bruce was pissed, stomping around the dugout and throwing his A2000 into the corner. Normally one of the more composed players on the team, the pounding he took in the inning had him fired up. Striding with determination to the plate, Bruce found a pitch to his liking and unleashed his anger onto the defenseless orb sending it towering into the night for his first ever home run. As Bruce left the batter's box for his trot around the bases, he fixed a defiant stare onto the pitcher for Covina. Around the bases he went, sharing a laser beam glance at every player on the diamond. The message was loud and clear but the Covina players were not the only ones on the call list. As we waited at home plate for him to finish his circuit we too receive the message…game on.

Bruce went to work, no, he went on a mission. Inning after inning, he reached into his bag of baseball hoodoo voodoo, spinning and slicing the air with hooks, drops, curves and hoppers. Sidearm, three-quarters, over the top, all arm angles; elbows, knees and hair flying to the plate.

For the next five innings, no Covina hitter could figure out what was coming or what to do with a ball that just wouldn't behave the way a ball was supposed to. One minute it was right where they wanted it, the next it dipped away and found a home nestled in Sammy's mitt. When the cocky kids from Cali did manage to put the ball in play it was usually an off-balance, half-defensive excuse-me swing which our rejuvenated defense gobbled up just like we had been doing game after game, week after week. Bruce worked his magic, unfortunately they had a competent magician on their side and he applied the same prestidigitation on us. Going into the top of the seventh the score was right where we left it in the second, Covina 3, Wilmette 2.

CHAPTER 69

GRADUATION DAY

The final game of the season has arrived; the final act of a long spring. All the speeches have been made, all the drills have been done, all the preparation completed. The boys are full of what I could impart for the short time we had together which seems to have lasted years. My part is done; time to turn them loose to play the last game, free and unencumbered from my critical eye. I am curious to see the boys apply the material without reminders and oversight. Take the field and have at it.

The boys know the significance of the game and wish to put their best foot forward. Attention is paid to preparing themselves for the conflict ahead with focused warm up and positive attitudes all around. We have gone through our pre-game prep fifteen times previous to today's game, and every single one of them seems to have been different.

The feel of each day, each game, each bus ride, and each warm up has had its own personality. The beauty of spending time with these young men is you never really know the makeup of the boys or the motivations they bring to the field. The chaos theory of a flapping butterfly wing in Indonesia affecting events halfway around the world truly applies to the teenage world. The fact that my leadoff hitter was out of Pop-tarts this morning will have an effect on his first period math teacher, who will take it out on my clean-up hitter in fifth period, who in turn will jokingly punch our pitcher in his throwing arm, which will lead to a Charlie horse, which causes stiffness in the third inning. There is no way to account for the variables of the teenage world and it is best not to delve too deeply into the problem when I go out to talk to my pitcher with the sore arm in the third inning.

I know the guys want to do well in their last game and that's what worries me. Anytime we try too hard in any sport, we end up getting in the way of ourselves and the flow of natural movement. All year we talked about getting away from thinking the game and start reacting to the game. We need to tune into the spirit of being on the field, and as much as I kid the guys about the baseball gods and not making them angry, it is still that underlying spirit which truly does affect our game. When we try to direct the "undirect-able," such as momentum, or if we go beyond our physical limits, we enter a choppy world that rarely allows for smooth movement and natural play.

Bad baseball karma is simply stretching past the natural state of our talent and operating without character and respect for the game. Coaches are always saying things like, "play within yourself," without really understanding the full meaning of the statement. A player who is fully within himself will understand his physical limits, and he will remain mentally in control of his emotions, not allowing the passion of the moment to dictate his behavior. Playing within yourself is to have respect for yourself as a player in the moment, at that time, at that place.

Today I am working hard to play within myself as a host of emotions run through my head. I wish the boys well and I ache for all that is to come. I have given them the world of baseball as a template for how to approach the many obstacles and joys they will encounter in their lives. The game will flash into their brains from time to time as they travel through life. The game will be an anchor and resource for them to which they can always come back. Baseball is not going away anytime soon, and it is a testament to the lessons the game can teach that it continues to survive and thrive in our culture.

The many fans of the game come back for various reasons but also for all the right reasons. I would like to think these guys will also come back and spend an afternoon in the sun and think about the games they played and the players and coaches who brought the game to life for them. I know the years of reflection and lessons applied will one day bring them to the moment when their children will also take to the fields. At that time, the value of time spent playing a sport will be clear to them, and they will be secure in the knowledge that the game was there to help them become better people.

CHAPTER 70
THE SEVENTH

The seventh inning of game two could be the final inning of our season. Up until this point in the long run of the tournaments, we had played twenty-two baseball games in which we had won nineteen and lost three. That's 154 innings plus the six we had just finished, making a grand total of 160 innings over the course of four weeks.

Inning 161 took place on a crystal-clear night in Springfield. The sky had been scrubbed clean from the storms earlier in the week and the fresh field smelled intoxicating. Looking up past the lights of the stadium, I could see the stars and the black infinity of the very last remnants of summer. Somewhere out there was high school and home and a world that knew nothing of what was happening right here. The big stage at hand suddenly felt so very small.

We needed one run to keep our dream world alive and stave off the encroaching responsibilities waiting over the outfield wall. Bruce, who had been single- handedly keeping the angry California horde at bay, made his way to the plate. We were down to a measly three outs in which to extend the game, the series, and the summer.

Bruce entered the batter's box, no doubt arm weary but no less angered and focused in his approach to the team he had personally taken on from the black and white picture lodged in his mind. Bruce has had to fight and slay every player in that team photo. Now with the game down to its nub, we could only sit and wait to see if we had anything left.

On the bench, we were all a bit stunned and disoriented. For so many of our games, we never really entertained the notion of losing. Never during games in which we were down or when the game was close did we ever think negative thoughts or feel like giving up. The guys around me were that unique blend of positives and negatives who balanced and cancelled each other out to the point where the final feeling and attitude was always a plus sum. All the energy, down to the electrons it seems, spun around the dugout, the field, and the coaches, whirling us toward some destiny. And with the colliding of all the up and down personalities, we ended up with a fusion of energy that seemed to always propel us forward rather than backward. No matter how bleak things appeared the Wilmette reactor always turned the tide and spun us onward. However, at this moment the coolant seemed to be leaking and we were not sure if we knew how to fix it. And then Bruce swung.

Up to this point in our journey Bruce had been a steady player contributing his share of hits, doing his part to win ball games. His home run in the second inning, like mine the night before, was an anomaly, his first in twenty-two games. Bruce swung, and again the determination, anger, and focus of his desire transferred into the arm weary muscles holding his bat and he sent another bullet rocketing into the sky at Memorial Stadium. The confusion we felt a moment before rocketed out of the park as payload on the ball sailing over the left field fence. Once again Bruce ran his bouncy self around the bases, eyes fixed, hair waving, determination in place. With that blast, we had tied the game at three and were back on track, all electrons back in orbit.

The game was back to even but the Covina boys still held last bats. All the California guys needed was one run and the game would be over, they would be the champs. In our mind the game simply became a good tussle which we did not want to lose. We had to think of it that way, otherwise we would shake ourselves apart with the anxiety and trepidation of a one inning contest.

The Covina boys were going for the kill. They could see the end of their long road and they wanted it; we could see it and we were trying hard to look away. As hard as we tried to manage the huge emotions at hand, as hard as we tried to keep the game small and simple, the fact was we were only fourteen and our hearts were in our throats.

Standing at shortstop, I felt like my saliva glands had completely stopped functioning. I could hear my pulse. I could see my chest move where my heart was pumping, working hard to bust out. Pacing around the turf I tenant shared with that damn Covina kid, I vibrated like I did after drinking three Mountain Dews. My body felt so physically out of whack right then that I didn't know whether I wanted us to lose and be done with it or win and have to go through this feeling all over again. All I could be sure of was that I needed for us to get this inning going so I could see how it played out. Bruce, please stop my mind from spinning. Please throw a pitch because I am dying to see what happens next, I need to see what happens next.

He walked the first batter. The one thing we didn't need in a tie game was for the leadoff hitter to get on and there he was. I knew Bruce was tired because we were all tired. Game after game, day after day, we had been playing a relentless schedule which seemed to be catching up with us. Not only were we physically tired, but mentally we were wearing down. As strong as Bruce's will was on that day, I could see he was starting to crack. With all the recent games, we were a little thin at the pitcher's spot, plus I think Coach Schachtel believed Bruce was our best chance given his determination on the day.

The next guy lashed a single to right. The runner at first advanced to third on the hit and now there were runners at first and third, with nobody out. Coach called a meeting at the mound to discuss the plan. Standing in a circle on the pitcher's mound the entire infield had convened to hear what possible strategy we could employ to get us out of this one. The winning run was 80 feet from the plate, they had no outs, our pitcher was running on fumes, and my head was about to explode. Coach Schachtel was as calm and positive as though we were playing at Locust field back in Wilmette. Yes, the situation was bleak, but we were still playing and we could control a few elements, so here is what we are going to do. The plan was to intentionally walk the next batter to set up a force at every base then draw the infield in and cut down any runner at the plate on a ground ball...simple. My head shrunk a bit and my chest cavity stopped its flexing. We had a plan.

Bruce issued the free pass and the infield became really crowded. Everywhere I turned I saw anxious faces in all colors of uniforms. I realized it was okay. At that moment, I saw the game.

The anxiety and excitement could not be any higher, but I still saw the game. All the variables the game possessed had created a moment of high drama, an ultimate baseball moment, and I had the privilege of being a part of it.

Looking around, I saw Howie at peak alert, and Ray at third with his praying mantis arms reaching for the ball to come to him. Mike at first did a little dance like he needed to go to the bathroom, and Bruce was on the hill locked into the zone he arrived in today. In center field Rick crouched ready to puma any ball hit far or near, and Larry in right stared down to the plate wanting to smother the hitter with a pillow. I could see it all and I smiled at the knowledge of being here, happy to be here on this night. And then the batter swung.

He didn't get all of it, in fact he only got a small sideways piece of the ball and it twisted off to the right side heading towards no man's land. Howie at second was playing in with the rest of the infield, and at contact spun and headed toward right field. Larry playing shallow in right field broke in on the quickly dying fly ball. Both players were converging on a spot that was not quite infield and not quite outfield. Because we were playing on a field that was not a Pony League field per se but a major league dimensions field, the cut of the grass at the outfield line was deeper than it would normally be on a regulation Pony field. Howie was sprinting back to this cut mark, Larry was thundering in to the cut mark, Coach Schachtel was bellowing for the infield fly rule.

The infield fly rule states that with less than two outs and runners on first and second any pop fly ball hit to the infield is an automatic out, and the runners may advance at their own risk. The rule is in place to keep a defensive team from faking a catch and intentionally dropping the ball to get a double play on the frozen runners. At that moment the rule was unclear because the way the field was cut brought into question where the infield itself ended. In order for the infield fly to be applied, it must be clear the ball is within the infield and that an infielder has a clear play on the ball. The ball off the Covina bat was coming down in no man's land.

I could see clearly that the calm of just a moment before was about to change. The band holding the moment in suspension had snapped and all the tension of a second ago had been released, one heading out the other coming in. Howie and Larry collided. The ball made its way to the ground but only for an instant as Larry scooped it up and hurled it in desperation to the plate. The ball sailed high and wide over the sky-reaching glove of our catcher Sam. The Covina player crossed the plate. The season was over, the summer came crashing down.

The shock lasted for the blink of an eye…and then the yelling began. Coach Schachtel had always been able to get his point across to us with minimal effort and moderate modulation. Only a few times had I seen him have to raise his voice and those occasions had been on bad calls or guys screwing around to excess. Coach was out of the dugout before the ball came to rest, and he was hot. A full-blown melee was in progress regarding the location of the pop fly and the lack of a call regarding the infield fly rule. All the emotions we as players felt over the last month must have been playing around in Coach Schachtel's mind as well because it looked like he needed to get a few things off his chest. However, as the argument wore on I could tell the result was going to remain the same.

Watching our coach plead for us, argue for us, stand up for us, was heartbreaking. The more emotional players could not hold back their frustration and they too poured out the anger and disappointment of losing on such a sour note. We played so many classic games in our run to that moment so to lose on a questionable call was more than some could take. The beauty of the game was gone at that moment. The victor was happy to win that way, but for the loser, we felt cheated and betrayed.

Baseball can be cruel. The ball doesn't always bounce the way it's supposed to; the other team may not respect the game as much as you, the umpires less invested, and the baseball gods are off to the fridge for another beer. Second out of 8000 teams sounds impressive, but when the last run scores on a quirk of baseball spatial judgment then all which has come before feels lost.

At fourteen, we were asked by Mr. Blesius to take it like men and hold our heads high. As a group we tried, but at fourteen we didn't understand. For a month we persevered, grew and played far beyond our abilities as baseball players, and now we were called on to act far beyond our years. The game called on us to learn a lesson in a way which could not have been more raw and painful. Not all fairy tales have happy endings. In life, events simply have endings and it is up to us to glean the value we can from each outcome.

That day the event was huge and the lesson we learned would take some time to discover. Standing on the field, the exposed nerves kept us from fully appreciating what we had accomplished, what we had learned, and the progress we had made. Covina jumped around, the stadium was stunned, and moms were dying to hug their boys.

CHAPTER 71
THE TROPHY

The trophy ceremony was nothing for us to be proud of. Many of us had a hard time holding our tongues as we were presented with the smallest second-out-of-8000-teams trophy you could imagine. For all the work, sweat, and heartache we endured, the hardware came up way short of what we thought we deserved. We were young and as much facial hair as some of us might have we were hurt and wanted to get off that field and find those hugs.

On the other hand we were not the same group of guys who showed up at Locust field for tryouts a month ago. Every single guy on that team had been affected by the experience including those who were already adults. The coaches had also grown along the way. Coach Schachtel announced he was retiring from coaching perhaps feeling the experience was the ultimate for him. Buddy Meyers' experience as manager had been more than he ever bargained for, what with watermelon felons and kids plunging to their deaths. Yet, listening to his conversations with the parents and seeing the excitement in his eyes it was easy to see how much fun he had and how proud he was of himself and in us. Coach Blesius was as stoic as ever, but he too swelled with pride, for he had worked tirelessly with Coach Schachtel to create a team philosophy and approach which took this ragtag group to the very edge of ultimate success.

All around there was success. Every red-eyed kid was better off for what occurred there that day. Would it have been nicer to win? You bet. Would we have gotten more out of it? I don't know, but I do know it would have been a very different lesson. Covina took away the win and the title. Their win at all cost and with any means available approach worked out for them, and they would have to learn to live with that kind of victory.

We would have to come to grips with our loss and with the knowledge that things do not always work out the way we want them to. Baseball is just a game, they say. Hold your head up, it's only a game. Well, that may be, but for the group of boys from Wilmette, on a warm night in August, 1975 on a baseball field in Springfield, Illinois, it was the end of their adolescence and the beginning of their journey down the road to maturity and manhood.

CHAPTER 72
FULL CIRCLE

Thirty-five years later, I am back on the baseball field as a coach of boys searching for some meaning in the throwing of a baseball. I certainly didn't find the meaning of life on that summer night in Springfield but I did find the edges of the puzzle that I have been working on ever since. The awakening of my adult sensibilities, better yet, my human attributes did occur during the summer of '75. I awoke from the coma of my youth into a world that demanded more than I ever thought possible.

Soon my parents would divorce, high school pressures would mount, and I would take a shot at trying to become a professional baseball player. Life's endless string of trials, tests, and lessons spooled out in front of me through my young life. Real and hard life lessons began to rain down all around me and they continue to this day. But in the summer of '75, I was tested and tried on the sport stage with a group of guys at my side who made the lessons learned easier to handle and all the more poignant for their shared intimacy.

The young men on the field today have already been faced with multiple assaults on their adolescence whether they are aware of them or not. As parents, we are hard pressed to keep the innocence-destroying influences of our society at bay much past the age of ten. I believe baseball is one of the pure vestiges of a sheltered world we all share from our youth. Putting our children on the path through the baseball youth leagues is a way to protect our children and show them a simple game that is pure in spirit and that can teach so much.

Baseball will never disappoint a parent who wishes to share the physical beauty of the sport or who wants their child to experience the first traces of what life has in store. The look on the face of a small child as the ball finally finds its way into the glove they control is priceless. Success and failure and a bonk on the nose by what is appropriately called a "hardball" are lessons doled out in a loving and graceful way by parents who fondly remember time spent in their youth learning the sting of the ball in their palm. The game will grow inside the child. They will always find satisfaction for the play well made or for the simple joy of catching that first ball.

Over time, baseball joy builds until the player surpasses the parent and becomes poised for the transition from simple game to life mirror. Then one day, the game and its gods will bring the player to his knees with a moment so rich in beauty, pain, and anguish that the player has no choice but to dig down deep and search for a way to handle the flood of emotions the moment has brought to him. From that moment on, the player is on his way, awake, aware, and in tune to the complexities of the game and the large amazing world he has in front of him.

CHAPTER 73
BECOMING

The boys who finish their last spring baseball game are all in various stages of growth and birth. I feel so privileged and excited each day to witness the awakening of these amazing young men. Every one of these guys has their own path to follow and their own pace in which to actualize their becoming.

Baseball has been a big part of these guys' lives for the past seven years. Seven years in which the game has revealed some of its secrets; seven years for coaches, parents, and other players to interact within the framework of baseball's simple constructs. I have given them my take on the game of baseball, and hopefully I have instilled in them the love and passion I feel for the game and what it has done for me.

Given all the messages that bombard these kids today, my only hope is that out here, isolated on a field of grass and dirt, the kids have allowed the game and the gods to talk to them, to help them drown out the noise of the day so they can hear the clearer messages baseball has to offer. The day is over, the work is done, and I walk away with all their voices still ringing clear.

www.ingramcontent.com/pod-product-compliance
Lightning Source LLC
Chambersburg PA
CBHW021352090426
42742CB00009B/826